An Australian

Being the Narrative of a Quiet Journey Across China to Burma

George Ernest Morrison

Alpha Editions

Copyright © 2018

ISBN : 9789352970704

Design and Setting By
Alpha Editions
email - alphaedis@gmail.com

All rights reserved. No part of this publication may be reproduced, distributed, or transmitted in any form or by means, including photocopying, recording, or other electronic or mechanical methods, without the prior written permission of the publisher.

The views and characters expressed in the book are of the author and his/her imagination and do not represent the views of the Publisher.

Contents

CHAPTER I.	- 1 -
CHAPTER II.	- 9 -
CHAPTER III.	- 18 -
CHAPTER IV.	- 27 -
CHAPTER V.	- 40 -
CHAPTER VI.	- 52 -
CHAPTER VII.	- 62 -
CHAPTER VIII.	- 79 -
CHAPTER IX.	- 86 -
CHAPTER X.	- 92 -
CHAPTER XI.	- 100 -
CHAPTER XII.	- 107 -
CHAPTER XIII.	- 117 -
CHAPTER XIV.	- 125 -
CHAPTER XV.	- 135 -
CHAPTER XVI.	- 146 -
CHAPTER XVII.	- 161 -

CHAPTER XVIII.	- 173 -
CHAPTER XIX.	- 186 -
CHAPTER XX.	- 196 -
CHAPTER XXI.	- 208 -
CHAPTER XXII.	- 215 -
CHAPTER XXIII.	- 224 -

CHAPTER I.

INTRODUCTORY—MAINLY ABOUT MISSIONARIES AND THE CITY OF HANKOW.

In the first week of February, 1894, I returned to Shanghai from Japan. It was my intention to go up the Yangtse River as far as Chungking, and then, dressed as a Chinese, to cross quietly over Western China, the Chinese Shan States, and Kachin Hills to the frontier of Burma. The ensuing narrative will tell how easily and pleasantly this journey, which a few years ago would have been regarded as a formidable undertaking, can now be done.

The journey was, of course, in no sense one of exploration; it consisted simply of a voyage of 1500 miles up the Yangtse River, followed by a quiet, though extended, excursion of another 1500 miles along the great overland highway into Burma, taken by one who spoke no Chinese, who had no interpreter or companion, who was unarmed, but who trusted implicitly in the good faith of the Chinese. Anyone in the world can cross over to Burma in the way I did, provided he be willing to exercise for a certain number of weeks or months some endurance—for he will have to travel many miles on foot over a mountainous country—and much forbearance.

I went to China possessed with the strong racial antipathy to the Chinese common to my countrymen, but that feeling has long since given way to one of lively sympathy and gratitude, and I shall always look back with pleasure to this journey, during which I experienced, while traversing provinces as wide as European kingdoms, uniform kindness and hospitality, and the most charming courtesy. In my case, at least, the Chinese did not forget their precept, "deal gently with strangers from afar."

I left Shanghai on Sunday, February 11th, by the Jardine Matheson's steamer *Taiwo*. One kind friend, a merchant captain who had seen life in every important seaport in the world, came down, though it was past midnight, to bid me farewell. We shook hands on the wharf, and for the last time. Already he had been promised the first vacancy in Jardine Matheson's. Some time after my departure, when I was in Western China, he was appointed one of the officers of the ill-fated *Kowshing*, and when this unarmed transport before the declaration of war was destroyed by a Japanese gunboat, he was among the slain—struck, I believe, by a Japanese bullet while struggling for life in the water.

I travelled as a Chinese, dressed in warm Chinese winter clothing, with a pigtail attached to the inside of my hat. I could not have been more comfortable. I had a small cabin to myself. I had of course my own bedding, and by paying a Mexican dollar a day to the Chinese steward, "foreign chow," was brought me from the saloon. The traveller who cares to travel in this way, to put his pride in his pocket and a pigtail down his back, need pay only one-fourth of what it would cost him to travel as a European in European dress.

But I was, I found, unwittingly travelling under false pretences. When the smart chief officer came for my fare he charged me, I thought, too little. I expressed my surprise, and said that I thought the fare was seven dollars. "So it is," he replied "but we only charge missionaries five dollars, and I knew you were a missionary even before they told me." How different was his acuteness from that of the Chinese compradore who received me on the China Merchants' steamer *Hsin Chi*, in which I once made a voyage from Shanghai to Tientsin, also in Chinese dress! The conversation was short, sharp, and emphatic. The compradore looked at me searchingly. "What pidgin belong you?" he asked—meaning what is your business? Humbly I answered, "My belong Jesus Christ pidgin"; that is, I am a missionary, to which he instantly and with some scorn replied, "No dam fear!"

We called at the river ports and reached Hankow on the 14th. Hankow, the Chinese say, is the mart of eight provinces and the centre of the earth. It is the chief distributing centre of the Yangtse valley, the capital city of the centre of China. The trade in tea, its staple export, is declining rapidly, particularly since 1886. Indian opium goes no higher up the river than this point; its importation into Hankow is now insignificant, amounting to only 738 piculs (44 tons) per annum. Hankow is on the left bank of the Yangtse, separated only by the width of the Han river from Hanyang, and by the width of the Yangtse from Wuchang; these three divisions really form one large city, with more inhabitants than the entire population of the colony of Victoria.

Wuchang is the capital city of the two provinces of Hunan and Hupeh; it is here that the Viceroy, Chang Chi Tung, resides in his official yamen and dispenses injustice from a building almost as handsome as the American mission-houses which overlook it. Chang Chi Tung is the most anti-foreign of all the Viceroys of China; yet no Viceroy in the Empire has ever had so many foreigners in his employ as he. "Within the four seas," he says, "all men are brothers"; yet the two provinces he rules over are closed against foreigners, and the missionaries are compelled to remain under the shelter of the foreign Concession in Hankow. With a public spirit unusual among Chinese Viceroys he has devoted the immense revenues of his office to the modern development of the resources of his vice-kingdom. He has erected a gigantic cotton-mill at Wuchang with thirty-five thousand spindles, covering six acres and lit with the electric light, and with a reservoir of three acres and a half. He has built a large mint. At Hanyang he has erected magnificent iron-works and blast furnaces which cover many acres and are provided with all the latest machinery. He has iron and coal mines, with a railway seventeen miles long from the mines to the river, and specially constructed river-steamers and special hoisting machinery at the river-banks. Money he has poured out like water; he is probably the only important official in China who will leave office a poor man.

Acting as private secretary to the Viceroy is a clever Chinese named Kaw Hong Beng, the author of *Defensio Populi*, that often-quoted attack upon missionary methods which appeared first in *The North China Daily News*. A linguist of unusual ability, who publishes in *The Daily News* translations from Heine in English verse, Kaw is gifted with a rare command over the resources of English. He is a Master of Arts of the University of Edinburgh. Yet, strange paradox, notwithstanding that he had the privilege of being trained in the most pious and earnest community in the United Kingdom, under the lights of the United Presbyterian Kirk, Free Kirk, Episcopalian Church, and *The* Kirk, not to mention a large and varied assortment of Dissenting Churches of more or less dubious orthodoxy, he is openly hostile to the introduction of Christianity into China. And nowhere in China is the opposition to the introduction of Christianity more intense than in the Yangtse valley. In this intensity many thoughtful missionaries see the greater hope of the ultimate conversion of this portion of China;

opposition they say is a better aid to missionary success than mere apathy.

During the time I was in China, I met large numbers of missionaries of all classes, in many cities from Peking to Canton, and they unanimously expressed satisfaction at the progress they are making in China. Expressed succinctly, their harvest may be described as amounting to a fraction more than two Chinamen per missionary per annum. If, however, the paid ordained and unordained native helpers be added to the number of missionaries, you find that the aggregate body converts nine-tenths of a Chinaman per worker per annum; but the missionaries deprecate their work being judged by statistics. There are 1511 Protestant missionaries labouring in the Empire; and, estimating their results from the statistics of previous years as published in the *Chinese Recorder*, we find that they gathered last year (1893) into the fold 3127 Chinese—not all of whom it is feared are genuine Christians—at a cost of £350,000, a sum equal to the combined incomes of the ten chief London hospitals.

Hankow itself swarms with missionaries, "who are unhappily divided into so many sects, that even a foreigner is bewildered by their number, let alone the heathen to whom they are accredited." (Medhurst.)

Dwelling in well-deserved comfort in and around the foreign settlement, there are members of the London Missionary Society, of the Tract Society, of the Local Tract Society, of the British and Foreign Bible Society, of the National Bible Society of Scotland, of the American Bible Society; there are Quaker missionaries, Baptist, Wesleyan, and Independent missionaries of private means; there are members of the Church Missionary Society, of the American Board of Missions, and of the American High Church Episcopal Mission; there is a Medical Mission in connection with the London Missionary Society, there is a flourishing French Mission under a bishop, the "*Missions étrangères de Paris*," a Mission of Franciscan Fathers, most of whom are Italian, and a Spanish Mission of the Order of St. Augustine.

The China Inland Mission has its chief central distributing station at Hankow, and here also are the headquarters of a Scandinavian Mission, of a Danish Mission, and of an unattached mission, most of the members of which are also Danish. Where there are so many missions, of so many different sects, and holding such widely divergent views, it is, I suppose, inevitable that each mission should look with some disfavour upon the work done by its neighbours, should have some doubts as to the expediency of their methods, and some reasonable misgivings as to the genuineness of their conversions.

The Chinese "Rice Christians," those spurious Christians who become converted in return for being provided with rice, are just those who profit by these differences of opinion, and who, with timely lapses from grace, are said to succeed in being converted in turn by all the missions from the Augustins to the Quakers.

Every visitor to Hankow and to all other open ports, who is a supporter of missionary effort, is pleased to find that his preconceived notions as to the hardships and discomforts of the open port missionary in China are entirely false. Comfort and pleasures of life are there as great as in any other country. Among the most comfortable residences in Hankow are the quarters of the missionaries; and it is but right that the missionaries should be separated as far as possible from all discomfort—missionaries who are sacrificing all for China, and who are prepared to undergo any reasonable hardship to bring enlightenment to this land of darkness.

I called at the headquarters of the Spanish mission of Padres Agustinos and smoked a cigarette with two of the Padres, and exchanged reminiscences of Valladolid and Barcelona. And I can well conceive, having seen the extreme dirtiness of the mission premises, how little the Spaniard has to alter his ways in order to make them conform to the more ancient civilisation of the Chinese.

In Hankow there is a large foreign concession with a handsome embankment lined by large buildings. There is a rise and fall in the river between summer and winter levels of nearly sixty feet. In the summer the river laps the edge of the embankment and may overflow into the concession; in the winter, broad steps lead down to the edge of the water which, even when shrunk into its bed, is still more than half a mile in width. Our handsome consulate is at one end of the embankment; at the other there is a remarkable municipal building which was designed by a former City constable, who was, I hope, more expert with the handcuffs than he was with the pencil.

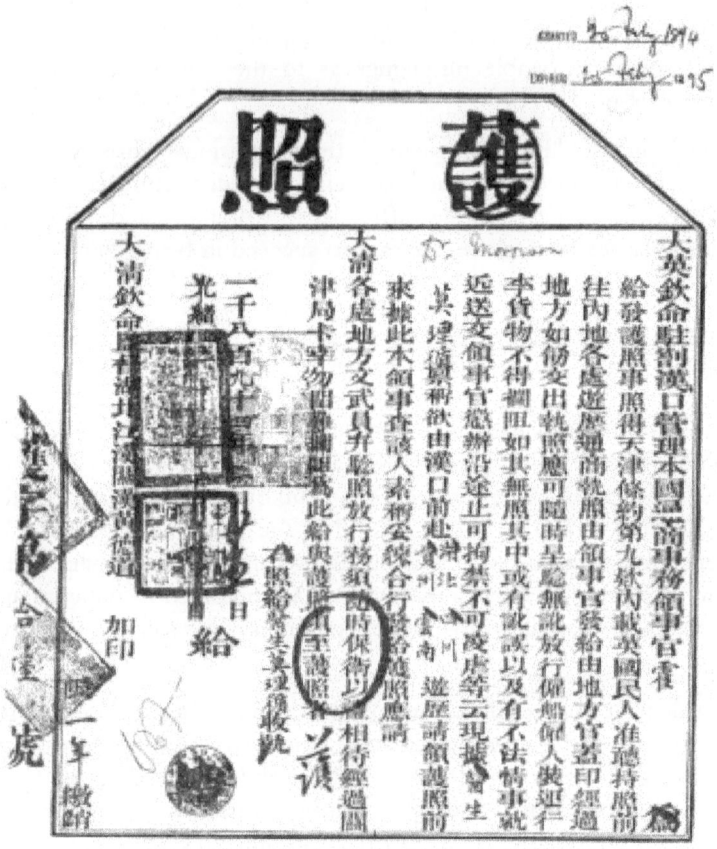

THE AUTHOR'S CHINESE PASSPORT.

Our interests in Hankow are protected by Mr. Pelham Warren, the Consul, one of the ablest men in the Service. I registered at the Consulate as a British subject and obtained a Chinese passport in terms of the Treaty of Tientsin for the four provinces Hupeh, Szechuen, Kweichow, and Yunnan, available for one year from the date of issue.

I had no servant. An English-speaking "boy," hearing that I was in need of one, came to me to recommend "his number one flend," who, he assured me, spoke English "all the same Englishman." But when the "flend" came I found that he spoke English all the same as I spoke Chinese. He was not abashed, but turned away wrath by saying to me, through an interpreter, "It is true that I cannot speak the foreign language, but the foreign gentleman is so clever that in one month he will speak Chinese beautifully." We did not come to terms.

At Hankow I embarked on the China Merchants' steamer *Kweili*, the only triple-screw steamer on the River, and four days later, on February 21st, I landed at Ichang, the most inland port on the Yangtse yet reached by steam. Ichang is an open port; it is the scene of the anti-foreign riot of September 2nd, 1891, when the foreign settlement was pillaged and burnt by the mob, aided by soldiers of the Chentai Loh-Ta-Jen, the head military official in charge at Ichang, "who gave the outbreak the benefit of his connivance." Pleasant zest is given to life here in the anticipation of another outbreak; it is the only excitement.

From Ichang to Chungking—a distance of 412 miles—the river Yangtse, in a great part of its course, is a series of rapids which no steamer has yet attempted to ascend, though it is contended that the difficulties of navigation would not be insuperable to a specially constructed steamer of elevated horse-power. Some idea of the speed of the current at this part of the river may be given by the fact that a junk, taking thirty to thirty-five days to do the upward journey, hauled most of the way by gangs of trackers, has been known to do the down-river journey in two days and a half.

Believing that I could thus save some days on the journey, I decided to go to Chungking on foot, and engaged a coolie to accompany me. We were to start on the Thursday afternoon; but about midnight on Wednesday I met Dr. Aldridge, of the Customs, who easily persuaded me that by taking the risk of going in a small boat (a *wupan*), and not in an ordinary passenger junk (a *kwatze*), I might, with luck, reach Chungking as soon by water as I could reach Wanhsien at half the distance by land. The Doctor was a man of surprising energy. He offered to arrange everything for me, and by 6 o'clock in the morning he had engaged a boat, had selected a captain (*laoban*), and a picked crew of four young men, who undertook to land me in Chungking in fifteen days, and had given them all necessary instructions for my journey. All was to be ready for a start the same evening.

During the course of the morning the written agreement was brought me by the laoban, drawn up in Chinese and duly signed, of which a Chinese clerk made me the following translation into English. I transcribe it literally:—

Yang Hsing Chung (the laoban) hereby contracts to convey Dr. M. to Chungking on the following conditions:—

1. The passage-money agreed upon is 28,000 cash (£2 16s.), which includes all charges.

2. If Chungking is reached in twelve days, Dr. M. will give the master 32,500 cash instead; if in thirteen days 31,000, and if in fifteen days 28,000.

3. If all goes well and the master does his duty satisfactorily, Dr. M. will give him 30,000 cash, even if he gets to Chungking in fifteen days.

4. The sum of 14,000 cash is to be advanced to the master before starting; the remainder to be paid on arrival at Chungking.

(Signed) YANG HSING CHUNG.

Dated the 17th day of the 2nd moon,
K, shui 20th year.

The Chinaman who wrote this in English speaks English better than many Englishmen.

CHAPTER II.

FROM ICHANG TO WANHSIEN, WITH SOME ACCOUNT OF CHINESE WOMEN AND THE RAPIDS OF THE YANGTSE KIANG.

The agreement was brought me in the morning; all the afternoon I was busy, and at 8 p.m. I embarked from the Customs pontoon. The boat was a wupan (five boards), 28 feet long and drawing 8 inches. Its sail was like the wing of a butterfly, with transverse ribs of light bamboo; its stern was shaped "like a swallow's wings at rest." An improvised covering of mats amidships was my crib; and with spare mats, slipt during the day over the boat's hood, coverings could be made at night for'ard for my three men and aft for the other two. It seemed a frail little craft to face the dangers of the cataracts, but it was manned by as smart a crew of young Chinese as could be found on the river. It was pitch dark when we paddled into the stream amidst a discharge of crackers. As we passed under the *Kweili*, men were there to wish me *bon voyage*, and a revolver was emptied into the darkness to propitiate the river god.

We paddled up the bank under the sterns of countless junks, past the walled city, and then, crossing to the other bank, we made fast and waited for the morning to begin our journey. The lights of the city were down the river; all was quiet; my men were in good heart, and there was no doubt whatever that they would make every effort to fulfil their contract.

At daylight we were away again and soon entered the first of the great gorges where the river has cleft its way through the mountains.

With a clear and sunny sky, the river flowing smoothly and reflecting deeply the lofty and rugged hills which fall steeply to the water's edge, a light boat, and a model crew, it was a pleasure to lie at ease wrapped in my Chinese pukai and watch the many junks lazily falling down the river, the largest of them "dwarfed by the colossal dimensions of the surrounding scenery to the size of sampans," and the fishing boats, noiseless but for the gentle creaking of the sheers and dip-net, silently working in the still waters under the bank.

At Ping-shan-pa there is an outstation of the Imperial Maritime Customs in charge of a seafaring man who was once a cockatoo farmer in South Australia, and drove the first team of bullocks to the Mount Brown diggings. He lives comfortably in a house-boat moored to the bank. He is one of the few Englishmen in China married in the English way, as distinct from the Chinese, to a Chinese girl. His wife is one of the prettiest girls that ever came out of Nanking, and talks English delightfully with a musical voice that is pleasant to listen to. I confess that I am one of those who agree with the missionary writer in regarding "the smile of a Chinese woman as inexpressibly charming." I have seen girls in China who would be considered beautiful in any capital in Europe. The attractiveness of the Japanese lady has been the theme of many writers, but, speaking as an impartial observer who has been both in Japan and China, I have never been able to come to any other decision than that in every feature the Chinese woman is superior to her Japanese sister. She is head and shoulders above the Japanese; she is more intellectual, or, rather, she is more capable of intellectual development; she is incomparably more chaste and modest. She is prettier, sweeter, and more trustworthy than the misshapen cackling little dot with black teeth that we are asked to admire as a Japanese beauty. The traveller in China is early impressed by the contrast between the almost entire freedom from apparent immorality of the Chinese cities, especially of Western China, and the flaunting indecency of the *Yoshiwaras* of Japan, with "their teeming, seething, busy mass of women, whose virtue is industry and whose industry is vice."

The small feet of the Chinese women, though admired by the Chinese and poetically referred to by them as "three-inch gold lilies," are in our eyes a very unpleasant deformity—but still, even with this deformity, the walk of the Chinese woman is more comely than the gait of the Japanese woman as she shambles ungracefully along with her little bent legs, scraping her wooden-soled slippers along the pavement with a noise that sets your teeth on edge. "Girls are like flowers," say the Chinese, "like the willow. It is very important that their feet should be bound short so that they can walk beautifully with mincing steps, swaying gracefully, and thus showing to all that they are persons of respectability." Apart from the Manchus, the dominant race, whose women do not bind their feet, all chaste Chinese girls have small feet. Those who have large feet are either, speaking generally, ladies of easy virtue or slave girls. And, of course, no Christian girl is allowed to have her feet bound.

ON A BALCONY IN WESTERN CHINA.

Leaving Ping-shan-pa with a stiff breeze in our favour we slowly stemmed the current. Look at the current side, and you would think we were doing eight knots an hour or more, but look at the shore side, close to which we kept to escape as far as possible from the current, and you saw how gradually we felt our way along.

At a double row of mat sheds filled with huge coils of bamboo rope of all thicknesses, my laoban went ashore to purchase a towline; he took with him 1000 cash (about two shillings), and returned with a coil 100 yards in length and 600 cash of change. The rope he brought was made of plaited bamboo, was as thick as the middle finger, and as tough as whalebone.

The country was more open and terraced everywhere into gardens. Our progress was most satisfactory. When night came we drew into the bank, and I coiled up in my crib and made myself comfortable. Space was cramped, and I had barely room to stretch my legs. My cabin was 5 feet 6 inches square and 4 feet high, open behind, but with two little doors in front, out of which I could just manage to squeeze myself sideways round the mast. Coir matting was next the floor boards, then a thick Chinese quilt (a *pukai*), then a Scotch plaid made in Geelong. My pillow was Chinese, and the hardest part of the bed; my portmanteau was beside me and served as a desk; a Chinese candle, more wick than wax, stuck into a turnip, gave me light.

This, our first day's journey, brought us to within sound of the worst rapid on the river, the Hsintan, and the roar of the cataract hummed in our ears all night.

Early in the morning we were at the foot of the rapid under the bank on the opposite side of the river from the town of Hsintan. It was an exciting scene. A swirling torrent with a roar like thunder was frothing down the cataract. Above, barriers of rocks athwart the stream stretched like a weir across the river, damming the deep still water behind it. The shore was strewn with boulders. Groups of trackers were on the bank squatting on the rocks to see the foreign devil and his cockleshell. Other Chinese were standing where the side-stream is split by the boulders into narrow races, catching fish with great dexterity, dipping them out of the water with scoop-nets.

We rested in some smooth water under shelter and put out our towline; three of my boys jumped ashore and laid hold of it; another with his bamboo boat-hook stood on the bow; the laoban was at the tiller; and I was cooped up useless in the well under the awning. The men started hauling as we pushed out into the sea of waters. The boat quivered, the water leapt at the bow as if it would engulf us; our three men were obviously too few. The boat danced in the rapid. My men on board shrieked excitedly that the towrope was fouling—it had caught in a rock—but their voices could not be heard; our trackers were brought to with a jerk; the hindmost saw the foul and ran back to free it, but he was too late, for the boat had come beam on to the current. Our captain frantically waved to let go, and the next moment we were tossed bodily into the cataract. The boat heeled gunwale under, and suddenly, but the bowman kept his feet like a Blondin, dropped the boat-hook, and jumped to unlash the halyard; a wave buried the boat nose under and swamped me in my kennel; my heart stopped beating, and, scared out of my wits, I began to strip off my sodden clothes; but before I had half done the sail had been set; both men had miraculously fended the boat from a rock, which, by a moment's hesitation, would have smashed us in bits or buried us in the boiling trough formed by the eddy below it, and, with another desperate effort, we had slid from danger into smooth water. Then my men laughed heartily. How it was done I do not know, but I felt keen admiration for the calm dexterity with which it had been done.

We baled the water out of the boat, paid out a second towrope—this one from the bow to keep the stern under control, the other being made fast to the mast, and took on board a licensed pilot. Extra trackers, hired for a few cash, laid hold of both towlines, and bodily—the water swelling and foaming under our bows—the boat was hauled against the torrent, and up the ledge of water that stretches across the river. We were now in smooth water at the entrance to the Mi Tsang Gorge. Two stupendous walls of rock, almost perpendicular, as bold and rugged as the Mediterranean side of the Rock of Gibraltar seem folded one behind the other across the river. "Savage cliffs are these, where not a tree and scarcely a blade of grass can grow, and where the stream, which is rather heard than seen, seems to be fretting in vain efforts to escape from its dark and gloomy prison." In the gorge itself the current was restrained, and boats could cross from bank to bank without difficulty. It was an eerie feeling to glide over the sunless water shut in by the stupendous sidewalls of rock. At a sandy spit to the west of the gorge we landed and put things in order. And here I stood and watched the junks disappear down the river one after the other, and I saw the truth of what Hosie had written that, as their masts are always unshipped in the down passage, the junks seem to be "passing with their human freight into eternity."

An immensely high declivity with a precipitous face was in front of us, which strained your eyes to look at; yet high up to the summit and to the very edge of the precipice, little farmsteads are dotted, and every yard of land available is under cultivation. So steep is it that the scanty soil must be washed away, you think, at the first rains, and only an adventurous goat could dwell there in comfort. My laoban, Enjeh, pointing to this mighty mass, said, "*Pin su chiao*;" but whether these words were the name of the place, or were intended to convey to me his sense of its magnificence, or dealt with the question of the precariousness of tenure so far above our heads, I had no means to determine.

My laoban knew twelve words of English, and I twelve words of Chinese, and this was the extent of our common vocabulary; it had to be carefully eked out with signs and gestures. I knew the Chinese for rice, flourcake, tea, egg, chopsticks, opium, bed, by-and-by, how many, charcoal, cabbage, and customs. My laoban could say in English, or pidgin English, chow, number one, no good, go ashore, sit down, by-and-by, to-morrow, match, lamp, alright, one piecee, and goddam. This last named exotic he had been led to consider as synonymous with "very good." It was not the first time I had known the words to be misapplied. I remember reading in the *Sydney Bulletin*, that a Chinese cook in Sydney when applying for a situation detailed to the mistress his undeniable qualifications, concluding with the memorable announcement, "My Clistian man mum; my eat beef; my say goddam."

There was a small village behind us. The villagers strolled down to see the foreigner whom children well in the background called "*Yang kweitze*" (foreign devil). Below on the sand, were the remains of a junk, confiscated for smuggling salt; it had been sawn bodily in two. Salt is a Government monopoly and a junk found smuggling it is confiscated on the spot.

Kueichow, on the left bank, is the first walled town we came to. Here we had infinite difficulty in passing the rapids, and crossed and recrossed the river several times. I sat in the boat stripped and shivering, for shipwreck seemed certain, and I did not wish to be drowned like a rat. For cool daring I never saw the equal of my boys, and their nicety of judgment was remarkable. Creeping along close to the bank, every moment in danger of having its bottom knocked out, the boat would be worked to the exact point from which the crossing of the river was feasible, balanced for a moment in the stream, then with sail set and a clipping breeze, and my men working like demons with the oars, taking short strokes, and stamping time with their feet, the boat shot into the current. We made for a rock in the centre of the river; we missed it, and my heart was in my mouth as I saw the rapid below us into which we were being drawn, when the boat mysteriously swung half round and glided under the lee of the rock. One of the boys leapt out with the bow-rope, and the others with scull and boat-hook worked the boat round to the upper edge of the rock, and then, steadying her for the dash across, pushed off again into the swirling current and made like fiends for the bank. Standing on the stern, managing the sheet and tiller, and with his bamboo pole ready, the laoban yelled and stamped in his excitement; there was the roar of the cataract below us, towards which we were fast edging stern on, destruction again threatened us and all seemed over, when in that moment we entered the back-wash and were again in good shelter. And so it went on, my men with splendid skill doing always the right thing, in the right way, at the right time, with unerring certainty.

At Yehtan rapid, which is said to be the worst on the river in the winter, as the Hsintan rapid is in summer, three of the boys went ashore to haul us up the ledge of water—they were plainly insufficient. While we were hanging on the cataract extra trackers appeared from behind the rocks and offered their services. They could bargain with us at an advantage. It was a case well known to all Chinese "of speaking of the price after the pig has been killed." But, when we agreed to their terms, they laid hold of the towrope and hauled us through in a moment. Here, as at other dangerous rapids on the river, an official lifeboat is stationed. It is of broad beam, painted red. The sailors are paid eighty cash (2*d*.) a day, and are rewarded with 1000 cash for every life they save, and 800 cash for every corpse.

Wushan Gorge, the "Witches' Gorge," which extends from Kuantukou to Wushan-hsien, a distance of twenty miles, is the longest gorge on the river.

Directly facing us as we emerged from the gorge was the walled town of Wushan-hsien. Its guardian pagoda, with its seven stories and its upturned gables, like the rim of an official hat, is downstream from the city, and thus prevents wealth and prosperity being swept by the current past the city.

Beyond there is a short but steep rapid. Before a strong wind with all sail set we boldly entered it and determined which was the stronger, the wind or the current. But, while we hung in the current calling and whistling for the wind, the wind flagged for a moment; tension being removed, the bow swung into the rocks; but the water was shallow, and in a trice two of the boys had jumped into the water and were holding the boat-sides. Then poling and pulling we crept up the rapid into smooth water. Never was there any confusion, never a false stroke. To hear my boys jabber in their unintelligible speech you pictured disorder, and disaster, and wild excitement; to see them act you witnessed such coolness, skill, and daring as you had rarely seen before. My boys were all young. The captain was only twenty, and was a model of physical grace, with a face that will gladden the heart of the Chinese maiden whom he condescends to select to be the mother of his children.

Junks were making slow progress up the river. The towpath is here on the left bank, sixty feet above the present level of the river. Barefooted trackers, often one hundred in a gang, clamber over the rocks "like a pack of hounds in full cry," each with the coupling over his shoulder and all singing in chorus, the junk they are towing often a quarter of a mile astern of them. When a rapid intervenes they strain like bondmen at the towrope; the line creaks under the enormous tension but holds fast. On board the junk, a drum tattoo is beaten and fire-crackers let off, and a dozen men with long ironshod bamboos sheer the vessel off the rocks as foot by foot it is drawn past the obstruction. Contrast with this toilsome slowness the speed of the junk bound down-stream. Its mast is shipped; its prodigious bow-sweep projects like a low bowsprit; the after deck is covered as far as midships with arched mat-roof; coils of bamboo rope are hanging under the awning; a score or more of boatmen, standing to their work and singing to keep time, work the yulos, as looking like a modern whaleback the junk races down the rapids.

Kweichou-fu, 146 miles from Ichang, is one of the largest cities on the Upper Yangtse. Just before it is the Feng-hsiang Gorge the "Windbox Gorge" where the mountains have been again cleft in twain to let pass the river; this is the last of the great gorges of the Yangtse.

We had left the province of Hupeh. Kweichou is the first prefectural city that the traveller meets in Szechuen; for that reason my laoban required me to give him my passport that he might take it ashore and have it viséed by the magistrate. While he was away two Customs officials searched my boat for contraband goods. When he returned, he had to pay a squeeze at the Customs station. We clawed with our hooked bamboos round the sterns of a hundred Szechuen junks, and were again arrested at a likin boat, and more cash passed from my laoban to the officials in charge. We went on again, when a third time we came face on to a likin-barrier, and a third time my laoban was squeezed. After this we were permitted to continue our journey. For the rest of the day whenever the laoban caught my eye he raised three fingers and with a rueful shake of the head said "Kweichou haikwan (customs) no good"; and then he swore, no doubt.

My little boat was the smallest on the river. In sailing it could hold its own with all but the long ferry boats or tenders which accompany the larger junks to land the trackers and towline. These boats carry a huge square sail set vertically from sheer legs, and are very fast. But in rowing, poling, and tracking we could beat the river.

Anping was passed—a beautiful country town in a landscape of red hills and rich green pastures, of groves of bamboo and cypress, of pretty little farmhouses with overhanging eaves and picturesque temples in wooded glens.

At Chipatzu there are the remains of a remarkable embankment built of huge blocks of dressed stone resting upon a noble brow of natural rock; deep Chinese characters are cut into the stone; but the glory is departed and there are now only a few straggling huts where there was once a large city.

The river was now at its lowest and at every point of sand and shingle, meagre bands of gold puddlers were at work washing for gold in cradle rockers. To judge, however, from the shabbiness of their surroundings there was little fear that their gains would disturb the equilibrium of the world's gold yield.

CHAPTER III.

THE CITY OF WANHSIEN, AND THE JOURNEY FROM WANHSIEN TO CHUNGKING.

At daylight, on March 1st, we were abreast of the many storied pagoda, whose lofty position, commanding the approach to the city, brings good fortune to the city of Wanhsien. A beautiful country is this—the chocolate soil richly tilled, the sides of the hills dotted with farmhouses in groves of bamboo and cedar, with every variety of green in the fields, shot through with blazing patches of the yellow rape-seed. The current was swift, the water was shallow where we were tracking, and we were constantly aground in the shingle; but we rounded the point, and Wanhsien was before us. This is the half-way city between Ichang and Chungking. My smart laoban dressed himself in his best to be ready to go ashore with me; he was jubilant at his skill in bringing me so quickly. "Sampan number one! goddam!" he said; and, holding up two hands, he turned down seven fingers to show that we had come in seven days. Then he pointed to other boats that we were passing, and counted on his fingers fifteen, whereby I knew he was demonstrating that, had I gone in any other boat but his, I should have been fifteen days on the way instead of seven.

An immense number of junks of all kinds were moored to the bank, bow on. Many of them were large vessels, with hulls like that of an Aberdeen clipper. Many carry foreign flags, by which they are exempt from the Chinese likin duties, so capricious in their imposition, and pay instead a general five per cent. *ad valorem* duty on their cargoes, which is levied by the Imperial Maritime Customs, and collected either in Chungking or Ichang. From one to the other, with boathooks and paddle, we crept past the outer wings of their balanced rudders till we reached the landing place. On the rocks at the landing a bevy of women were washing, beating their hardy garments with wooden flappers against the stones; but they ceased their work as the foreign devil, in his uncouth garb, stepped ashore in their midst. Wanhsien is not friendly to foreigners in foreign garb. I did not know this, and went ashore dressed as a European. Never have I received such a spontaneous welcome as I did in this city; never do I wish to receive such another. I landed at the mouth of the small creek which separates the large walled city to the east from the still larger city beyond the walls to the west. My laoban was with me. We passed through the washerwomen. Boys and ragamuffins hanging about the shipping saw me, and ran towards me, yelling: "*Yang kweitze, Yang kweitze*" (foreign devil, foreign devil).

Behind the booths a story-teller had gathered a crowd; in a moment he was alone and the crowd were following me up the hill, yelling and howling with a familiarity most offensive to a sensitive stranger. My sturdy boy wished me to produce my passport which is the size of an admiral's ensign, but I was not such a fool as to do so for it had to serve me for many months yet. With this taunting noisy crowd I had to walk on as if I enjoyed the demonstration. I stopped once and spoke to the crowd, and, as I knew no Chinese, I told them in gentle English of the very low opinion their conduct led me to form of the moral relations of their mothers, and the resignation with which it induced me to contemplate the hyperpyretic surroundings of their posthumous existence; and, borrowing the Chinese imprecation, I ventured to express the hope that when their souls return again to earth they may dwell in the bodies of hogs, since they appeared to me the only habitations meet for them.

But my words were useless. With a smiling face, but rage at my heart, I led the procession up the creek to a stone bridge where large numbers left me, only to have their places taken on the other bank by a still more enthusiastic gathering. I stopped here a moment in the jostling crowd to look up-stream at that singular natural bridge, which an enormous mass of stone has formed across the creek, and I could see the high arched bridge beyond it, which stretches from bank to bank in one noble span, and is so high above the water that junks can pass under it in the summer time when the rains swell this little stream into a broad and navigable river.

Then we climbed the steep bank into the city and entering by a dirty narrow street we emerged into the main thoroughfare, the crowd still following and the shops emptying into the street to see me. We passed the Mohammedan Mosque, the Roman Catholic Mission, the City Temple, to a Chinese house where I was slipped into the court and the door shut, and then into another to find that I was in the home of the China Inland Mission, and that the pigtailed celestial receiving me at the steps was Mr. Hope Gill. It was my clothes I then learnt that had caused the manifestation in my honour. An hour later, when I came out again into the street, the crowd was waiting still to see me, but it was disappointed to see me now dressed like one of themselves. In the meantime I had resumed my Chinese dress. "Look," the people said, "at the foreigner; he had on foreign dress, and now he is dressed in Chinese even to his queue. Look at his queue, it is false." I took off my hat to scratch my head. "Look," they shouted again, "at his queue; it is stuck to the inside of his hat." But they ceased to follow me.

There are three Missionaries in Wanhsien of the China Inland Mission, one of whom is from Sydney. The mission has been opened six years, and has been fairly successful, or completely unsuccessful, according to the point of view of the inquirer.

Mr. Hope Gill, the senior member of the mission, is a most earnest good man, who works on in his discouraging task with an enthusiasm and devotion beyond all praise. A Premillennialist, he preaches without ceasing throughout the city; and his preaching is earnest and indiscriminate. His method has been sarcastically likened by the Chinese, in the words of one of their best-known aphorisms, to the unavailing efforts of a "blind fowl picking at random after worms." Nearly all the Chinese in Wanhsien have heard the doctrine described with greater or less unintelligibility, and it is at their own risk if they still refuse to be saved.

During the cholera epidemic this brave man never left his post; he never refused a call to attend the sick and dying, and, at the risk of his own, saved many lives. And what is his reward? This work he did, the Chinese say, not from a disinterested love of his fellows, which was his undoubted motive, but to accumulate merit for himself in the invisible world beyond the grave. "Gratitude," says this missionary, and it is the opinion of many, "is a condition of heart, or of mind, which seems to be incapable of existence in the body of a Chinaman." Yet other missionaries tell me that no man can possess a livelier sense of gratitude than a Chinaman, or manifest it with more sincerity. "If our words are compared to the croaking of the frog, we heed it not, but freely express the feelings of our heart," are actual words addressed by a grateful Chinese patient to the first medical missionary in China. And the Chinaman himself will tell you, says Smith, "that it does not follow that, because he does not exhibit gratitude he does not feel it. When the dumb man swallows a tooth he may not say much about it, but it is all inside."

Since its foundation in 1887, the Inland Mission of Wanhsien has been conducted with brave perseverance. There are, unfortunately, no converts, but there are three hopeful "inquirers," whose conversion would be the more speedy the more likely they were to obtain employment afterwards. They argue in this way; they say, to quote the words used by the Rev. G. L. Mason at the Shanghai Missionary Conference of 1890, "if the foreign teacher will take care of our bodies, we will do him the favour to seek the salvation of our souls." This question of the employment of converts is one of the chief difficulties of the missionary in China. "The idea (derived from Buddhism) is universally prevalent in China," says the Rev. C. W. Mateer, "that everyone who enters any sect should live by it.... When a Chinaman becomes a Christian he expects to live by his Christianity."

One of the three inquirers was shown me; he was described as the most advanced of the three in knowledge of the doctrine. Now I do not wish to write unkindly, but I am compelled to say that this man was a poor, wretched, ragged coolie, who sells the commonest gritty cakes in a rickety stall round the corner from the mission, who can neither read nor write, and belongs to a very humble order of blunted intelligence. The poor fellow is the father of a little girl of three, an only child, who is both deaf and dumb. And there is the fear that his fondness for the little one tempts him to give hope to the missionaries that in him they are to see the first fruit of their toil, the first in the district to be saved by their teaching, while he nurses a vague hope that, when the foreign teachers regard him as adequately converted, they may be willing to restore speech and hearing to his poor little offspring. It is a scant harvest.

After a Chinese dinner the missionary and I went for a walk into the country. In the main street we met a troop of beggars, each with a bowl of rice and garbage and a long stick, with a few tattered rags hanging round his loins—they were the poorest poor I had ever seen. They were the beggars of the city, who had just received their midday meal at the "Wanhsien Ragged Homes."

There are three institutions of the kind in the city for the relief of the destitute; they are entirely supported by charity, and are said to have an average annual income of 40,000 taels. Wanhsien is a very rich city, with wealthy merchants and great salt hongs. The landed gentry and the great junk owners have their town houses here. The money distributed by the townspeople in private charity is unusually great even for a Chinese city. Its most public-spirited citizen is Ch'en, one of the merchant princes of China whose transactions are confined exclusively to the products of his own country. Starting life with an income of one hundred taels, bequeathed him by his father, Ch'en has now agents all over the empire, and mercantile dealings which are believed to yield him a clear annual income of a quarter of a million taels. His probity is a by-word; his benefactions have enriched the province. That cutting in the face of the cliff in the Feng-hsiang Gorge near Kweichou-fu, where a pathway for trackers has been hewn out of the solid rock, was done at his expense, and is said to have cost one hundred thousand taels. Not only by his benefactions has Ch'en laid up for himself merit in heaven, but he has already had his reward in this world. His son presented himself for the M.A. examination for the Hanlin degree, the highest academical degree in the Empire. Everyone in China knows that success in this examination is dependent upon the favour of Wunchang-te-keun, the god of literature (Taoist) "who from generation to generation hath sent his miraculous influence down upon earth", and, as the god had seen with approbation the good works done by the father, he gave success to the son. When the son returned home after his good fortune, he was met beyond the walls and escorted into the city with royal honours; his success was a triumph for the city which gave him birth.

A short walk and we were out of the city, following a flagged path with flights of steps winding up the hill through levelled terraces rich with every kind of cereal, and with abundance of poppy. Splendid views of one of the richest agricultural regions in the world are here unfolded. Away down in the valley is the palatial family mansion of Pien, one of the wealthiest yeomen in the province. Beyond you see the commencement of the high road, a paved causeway eight feet wide, which extends for hundreds of miles to Chentu, the capital of the province, and takes rank as the finest work of its kind in the empire. On every hill-top is a fort.

That bolder than the rest commanding the city at a distance of five miles, is on the "Hill of Heavenly Birth." It was built, says Hobson, during the Taiping Rebellion; it existed, says the missionary, before the present dynasty; discrepant statements characteristic of this country of contradictions. But, whether thirty or two hundred and fifty years old, the fort is now one in name only, and is at present occupied by a garrison of peaceful peasantry.

Chinamen that we met asked us politely "if we had eaten our rice," and "whither were we going." We answered correctly. But when with equal politeness we asked the wayfarer where he was going, he jerked his chin towards the horizon and said, "a long way."

We called at the residence of a rich young Chinese, who had lately received it in his inheritance, together with 3000 acres of farmland, which, we were told, yield him an annual income of 70,000 taels. In the absence of the master, who was away in the country reading with his tutor for the Hanlin degree, we were received by the caretakers, who showed us the handsome guest chambers, the splendid gilded tablet, the large courts, and garden rockeries. A handsome residence is this, solidly built of wood and masonry, and with the trellis work carved with much elaboration.

It was late when we returned to the mission, and after dark when I went on board my little wupan. My boys had not been idle. They had bought new provisions of excellent quality, and had made the boat much more comfortable. The three kind missionaries came down to wish me Godspeed. Brave men! they deserve a kinder fortune than has been their fate hitherto. We crossed the river and anchored above the city, ready against an early start in the morning.

The day after leaving Wanhsien was the first time that we required any assistance on our journey from another junk; it was cheerfully given. Our towrope had chafed through, and we were in a difficulty, attempting to pass a bad rapid among the rocks, when a large junk was hauled bodily past us, and, seeing our plight, hooked on to us and towed us with them out of danger. On this night we anchored under the Sentinel Rock (Shih-pao-chai), perhaps the most remarkable landmark on the river. From two hundred to three hundred feet high, and sixty feet wide at the base, it is a detached rock, cleft vertically from a former cliff. A nine-storied pagoda has been inset into the south-eastern face, and temple buildings crown the summit.

It was surprising how well my men lived on board the boat. They had three good meals a day, always with rice and abundance of vegetables, and frequently with a little pork. Cooking was done while we were under way; for the purpose we had two little earthenware stoves, two pans, and a kettle. All along the river cabbages and turnips are abundant and cheap. Bumboats, laden to the rail, waylay the boats *en route*, and offer an armful of fresh vegetables for the equivalent in copper cash of three-eighths of a penny. Other boats peddle firewood, cut short and bound in little bundles, and sticks of charcoal. Coal is everywhere abundant, and there are excellent briquettes for sale, made of a mixture of clay and coal-dust.

All day long now for the rest of our voyage we sailed through a beautiful country. From the hill tops to the water's edge the hillsides are levelled into a succession of terraces; there are cereals and the universal poppy, pretty hamlets, and thriving little villages; a river half a mile wide thronged with every kind of river craft, and back in the distance snow-clad mountains. There are bamboo sheds at every point, with coils of bamboo towrope, mats, and baskets, and huge Szechuen hats as wide as an umbrella.

On the morning of March 5th I was awakened by loud screaming and yelling ahead of us. I squeezed out of my cabin, and saw a huge junk looming down upon us. In an awkward rapid its towline had parted, and the huge structure tumbling uncontrolled in the water, was bearing down on us, broadside on. It seemed as if we should be crushed against the rocks, and we must have been, but for the marvellous skill with which the sailors on the junk, just at the critical time, swung their vessel out of danger. They were yelling with discord, but worked together as one man.

In the afternoon we were at Feng-tu-hsien, a flourishing river port, one of the principal outlets of the opium traffic of the Upper Yangtse. Next day we were at Fuchou, the other opium port, whose trade in opium is greater still than that of Feng-tu-hsien. It is at the junction of a large tributary—the Kung-t'-an-ho, which is navigable for large vessels for more than two hundred miles. Large numbers of the Fuchou junks were moored here, which differ in construction from all other junks on the river Yangtse in having their great sterns twisted or wrung a quarter round to starboard, and in being steered by an immense stern sweep, and not by the balanced rudder of an ordinary junk.

The following day, after a long day's work, we moored beyond the town of Chang-show-hsien. Here I paid the laoban 2000 cash, whereupon he paid his men something on account, and then blandly suggested a game of cards. He was fast winning back his money, when I intervened and bade them turn in, as I wished to make an early start in the morning. The river seemed to get broader, deeper, and more rapid as we ascended; the trackers, on the contrary, became thinner, narrower, and more decrepit.

On March 8th, our fourteenth day out, disaster nearly overtook us when within a day's sail of our destination. Next day we reached Chungking safely, having done by some days the fastest journey on record up the Yangtse rapids. My captain and his young crew had finished the journey within the time agreed upon.

THE RIVER YANGTSE AT TUNG-LO-HSIA.

MEMORIAL ARCHWAY AT THE FORT OF FU-TO-KUAN.

CHAPTER IV.

THE CITY OF CHUNGKING—THE CHINESE CUSTOMS—THE FAMOUS MONSIEUR HAAS, AND A FEW WORDS ON THE OPIUM FALLACY.

After passing through the gorge known as Tung-lo-hsia ten miles from Chungking, the laoban tried to attract my attention, calling me from my crib and pointing with his chin up the river repeating "Haikwan one piecee," which I interpreted to mean that there was an outpost of the customs here in charge of one white man; and this proved to be the case. The customs kuatze or houseboat was moored to the left bank; the Imperial Customs flag floated gaily over an animated collection of native craft. We drew alongside the junk and an Englishman appeared at the window.

"Where from?" he asked, laconically.

"Australia."

"The devil, so am I. What part?"

"Victoria."

"So am I. Town?"

"Last from Ballarat."

"My native town, by Jove! Jump up."

I gave him my card. He looked at it and said, "When I was last in Victoria I used to follow with much interest a curious walk across Australia, from the Gulf of Carpentaria to Melbourne done by a namesake. Any relation? The same man! I'm delighted to see you." Here then at the most inland of the customs stations in China, 1500 miles from the sea, I met my fellow countryman who was born near my home and whose father was a well-known Mayor of Ballarat City.

Like myself he had formerly been a student of Melbourne University, but I was many years his senior. What was his experience of the University I forgot to inquire, but mine I remember vividly enough; for it was not happy. In the examination for the Second-year Medicine, hoping the more to impress the Professors, I entered my name for honours—and they rejected me in the preliminary pass. It seems that in the examination in Materia Medica, I had among other trifling lapses prescribed a dose of Oleum Crotonis of "one half to two drachms *carefully increased.*" I confess that I had never heard of the wretched stuff; the question was taken from far on in the text book and, unfortunately, my reading had not extended quite so far. When a deputation from my family waited upon the examiner to ascertain the cause of my misadventure, the only satisfaction we got was the obliging assurance "that you might as well let a mad dog loose in Collins Street" as allow me to become a doctor. And then the examiner produced my prescription. But I thought I saw a faint chance of escape. I pointed a nervous finger to the two words "carefully increased," and pleaded that that indication of caution ought to save me. "Save *you* it might," he shouted with unnecessary vehemence; "but, God bless my soul, man, it would not save your patient." The examiner was a man intemperate of speech; so I left the University. It was a severe blow to the University, but the University survived it.

My countryman had been five years in China in the customs service, that marvellous organisation which is more impartially open to all the world than any other service in the world. As an example, I note that among the Commissioners of Customs at the ports of the River Yangtse alone, at the time of my voyage the Commissioner at Shanghai was an Austrian, at Kiukiang a Frenchman, at Hankow an Englishman, at Ichang a Scandinavian, and at Chungking a German.

The Australian had been ten months at Chungking. His up-river journey occupied thirty-eight days, and was attended with one moving incident. In the Hsintan rapid the towline parted, and his junk was smashed to pieces by the rocks, and all that he possessed destroyed. It was in this rapid that my boat narrowly escaped disaster, but there was this difference in our experiences, that at the time of his accident the river was sixty feet higher than on the occasion of mine.

Tang-chia-to, the customs out-station, is ten miles by river from Chungking, but not more than four miles by land. So I sent the boat on, and in the afternoon walked over to the city. A customs coolie came with me to show me the way. My friend accompanied me to the river crossing, walking with me through fields of poppy and sugarcane, and open beds of tobacco. At the river side he left me to return to his solitary home, while I crossed the river in a sampan, and then set out over the hills to Chungking. It was more than ever noticeable, the poor hungry wretchedness of the river coolies. For three days past all the trackers I had seen were the most wretched in physique of any I had met in China. Phthisis and malaria prevail among them; their work is terribly arduous; they suffer greatly from exposure; they appear to be starving in the midst of abundance. My coolie showed well by contrast with the trackers; he was sleek and well fed. A "chop dollar," as he would be termed down south, for his face was punched or chopped with the small-pox, he swung along the paved pathway and up and down the endless stone steps in a way that made me breathless to follow. We passed a few straggling houses and wayside shrines and tombstones. All the dogs in the district recognised that I was a stranger, and yelped consumedly, like the wolfish mongrels that they are. From a hill we obtained a misty view of the City of Chungking, surrounded on two sides by river and covering a broad expanse of hill and highland. I was taken to the customs pontoon on the south bank of the river, and then up the steep bank by many steps to the basement of an old temple where the two customs officers have their pleasant dwelling. I was kindly received, and stayed the night. We were an immense height above the water; the great city was across the broad expanse of river, here more than seven hundred yards in width. Away down below us, moored close to the bank, and guarded by three Chinese armed junks or gunboats, was the customs hulk, where the searching is done, and where the three officers of the outdoor staff have their offices. There is at present but little smuggling, because there are no Chinese officials. Smuggling may be expected to begin in earnest as soon as Chinese officials are introduced to prevent it. Chinese searchers do best who use their eyes not to see—best for themselves, that is. The gunboats guarding this Haikwan Station have a nominal complement of eighty men, and an actual complement of twenty-four; to avoid, however, unnecessary explanation, pay is drawn by the commanding officer, not for the actual twenty-four, but for the nominal eighty.

THE CITY OF CHUNGKING, AS SEEN FROM THE OPPOSITE BANK OF THE RIVER YANGTSE.

My two companions in the temple were tidewaiters in the Customs. There are many storied lives locked away among the tidewaiters in China. Down the river there is a tidewaiter who was formerly professor of French in the Imperial University of St. Petersburg; and here in Chungking, filling the same humble post, is the godson of a marquis and the nephew of an earl, a brave soldier whose father is a major-general and his mother an earl's daughter, and who is first cousin to that enlightened nobleman and legislator the Earl of C. Few men so young have had so many and varied experiences as this sturdy Briton. He has humped his swag in Australia, has earned fifteen shillings a day there as a blackleg protected by police picquets on a New South Wales coal mine. He was at Harrow under Dr. Butler, and at Corpus Christi, Cambridge. He has been in the Dublin Fusiliers, and a lieutenant in Weatherby's Horse, enlisted in the 5th Lancers, and rose from private to staff-sergeant, and ten months later would have had his commission. He served with distinction in the Soudan and Zululand, and has three medals with four clasps. He was present at

El Teb, and at the disaster at Tamai, when McNeill's zareeba was broken. He was at Tel-el-kebir; saw Burnaby go forth to meet a coveted death at Abu-klea, and was present at Abu-Kru when Sir Herbert Stewart received his death-wound. He was at Rorke's Drift, and appears with that heroic band in Miss Elizabeth Thompson's painting. Leaving the army, C. held for a time a commission in the mounted constabulary of Madras, and now he is a third class assistant tidewaiter in the Imperial Maritime Customs of China, with a salary as low as his spirits are high.

Chungking is an open port, which is not an open port. By the treaty of Tientsin it is included in the clause which states that any foreign steamer going to it, a closed port, shall be confiscated. Yet by the Chefoo Convention, Chungking is to become an open port as soon as the first foreign steamer shall reach there. This reminds one of the conflicting instructions once issued by a certain government in reference to the building of a new gaol. The instructions were explicit:—

Clause I.—The new gaol shall be constructed out of the materials of the old.

Clause II.—The prisoners shall remain in the old gaol till the new gaol is constructed.

In Chungking the Commissioner of Customs is Dr. F. Hirth, whose Chinese house is on the highest part of Chungking in front of a temple, which, dimly seen through the mist, is the crowning feature of the city. A distinguished sinologue is the doctor, one of the finest Chinese scholars in the Empire, author of "China and the Roman Orient," "Ancient Porcelain," and an elaborate "Textbook of Documentary Chinese," which is in the hands of most of the Customs staff in China, for whose assistance it was specially written. Dr. Hirth is a German who has been many years in China. He holds the third button, the transparent blue button, the third rank in the nine degrees by which Chinese Mandarins are distinguished.

The best site in Chungking has been fortunately secured by the Methodist Episcopalian Mission of the United States. Their missionaries dwell with great comfort in the only foreign-built houses in the city in a large compound with an ample garden. Their Mission hospital is a well-equipped Anglo-Chinese building attached to the city wall, and overlooking from its lofty elevation the Little River, and the walled city beyond it.

The wards of the hospital are comfortable and well lit; the floors are varnished; the beds are provided with spring mattresses; indeed, in the comfort of the hospital the Chinese find its chief discomfort. A separate compartment has been walled off for the treatment of opium-smokers who desire by forced restraint to break off the habit. Three opium-smokers were in durance at the time of my visit; they were happy and contented and well nourished, and none but the trained eye of an expert, who saw what he wished to see, could have guessed that they were addicted to the use of a drug which has been described in exaggerated terms as "more deadly to the Chinese than war, famine, and pestilence combined." (Rev. A. H. Smith, "Chinese Characteristics," p. 187.)

Not long ago three men were admitted into the hospital suffering, on their own confession, from the opium habit. They freely expressed the desire of their hearts to be cured, and were received with welcome and placed in confinement. Every effort was made to wean them from the habit which, they alleged, had "seized them in a death grip." Attentive to the teacher and obedient to the doctor, they gave every hope of being early admitted into Church fellowship. But one night the desire to return to the drug became irresistible, and, strangely, the desire attacked all three men at the same time on the same night; and they escaped together. Sadly enough there was in this case marked evidence of the demoralising influence of opium, for when they escaped they took with them everything portable that they could lay their hands on. It was a sad trial.

Excellent medical work is done in the hospital. From the first annual report just published by the surgeon in charge, an M.D. from the United States, I extract the two following pleasing items.

Medical Work.—"Mr. Tsang Taotai, of Kuei-Iang-fu, was an eye witness to several operations, as well as being operated upon for Internal Piles" (the last words in large capitals).

Evangelistic Work.—"Mrs. Wei, in the hospital for suppurating glands of the neck, became greatly interested in the truth while there, left a believer, and attends Sunday service regular (*sic*), walking from a distant part of the city each Sunday. We regard her as very hopeful, and she is reported by the Chinese as being very warm-hearted. She will be converted when the first vacancy occurs in the nursing staff."

During my stay in Chungking I frequently met the French Consul "*en commission*," Monsieur Haas, who had lately arrived on a diplomatic mission, which was invested with much secrecy. It was believed to have for its object the diversion of the trade of Szechuen from its natural channel, the Yangtse River, southward through Yunnan province to Tonquin. Success need not be feared to attend his mission. "*Ils perdront et leur temps et leur argent.*" Monsieur Haas has helped to make history in his time. The most gentle-mannered of men, he writes with strange rancour against the perfidious designs of Britain in the East. In his diplomatic career Monsieur Haas suffered one great disappointment. He was formerly the French Chargé d'Affaires and Political Resident at the court of King Theebaw in Mandalay. And it was his "Secret Treaty" with the king which forced the hand of England and led to her hasty occupation of Upper Burma. The story is a very pretty one. By this treaty French influence was to become predominant in Upper Burma; the country was to become virtually a colony of France, with a community of interest with France, with France to support her in any difficulty with British Burma. Such a position England could not tolerate for one moment. Fortunately for us French intrigue outwitted itself, and the Secret Treaty became known. It was in this way. Draft copies of the agreement drawn up in French and Burmese were exchanged between Monsieur Haas and King Theebaw. But Monsieur Haas could not read Burmese, and he distrusted the King. A trusted interpreter was necessary, and there was only one man in Mandalay that seemed to him sufficiently trustworthy. To Signor A—— then, the Italian Chargé d'Affaires and Manager of the Irrawaddy Flotilla Company, Monsieur Haas went and, pledging him to secrecy, sought his assistance as interpreter.

As Monsieur Haas had done, so did his Majesty the King. Two great minds were being guided by the same spirit. Theebaw could not read French, and he distrusted Monsieur Haas. An interpreter was essential, and, casting about for a trusted one, he decided that no one could serve him so faithfully as Signor A——, and straightway sought his assistance, as Monsieur Haas had done.

Their fates were in his hands; which master should the Italian serve, the French or the Burmese? He did not hesitate—he betrayed them both. Within an hour the Secret Treaty was in possession of the British Resident. Action was taken with splendid promptitude. "M. de Freycinet, when pressed on the subject, repudiated any intention of acquiring for France a political predominance in Burma." An immediate pretext was found to place Theebaw in a dilemma; eleven days later the British troops had crossed the frontier, and Upper Burma was another province of our Indian Empire.

Monsieur Haas was recalled, and his abortive action repudiated. He had acted, of course, without orders, he had erred from too much zeal. Signor A—— was also recalled, but did not go because the order was not accompanied with the customary cheque to defray the cost of his passage. His services to England were rewarded, and he retained his engagement as Manager of the Flotilla Company; but he lost his appointment as the Representative of Italy—an honourable post with a dignified salary paid by the Italian Government in I.O.U.'s.

Chungking is an enormously rich city. It is built at the junction of the Little River and the Yangtse, and is, from its position, the great river port of the province of Szechuen. Water-ways stretch from here an immense distance inland. The Little River is little only in comparison with the Yangtse, and in any other country would be regarded as a mighty inland river. It is navigable for more than 2000 li (600 miles). The Yangtse drains a continent; the Little River drains a province larger than a European kingdom. Chungking is built at a great height above the present river, now sixty feet below its summer level. Its walls are unscalable. Good influences are directed over the city from a lofty pagoda on the topmost hill in the vicinity. Temples abound, and spacious yamens and rich buildings, the crowning edifice of all being the Temple to the God of Literature. Distances are prodigious in Chungking, and the streets so steep and hilly, with flights of stairs cut from the solid rock, that only a mountaineer can live here in comfort. All who can afford it go in chairs; stands of sedan chairs are at every important street corner.

A TEMPLE THEATRE IN CHUNGKING.

During the day the city vibrates with teeming traffic; at night the streets are deserted and dead, the stillness only disturbed by a distant watchman springing his bamboo rattle to keep himself awake and warn robbers of his approach. In no city in Europe is security to life and property better guarded than in this, or, indeed, in any other important city in China. It is a truism to say that no people are more law-abiding than the Chinese; "they appear," says Medhurst, "to maintain order as if by common consent, independent of all surveillance."

Our Consul in Chungking is Mr. E. H. Fraser, an accomplished Chinese scholar, who fills a difficult post with rare tact and complete success. Consul Fraser estimates the population of Chungking at 200,000; the Chinese, he says, have a record of 35,000 families within the walls. Of this number from forty to fifty per cent. of all men, and from four to five per cent. of all women, indulge in the opium pipe. The city abounds in opium-shops— shops, that is, where the little opium-lamps and the opium-pipes are stacked in hundreds upon hundreds. Opium is one of the staple products of this rich province, and one of the chief sources of wealth of this flourishing city.

During the nine months that I was in China I saw thousands of opium-smokers, but I never saw one to whom could be applied that description by Lay (of the British and Foreign Bible Society), so often quoted, of the typical opium-smoker in China "with his lank and shrivelled limbs, tottering gait, sallow visage, feeble voice, and death-boding glance of eye, proclaiming him the most forlorn creature that treads upon the ground."

This fantastic description, paraded for years past for our sympathy, can be only applied to an infinitesimal number of the millions in China who smoke opium. It is a well-known fact that should a Chinese suffering from the extreme emaciation of disease be also in the habit of using the opium-pipe, it is the pipe and not the disease that in ninety-nine cases out of a hundred will be wrongly blamed as the cause of the emaciation.

During the year 1893 4275 tons of Indian opium were imported into China. The Chinese, we are told, plead to us with "outstretched necks" to cease the great wrong we are doing in forcing them to buy our opium. "Many a time," says the Rev. Dr. Hudson Taylor, "have I seen the Chinaman point with his thumb to Heaven, and say, 'There is Heaven up there! There is Heaven up there!' What did he mean by that? You may bring this opium to us; you may force it upon us; we cannot resist you, but there is a Power up there that will inflict vengeance." (*National Righteousness*, Dec. 1892, p. 13.)

But, with all respect to Dr. Hudson Taylor and his ingenious interpretation of the Chinaman's gesture, it is extremely difficult for the traveller in China to believe that the Chinese are sincere in their condemnation of opium and the opium traffic. "In some countries," says Wingrove Cooke, "words represent facts, but this is never the case in China." Li Hung Chang, the Viceroy of Chihli, in the well-known letter that he addressed to the Rev. F. Storrs Turner, the Secretary of the Society for the Suppression of the Opium Trade, on May 24th, 1881, a letter still widely circulated and perennially cited, says, "the poppy is certainly surreptitiously grown in some parts of China, notwithstanding the laws and frequent Imperial edicts prohibiting its cultivation."

Surreptitiously grown in some parts of China! Why, from the time I left Hupeh till I reached the boundary of Burma, a distance of 1700 miles, I never remember to have been out of sight of the poppy. Li Hung Chang continues, "I earnestly hope that your Society, and all right-minded men of your country, will support the efforts China is now making to escape from the thraldom of opium." And yet you are told in China that the largest growers of the poppy in China are the family of Li Hung Chang.

The Society for the Suppression of Opium has circulated by tens of thousands a petition which was forwarded to them from the Chinese—spontaneously, per favour of the missionaries. "Some tens of millions," this petition says, "some tens of millions of human beings in distress are looking on tiptoe with outstretched necks for salvation to come from you, O just and benevolent men of England! If not for the good or honour of your country, then for mercy's sake do this good deed now to save a people, and the rescued millions shall themselves be your great reward." (*China's Millions*, iv., 156.)

Assume, then, that the Chinese do not want our opium, and unavailingly beseech us to stay this nefarious traffic, which is as if "the Rivers Phlegethon and Lethe were united in it, carrying fire and destruction wherever it flows, and leaving a deadly forgetfulness wherever it has passed." (The Rev. Dr. Wells Williams. "The Middle Kingdom," i., 288.)

They do not want our opium, but they purchase from us 4275 tons per annum.

Of the eighteen provinces of China four only, Kiangsu, Chehkiang, Fuhkien, and Kuangtung use Indian opium, the remaining fourteen provinces use exclusively home-grown opium. Native-grown opium has entirely driven the imported opium from the markets of the Yangtse Valley; no Indian opium, except an insignificant quantity, comes up the river even as far as Hankow. The Chinese do not want our opium—it competes with their own. In the three adjoining provinces of Szechuen, Yunnan, and Kweichow they grow their own opium; but they grow more than they need, and have a large surplus to export to other parts of the Empire. The amount of this surplus can be estimated, because all exported opium has to pay customs and likin dues to the value of two shillings a pound, and the amount thus collected is known. Allowing no margin for opium that has evaded customs dues, and there are no more scientific smugglers than the Chinese, we still find that during the year 1893 2250 tons of opium were exported from the province of Szechuen, 1350 tons from Yunnan, and 450 tons from Kweichow, a total of 4050 tons exported by the rescued millions of three provinces only for the benefit of their fellow-countrymen, who, with outstretched necks, plead to England to leave them alone in their monopoly.

Edicts are still issued against the use of opium. They are drawn up by Chinese philanthropists over a quiet pipe of opium, signed by opium-smoking officials, whose revenues are derived from the poppy, and posted near fields of poppy by the opium-smoking magistrates who own them.

In the City Temple of Chungking there is a warning to opium-eaters. One of the fiercest devils in hell is there represented gloating over the crushed body of an opium-smoker; his protruding tongue is smeared with opium put there by the victim of "*yin*" (the opium craving), who wishes to renounce the habit. The opium thus collected is the perquisite of the Temple priests, and at the gate of the Temple there is a stall for the sale of opium fittings.

Morphia pills are sold in Chungking by the Chinese chemists to cure the opium habit. This profitable remedy was introduced by the foreign chemists of the coast ports and adopted by the Chinese. Its advantage is that it converts a desire for opium into a taste for morphia, a mode of treatment analogous to changing one's stimulant from colonial beer to methylated spirit. In 1893, 15,000 ounces of hydrochlorate of morphia were admitted into Shanghai alone.

The China Inland Mission have an important station at Chungking. It was opened seventeen years ago, in 1877, and is assisted by a representative of the Horsburgh Mission. The mission is managed by a charming English gentleman, who has exchanged all that could make life happy in England for the wretched discomfort of this malarious city. Every assistance I needed was given me by this kindly fellow who, like nearly all the China Inland Mission men, deserves success if he cannot command it. A more engaging personality I have rarely met, and it was sad to think that for the past year, 1893, no new convert was made by his Mission among the Chinese of Chungking. (*China's Millions*, January, 1894.) The Mission has been working short-handed, with only three missionaries instead of six, and progress has been much delayed in consequence.

The London Missionary Society, who have been here since 1889, have two missionaries at work, and have gathered nine communicants and six adherents. Their work is largely aided by an admirable hospital under Cecil Davenport, F.R.C.S., a countryman of my own. "Broad Benevolence" are the Chinese characters displayed over the entrance to the hospital, and they truthfully describe the work done by the hospital. In the chapel adjoining, a red screen is drawn down the centre of the church, and separates the men from the women—one of the chief pretexts that an Englishman has for going to church is thus denied the Chinaman, since he cannot cast an ogling eye through a curtain.

CHAPTER V.

THE JOURNEY FROM CHUNGKING TO SUIFU—CHINESE INNS.

I left the boat at Chungking and started on my land journey, going west 230 miles to Suifu. I had with me two coolies to carry my things, the one who received the higher pay having also to bring me my food, make my bed, and pay away my copper cash. They could not speak a single word of English. They were to be paid for the journey one 4*s*. 10*d.* and the other 5*s*. 7*d.* They were to be entitled to no perquisites, were to find themselves on the way, and take their chance of employment on the return journey. They were to lead me into Suifu on the seventh day out from Chungking. All that they undertook to do they did to my complete satisfaction.

On the morning of March 14th I set out from Chungking to cross 1600 miles over Western China to Burma. Men did not speak hopefully of my chance of getting through. There were the rains of June and July to be feared apart from other obstacles.

Père Lorain, the Procureur of the French Mission, who spoke from an experience of twenty-five years of China, assured me that, speaking no Chinese, unarmed, unaccompanied, except by two poor coolies of the humblest class, and on foot, I would have *les plus grandes difficultés*, and Monsieur Haas, the Consul *en commission*, was equally pessimistic. The evening before starting, the Consul and my friend Carruthers (one of the *Inverness Courier* Carruthers) gave me a lesson in Chinese. "French before breakfast" was nothing to this kind of cramming. I learnt a dozen useful words and phrases, and rehearsed them in the morning to a member of the Inland Mission, who cheered me by saying that it would be a clever Chinaman indeed who could understand Chinese like mine.

I left on foot by the West Gate, being accompanied so far by A. J. Little, an experienced traveller and authority on China, manager in Chungking of the Chungking Transport Company (which deals especially with the transport of cargo from Ichang up the rapids), whose book on "The Yangtse Gorges" is known to every reader of books on China.

I was dressed as a Chinese teacher in thickly-wadded Chinese gown, with pants, stockings, and sandals, with Chinese hat and pigtail. In my dress I looked a person of weight. I must acknowledge that my outfit was very poor; but this was not altogether a disadvantage, for my men would have the less temptation to levy upon it. Still it would have been awkward if my men had taken it into their heads to walk off with my things, because I could not have explained my loss. My chief efforts, I knew, throughout my journey would be applied in the direction of inducing the Chinese to treat me with the respect that was undoubtedly due to one who, in their own words, had done them the "exalted honour" of visiting "their mean and contemptible country." For I could not afford a private sedan chair, though I knew that Baber had written that "no traveller in Western China who possesses any sense of self-respect should journey without a sedan chair, not necessarily as a conveyance, but for the honour and glory of the thing. Unfurnished with this indispensable token of respectability he is liable to be thrust aside on the highway, to be kept waiting at ferries, to be relegated to the worst inn's worst room, and generally to be treated with indignity, or, what is sometimes worse, with familiarity, as a peddling footpad who, unable to gain a living in his own country, has come to subsist on China." ("Travels and Researches in Western China," p. 1.)

Six li out (two miles), beyond the gravemounds there is a small village where ponies are kept for hire. A kind friend came with me as far as the village to act as my interpreter, and here he engaged a pony for me. It was to carry me ten miles for fourpence. It was small, rat-like and wiry, and was steered by the "mafoo" using the tail like a tiller. Mounted then on this small beast, which carried me without wincing, I jogged along over the stone-flagged pathway, down hill and along valley, scaling and descending the long flights of steps which lead over the mountains. The bells of the pony jingled merrily; the day was fine and the sun shone behind the clouds. My two coolies sublet their contracts, and had their loads borne for a fraction of a farthing per mile by coolies returning empty-handed to Suifu.

ON THE MAIN ROAD TO SUIFU.

Fu-to-kuan four miles from Chungking is a powerful hill-fort that guards the isthmus where the Yangtse and the Little River come nearly together before encircling Chungking. Set in the face of the cliff is a gigantic image of Buddha. Massive stone portals, elaborately carved, and huge commemorative tablets cut from single blocks of stone and deeply engraved, here adorn the highway. The archways have been erected by command of the Emperor, but at the expense of their relatives, to the memory of virtuous widows who have refused to remarry, or who have sacrificed their lives on the death of their husbands. Happy are those whose names are thus recorded, for not only do they obtain ten thousand merits in heaven, as well as the Imperial recognition of the Son of Heaven on earth; but as an additional reward their souls may, on entering the world a second time, enjoy the indescribable felicity of inhabiting the bodies of men.

Cases where the widow has thus brought honour to the family are constantly recorded in the pages of the *Peking Gazette*. One of more than usual merit is described in the *Peking Gazette* of June 10th, 1892. The story runs:—

"The Governor of Shansi narrates the story of a virtuous wife who destroyed herself after the death of her husband. The lady was a native of T'ienmen, in Hupeh, and both her father and grandfather were officials who attained the rank of Taotai. When she was little more than ten years old her mother fell ill. The child cut flesh from her body and mixed it with the medicines and thus cured her parent. The year before last she was married to an expectant magistrate. Last autumn, just after he had obtained an appointment, he was taken violently ill. She mixed her flesh with the medicine but it was in vain, and he died shortly afterwards. Overcome with grief, and without parents or children to demand her care, she determined that she would not live. Only waiting till she had completed the arrangements for her husband's interment, she swallowed gold and powder of lead. She handed her trousseau to her relatives to defray her funeral expenses, and made presents to the younger members of the family and the servants, after which, draped in her state robes, she sat waiting her end. The poison began to work and soon all was over. The memorialist thinks that the case is one which should be recorded in the erection of a memorial arch, and he asks the Emperor to grant that honour to the deceased lady." ("*Granted.*")

Near the base of the rock upon which the hill-fort is built, and between it and the city, the Methodist Episcopalian Mission of the U.S.A. commenced in 1886 to build what the Chinese, in their ignorance, feared was a foreign fort, but what was nothing more than a mission house in a compound surrounded by a powerful wall. The indiscreet mystery associated with its erection was the exciting cause of the anti-foreign riot of July, 1886.

From the fort the pathway led us through a beautiful country. We met numbers of sedan chairs, borne by two coolies, or three, according to the importance of the traveller. There were Chinese gentlemen mounted on ponies or mules; there were strings of coolies swinging along under prodigious loads of salt and coal, and huge bales of raw cotton. Buffaloes with slow and painful steps were ploughing the paddy fields, the water up to their middles—the primitive plough and share guided by half-naked Chinamen. Along the road there are inns and tea-houses every mile or two, for this is one of the most frequented roadways of China. At one good-sized village my cook signed to me to dismount; the mafoo and pony were paid off, and I sat down in an inn, and was served with an excellent dish of rice and minced beef. The inn was crowded and open to the street. Despite my Chinese dress anyone could see that I was a foreigner, but I was not far enough away from Chungking to excite much curiosity. The other diners treated me with every courtesy; they offered me of their dishes, and addressed me in Chinese—a compliment which I repaid by thanking them blandly in English.

Now I went on, on foot, though I had difficulty in keeping pace with my men. Behind the village we climbed a very steep hill by interminable steps, and passed under an archway at the summit. Descending the hill, my cook engaged in a controversy with a thin lad whom he had hired to carry his load a stage. The dispute waxed warm, and, while they stopped to argue it out at leisure, I went on. My cook, engaged through the kind offices of the Inland Mission, was a man of strong convictions; and in the last I saw of the dispute he was pulling the unfortunate coolie downhill by the pigtail. When he overtook me he was alone and smiling cheerfully, well satisfied with himself for having settled *that* little dispute. The road became more level, and we got over the ground quickly.

Late in the evening I was led into a crowded inn in a large village, where we were to stay the night. We had come twenty-seven miles, and had begun well. I was shown into a room with three straw-covered wooden bedsteads, a rough table, lit by a lighted taper in a saucer of oil, a rough seat, and the naked earth floor. Hot water was brought me to wash with and tea to drink, and my man prepared me an excellent supper. My baggage was in the corner; it consisted of two light bamboo boxes with Chinese padlocks, a bamboo hamper, and a roll of bedding covered with oilcloth. An oilcloth is indispensable to the traveller in China, for placed next the straw on a Chinese bed it is impassable to bugs. And during all my journey in China I was never disturbed in my sleep by this unpleasant pest. Bugs in China are sufficiently numerous, but their numbers cannot be compared with the gregarious hosts that disturb the traveller in Spain.

My last night in Spain was spent in Cadiz, the most charming city in the peninsula. I had lost the last boat off to the steamer, on which I was a passenger; it was late at night, and I knew of no inn near the landing. At midnight, as I was walking in the Plaza, called after that revered monarch, Queen Isabel II., I was spoken to at the door of a fonda, and asked if I wanted a bedroom. It was the taberna "La Valenciana." I was delighted; it was the very thing I was looking for, I said. The innkeeper had just one room unoccupied, and he showed me upstairs into a plain, homely apartment, which I was pleased to engage for the night. "*Que usted descanse bien*" (may you sleep well), said the landlord, and left me. Keeping the candle burning I tumbled into bed, for I was very tired, but jumped out almost immediately, despite my fatigue. I turned down the clothes, and saw the bugs gathering in the centre from all parts of the bed. I collected a dozen or two, and put them in a basin of water, and, dressing myself, went out on the landing and called the landlord.

He came up yawning.

"Sir," he said, "do you wish anything?"

"Nothing; but it is impossible, absolutely impossible, for me to sleep in that bed."

"But why, señor?"

"Because it is full of bugs."

"Oh no, sir, that cannot be, that cannot be; there is not a bug in the house."

"But I have seen them."

"You must be mistaken; it is impossible that there can be a bug in the house."

"But I have caught some."

"It makes twenty years that I live in this house, and never have I seen such a thing."

"Pardon me, but will you do me the favour to look at this basin?"

"Sir, you are right, you are completely right; it is the weather; *every bed in Cadiz is now full of them.*"

In the morning, and every morning, we were away at daylight, and walked some miles before breakfast. All the way to Suifu the road is a paved causeway, 3 feet 6 inches to 6 feet wide, laid down with dressed flags of stone; and here, at least, it cannot be alleged, as the Chinese proverb would have it, that their roads are "good for ten years and bad for ten hundred." There are, of course, no fences; the main road picks its way through the cultivated fields; no traveller ever thinks of trespassing from the roadway, nor did I ever see any question of trespass between neighbours. In this law-abiding country the peasantry conspicuously follow the Confucian maxim taught in China four hundred years before Christ, "Do not unto others what you would not have others do unto you." Every rood of ground is under tillage.

Hills are everywhere terraced like the seats of an amphitheatre, each terrace being irrigated from the one below it by a small stream of water, drawn up an inclined plain by a continuous chain bucket, worked with a windlass by either hand or foot. The poppy is everywhere abundant and well tended; there are fields of winter wheat, and pink-flowered beans, and beautiful patches of golden rape-seed. Dotted over the landscape are pretty Szechuen farmhouses in groves of trees. Splendid banyan trees give grateful shelter to the traveller. Of this country it could be written as a Chinese traveller wrote of England, "their fertile hills, adorned with the richest luxuriance, resemble in the outline of their summits the arched eyebrows of a fair woman."

The country is well populated, and a continuous stream of people is moving along the road. Grand memorial arches span the roadway, many of them notable efforts of monumental skill, with columns and architraves carved with elephants and deer, and flowers and peacocks, and the Imperial seven-tailed dragon of China. Chinese art is seen at its best in this rich province.

CULTIVATION IN TERRACES.
In the foreground the poppy in bloom.

SCENE IN SZECHUEN.

I lived, of course, in the common Chinese inn, ate Chinese food, and was everywhere treated with courtesy and good nature; but at first I found it trying to be such an object of curiosity; to have to do all things in unsecluded publicity; to have to push my way through streets thronged by the curious to see the foreigner. My meals I ate in the presence of the street before gaping crowds. When they came too close I told them politely in English to keep back a little, and they did so if I illustrated my words by gesture. When I scratched my head and they saw the spurious pigtail, they smiled; when I flicked the dust off the table with my pigtail, they laughed hilariously.

The wayside inns are usually at the side of an arcade of grass and bamboo stretched above the main road. Two or three ponies are usually waiting here for hire, and expectant coolies are eager to offer their services. In engaging a pony you make an offer casually, as if you had no desire in the world of its being accepted, and then walk on as if you had no intention whatever of riding for the next month. The mafoo demands more, but will come down; you stick to your offer, though prepared to increase it; so demand and offer you exchange with the mafoo till the width of the village is between you, and your voices are almost out of hearing, when you come to terms.

Suppose I wanted a chair to give me a rest for a few miles—it was usually slung under the rafters—Laokwang (my cook) unobserved by anyone but me pointed to it with his thumb inquiringly. I nodded assent and apparently nothing more happened and the conversation, of which I was quite ignorant, continued. We left together on foot, my man still maintaining a crescendo conversation with the inn people till well away. When almost out of hearing he called out something and an answer came faintly back from the distance. It was his ultimatum as regards price and its acceptance—they had been bargaining all the time. My man motioned to me to wait, said the one word "*chiaodza*" (sedan chair) and in a few moments the chair of bamboo and wicker came rapidly down the road carried by two bearers. They put down the chair before me and bowed to me; I took my seat and was borne easily and pleasantly along at four miles an hour at a charge of less than one penny a mile.

My men received nearly 400 cash a day each; but from time to time they sweated their contract to unemployed coolies and had their loads carried for so little as sixty cash (one penny halfpenny), for two-thirds of a day's journey.

At nightfall we always reached some large village or town where my cook selected the best inn for my resting place, the best inn in such cases being usually the one which promised him the largest squeeze. All the towns through which the road passes swarm with inns, for there is an immense floating population to provide for. Competition is keen. Touts stand at the doorway of every inn, who excitedly waylay the traveller and cry the merits of their houses. At the counter inside the entrance, piles of pukais (the warm Chinese bedding), are stacked for hire—few of the travellers carry their own bedding. The inns are sufficiently comfortable. The bedrooms are in one or two stories and are arranged round one or more, or a succession of courts. The cheapness is to be commended. For supper, bed, and light, tea during the night and tea before starting in the morning, and various little comforts, such as hot water for washing, the total charge for the six nights of my journey from Chungking to Suifu was 840 cash (1*s.* 9*d.*).

Rice was my staple article of diet; eggs, fowls, and vegetables were also abundant and cheap; but I avoided pork which is the flesh universally eaten throughout China by all but the Mohammedans and vegetarians. In case of emergency I had a few tins of foreign stores with me. I made it a point never to drink water—I drank tea. No Chinaman ever drinks anything cold. Every half hour or hour he can reach an inn or teahouse where tea can be infused for him in a few minutes. The price of a bowl of tea with a pinch of tea-leaves, filled and refilled with hot water *ad lib*, is two cash—equal to the twentieth part of one penny. Pork has its weight largely added to by being injected with water, the point of the syringe being passed into a large vein; this is usually described as the Chinese method of "watering stock."

On the third day we were at Yuenchuan, sixty-three miles from Chungking. On the 5th, we passed through Luchow, one of the richest and most populous cities on the Upper Yangtse, and at noon next day we again reached the Yangtse at the Temple of the Goddess of Mercy, two miles down the river from the large town of Lanchihsien. According to my interpretation of the gesticulations of Laokwang, we were then forty miles from Suifu, and a beautiful sunny afternoon before us, in which to easily cover one half the distance. But I must reckon with my guide. He wished to remain here; I wished to go on; but as I could not understand his Chinese explanation, nor advance any protest except in English, of which he was innocent, I could only look aggrieved and make a virtue of a necessity. He did, however, convey to me his solemn assurance that to-morrow (*ming tien*) he would conduct me into Suifu before sunset. An elderly Chinaman, who had given us the advantage of his company at various inns during the last three days, here entered into the conversation, produced his watch, and, with his hand over his heart, which, in a Chinaman, is in the centre of the breast-bone, added his sacred asseveration to my guide's. So I stayed. We were quite a friendly party travelling together.

In the middle of the night a light was flashed into our room and a voice pealed out an alarm that awoke even my two Chinese, who always obligingly slept in the same room with me. I had protested against their doing so, but they mistook my expostulation for approbation. We rose at once, and came down the steep bank to a boat that was lying stern to shore showing a light. I was charmed to get such an early start, and construed the indications into a ferry boat to take me across the river, whence we would go by a short route into Suifu. The boat was loaded with sugar and had a crew of two men and three boys. There was an awning over the cargo, but most of the space under it was already occupied by twelve amiable Chinese, among whom were six promiscuous friends, who had kept with us for several stages, and had, I imagine, derived some pecuniary advantages from my company. Yet this was not a ferry boat, but a passenger boat engaged especially for me to carry me to Suifu before nightfall. The Chinese passengers had courteously projected their companionship upon the inarticulate stranger. An elderly gentleman, with huge goggles and long nails, whose fingers were stained with opium, was the pacificator of the party, and calmed the frequent wranglings in which the other eighteen Chinese engaged with much earnestness.

Well, this boat—a leaky, heavy, old tub that had to be tracked nearly all the way—carried me the forty miles to Suifu within contract time. The boatmen on board worked sixteen hours without any rest except at two hasty meals; the frayed towrope never parted at any rapid, and only once did our boat get entangled with any other. Towards sundown we were abreast of the fine pagoda of Suifu, and a little later were at the landing. The city is on a high, level shelf of land with high hills behind it. It lies in the angle of bifurcation formed by the Yangtse river (here known as the "River of Golden Sand"), going west, and the Min, or Chentu river, going north to Chentu, the capital city of the province. I landed below the southern wall, and said good-bye to my companions. Climbing up the bank into the city, I passed by a busy thoroughfare to the pretty home of the Inland Mission, where I received a kind welcome from the gentleman and lady who conduct the mission, and a charming English girl, also in the mission, who lives with them.

CHAPTER VI.

THE CITY OF SUIFU—THE CHINA INLAND MISSION, WITH SOME GENERAL REMARKS ABOUT MISSIONARIES IN CHINA.

At Suifu I rested a day in order to engage new coolies to go with me to Chaotong in Yunnan Province, distant 290 miles. Neither of my two Chungking men would re-engage to go further. Yet in Chungking Laokwang the cook had declared that he was prepared to go with me all the way to Talifu. But now he feared the loneliness of the road to Chaotong. The way, he said, was mountainous and little trodden, and robbers would see the smallness of our party and "come down and stab us." I was then glad that I had not paid him the retaining fee he had asked in Chungking to take me to Tali.

I called upon the famous Catholic missionaries, the Provicaire Moutot and Père Béraud, saw the more important sights and visited some newly-arrived missionaries of the American Board of Missions. Four of the Americans were living together. I called with the Inland missionary at a time when they were at dinner. We were shown into the drawing-room, where the most conspicuous ornament was a painted scroll with a well executed drawing of the poppy in flower, a circumstance which would confirm the belief of the Chinese who saw it, that the poppy is held in veneration by foreigners. While we waited we heard the noise of dinner gradually cease, and then the door opened and one of the single ladies entered. She was fierce to look at, tall as a grenadier, with a stride like a camel; she was picking her teeth with a hairpin. She courteously expressed her regret that she could not invite us to dinner. "Waal now," she said, looking at us from under her spectacles, "ahm real sorry I caan't ask you to have somethin' to eat, but we've just finished, and I guess there ain't nothin' left."

Fourteen American missionaries were lately imported into Suifu in one shipment. Most of them are from Chicago. One of their earliest efforts will be to translate into Chinese Mr. Stead's "If Christ came to Chicago," in order the better to demonstrate to the Chinese the lofty standard of morality, virtue, probity, and honour attained by the Christian community that sent them to China to enlighten the poor benighted heathen in this land of darkness.

Szechuen is a Catholic stronghold. There are nominally one hundred thousand Catholics in the province, representing the labours of many French missionaries for a period of rather more than two hundred years. Actually, however, there are only sixty thousand Chinese in the province who could be called Catholics. To use the words of the Provicaire, the Chinese are "*trôp matèrialistes*" to become Christian, and, as they are all "liars and robbers," the faith is not easily propagated amongst them. Rarely have I met two more charming men than these brave missionaries. French, they told me, I speak with the "*vrai accent parisien*," a compliment which I have no doubt is true, though it conflicts with my experience in Paris, where most of the true Parisians to whom I spoke in their own language gave me the same look of intelligence that I observe in the Chinaman when I address him in English. Père Moutot has been twenty-three years in China—six years at the sacred Mount Omi, and seventeen years in Suifu; Père Béraud has been twenty-three years in Suifu. They both speak Chinese to perfection, and have been co-workers with the bishop in the production of a Mandarin-French dictionary just published at Sicawei; they dress as Chinese, and live as Chinese in handsome mission premises built in Chinese style. There is a pretty chapel in the compound with scrolls and memorial tablets presented by Chinese Catholics, a school for boys attended by fifty ragamuffins, a nunnery and girls' school, and a fit residence for the venerable bishop. When showing me the chapel, the Provicaire told me of the visit of one of Our Lord's Apostles to Suifu. He seemed to have no doubt himself of the truth of the story. Tradition says that St. Thomas came to China, and, if further proof were wanting, there is the black image of Tamo worshipped to this day in many of the temples of Szechuen. Scholars, however, identify this image and its marked Hindoo features with that of the Buddhist evangelist Tamo, who is known to have visited China in the sixth century.

In Suifu there is a branch of the China Inland Mission under an enthusiastic young missionary, who was formerly a French polisher in Hereford. He is helped by an amiable wife and by a charming English girl scarcely out of her teens. The missionary's work has, he tells me, been "abundantly blessed,"—he has baptised six converts in the last three years. A fine type of man is this missionary, brave and self-reliant, sympathetic and self-denying, hopeful and self-satisfied. His views as a missionary are well-defined. I give them in his own words:—"Those Chinese who have never heard the Gospel will be judged by the Almighty as He thinks fit"—a contention which does not admit of dispute—"but those Chinese who have heard the Christian doctrine, and still steel their hearts against the Holy Ghost, will assuredly go to hell; there is no help for them, they can believe and they won't; had they believed, their reward would be eternal; they refuse to believe and their punishment will be eternal." But the destruction that awaits the Chinese must be pointed out to them with becoming gentleness, in accordance with the teaching of the Rev. S. F. Woodin, of the American Baptist Mission, Foochow, who says:—"There are occasions when we must speak that awful word 'hell,' but this should always be done in a spirit of earnest love." (*Records* of the Shanghai Missionary Conference, 1877, p. 91.) It was a curious study to observe the equanimity with which this good-natured man contemplates the work he has done in China, when to obtain six dubious conversions he has on his own confession sent some thousands of unoffending Chinese *en enfer bouillir éternellement*.

But, if the teaching of this good missionary is unwelcome to the Chinese, and there are hundreds in China who teach as he does, how infinitely more distasteful must be the teaching of both the Founder and the Secretary of the Mission which sent him to China.

"They are God's lost ones who are in China," says Mr. C. L. Morgan, editor of *The Christian*, "and God cares for them and yearns over them." (*China's Millions*, 1879, p. 94.) "The millions of Chinese," (who have never heard the Gospel,) says Mr. B. Broomhall, secretary of the China Inland Mission, and editor of *China's Millions*, "where are they going, what is to be their future? What is to be their condition beyond the grave? Oh, tremendous question! It is an awful thing to contemplate—but they perish; that is what God says." ("Evangelisation of the World," p. 70.) "The heathen are all guilty in God's eyes; as guilty they perish." (*Id.*, 101.) "Do we believe that these millions are without hope in the next world? We turn the leaves of God's Word in vain, for there we find no hope; not only that, but positive words to the contrary. Yes! we believe it." (*Id.*, p. 199.)

The Rev. Dr. Hudson Taylor, the distinguished Founder of the Mission, certainly believes it, and has frequently stated his belief in public. Ancestral worship is the keystone of the religion of the Chinese; "the keystone also of China's social fabric." And "the worship springs," says the Rev. W. A. P. Martin, D.D., LL.D., of the Tung Wen College, Peking, "from some of the best principles of human nature. The first conception of a life beyond the grave was, it is thought, suggested by a desire to commune with deceased parents." ("The Worship of Ancestors—a plea for toleration.") But Dr. Hudson Taylor condemned bitterly this plea for toleration. "Ancestral worship," he said (it was at the Shanghai Missionary Conference of May, 1890), "Ancestral worship is idolatry from beginning to end, the whole of it, and everything connected with it." China's religion is idolatry, the Chinese are universally idolatrous, and the fate that befalls idolaters is carefully pointed out by Dr. Taylor:—"Their part is in the lake of fire."

"These millions of China," I quote again from Dr. Taylor, "These millions of China" (who have never heard the Gospel), "are unsaved. Oh! my dear friends, may I say one word about that condition? The Bible says of the heathen, that they are without hope; will you say there is good hope for them of whom the Word of God says, 'they are without hope, without God in the world'?" (Missionary Conference of 1888, *Records*, i., 176.)

"There are those who know more about the state of the heathen than did the Apostle Paul, who wrote under the inspiration of the Holy Ghost, 'They that sin without law, perish without law,' nay, there are those who are not afraid to contradict the revelation of Jesus Christ, which God gave unto Him to shew unto His servants, in which He solemnly affirms that 'idolators and all liars, their part shall be in the lake that burneth with fire and brimstone.' Such being the state of the unsaved of China, do not their urgent needs claim from us that with *agonising eagerness* we should hasten to proclaim everywhere the message through which alone deliverance can be found?" (*Ut supra*, ii., 31.)

Look then at the enormous difficulty which the six hundred and eleven missionaries, of the China Inland Mission, raise up against themselves, the majority of whom are presumably in agreement with the teaching of their director, Dr. Hudson Taylor. They tell the Chinese inquirer that his unconverted father, who never heard the Gospel, has, like Confucius, perished eternally. But the chief of all virtues in China is filial piety; the strongest emotion that can move the heart of a Chinaman is the supreme desire to follow in the footsteps of his father. Conversion with him means not only eternal separation from the father who gave him life, but the "immediate liberation of his ancestors to a life of beggary, to inflict sickness and all manner of evil on the neighbourhood."

I believe that it is now universally recognised that the most difficult of all missionary fields—incomparably the most difficult—is China. Difficulties assail the missionary at every step; and every honest man, whether his views be broad or high or low, must sympathise with the earnest efforts the missionaries are making for the good and advancement of the Chinese.

Look for example at the difficulty there is in telling a Chinese, who has been taught to regard the love of his parents as his chief duty, as his forefathers have been taught for hundreds of generations before him—the difficulty there is in explaining to him, in his own language, the words of Christ, "If any man come to Me and hate not his father, he cannot be My disciple. For I am come to set a man at variance against his father."

In the patriarchal system of government which prevails in China, the most awful crime that a son can commit, is to kill his parent, either father or mother. And this is said to be, though the description is no doubt abundantly exaggerated, the punishment of his crime. He is put to death by the "*Ling chi*," or "degrading and slow process," and his younger brothers are beheaded; his house is razed to the ground and the earth under it dug up several feet deep; his neighbours are severely punished; his principal teacher is decapitated; the district magistrate is deprived of his office; and the higher officials of the province degraded three degrees in rank.

Such is the enormity of the crime of parricide in China; yet it is to the Chinese who approves of the severity of this punishment that the missionary has to preach, "And the children shall rise up against their parents and cause them to be put to death."

The China Inland Mission, as a body of courageous workers, brave travellers, unselfish and kindly men endowed with every manly virtue that can command our admiration, is worthy of all the praise that can be bestowed on it. Most of its members are men who have been saved after reaching maturity, and delicately-nurtured emotional girls with heightened religious feelings.

Too often entirely ignorant of the history of China, a mighty nation which has "witnessed the rise to glory and the decay of Egypt, Assyria, Babylonia, Persia, Greece, and Rome, and still remains the only monument of ages long bygone," of its manners and polity, customs and religions, and of the extraordinary difficulties in the acquirement of its language, too often forgetful that the Chinese are a people whose "prepossessions and prejudices and cherished judgments are the growth of millenniums," they come to China hoping that miraculous assistance will aid them in their exposition of the Christian doctrine, in language which is too often impenetrable darkness to its hearers.

"They are God's lost ones who are in China, and God cares for them and yearns over them," and men who were in England respectable artisans, with an imperfect hold of their own language, come to China, in response to the "wail of the dying millions," to stay this "awful ruin of souls," who, at the rate of 33,000 a day, are "perishing without hope, having sinned without law."

Six months after their arrival they write to *China's Millions*: "Now for the news! Glorious news this time! Our services crowded! Such bright intelligent faces! So eager to hear the good news! They seemed to drink in every word, and to listen as if they were afraid that a word might be lost." Five years later they write: "The first convert in Siao Wong Miao was a young man named Sengleping, a matseller. He was very earnest in his efforts to spread the Gospel, but about the beginning of the year he became insane. The poor man lost his reason, but not his piety." (*China's Millions*, iv., 5, 95, and 143).

A young English girl at this mission, who has been more than a year in China, tells me that she has never felt the Lord so near her as she has since she came to China, nor ever realised so entirely His abundant goodness. Poor thing, it made me sad to talk to her. In England she lived in a bright and happy home with brothers and sisters, in a charming climate. She was always well and full of life and vigour, surrounded by all that can make life worth living. In China she is never well; she is almost forgetting what is the sensation of health; she is anæmic and apprehensive; she has nervous headaches and neuralgia; she can have no pleasure, no amusement whatever; her only relaxation is taking her temperature;

her only diversion a prayer meeting. She is cooped up in a Chinese house in the unchanging society of a married couple—the only exercise she can permit herself is a prison-like walk along the top of the city at the back of the mission. Her lover, a refined English gentleman who is also in the mission, lives a week's journey away, in Chungking, a depressing fever-stricken city where the sun is never seen from November to June, and blazes with unendurable fierceness from July to October. In England he was full of strength and vigour, fond of boating and a good lawn-tennis player. In China he is always ill, anæmic, wasted, and dyspeptic, constantly subject to low forms of fever, and destitute of appetite. But more agonising than his bad health is the horrible reality of the unavailing sacrifice he is making—no converts but "outcasts subsidised to forsake their family altars;" no reward but the ultimate one which his noble self-devotion is laying up for himself in Heaven. No man with a healthy brain can discern "Blessing" in the work of these two missionaries, nor be blind to the fact that it is the reverse of worshipful to return effusive thanks to the great Almighty, "who yearns over the Chinese, His lost ones," for "vouchsafing the abundant mercies" of a harvest of six doubtful converts as the work of three missionaries for three years.

There are 180,000 people in Suifu, and, as is the case with Chinese cities, a larger area than that under habitation is occupied by the public graveyard outside the city, which covers the hill slopes for miles and miles. The number of opium-smokers is so large that the question is not, who does smoke opium, but who doesn't. In the mission street alone, besides the Inland Mission, the Buddhist Temple, Mohammedan Mosque, and Roman Catholic Mission, there are eight opium-houses. Every bank, silk shop, and hong, of any pretension whatever, throughout the city, has its opium-room, with the lamp always lit ready for the guest. Opium-rooms are as common as smoking rooms are with us. A whiff of opium rather than a nip of whisky is the preliminary to business in Western China.

OPIUM-SMOKING.

An immensely rich city is Suifu with every advantage of position, on a great waterway in the heart of a district rich in coal and minerals and inexhaustible subterranean reservoirs of brine. Silks and furs and silverwork, medicines, opium and whitewax, are the chief articles of export, and as, fortunately for us, Western China can grow but little cotton, the most important imports are Manchester goods.

Szechuen is by far the richest province of the eighteen that constitute the Middle Kingdom. Its present Viceroy, Liu, is a native of Anhwei; he is, therefore, a countryman of Li Hung Chang to whom he is related by marriage, his daughter having married Li Hung Chang's nephew. Its provincial Treasurer is believed to occupy the richest post held by any official in the empire. It is worth noticing that the present provincial Treasurer, Kung Chao-yuan, has just been made (1894) Minister Plenipotentiary to Great Britain, France, Italy, Belgium, Sweden and Norway, and one can well believe how intense was his chagrin when he received this appointment from the "Imperial Supreme" compelling him, as it did, to forsake the tombs of his ancestors—to leave China for

England on a fixed salary, and vacate the most coveted post in the empire, a post where the opportunities of personal enrichment are simply illimitable.

In Suifu there are two magistrates, both with important yamens. The Fu magistrate is the "Father of the City," the Hsien magistrate is the "Mother of the City;" and the "Mother of the City" largely favours the export opium trade. When Protestant missionaries first came to the city in 1888 and 1889 there was little friendliness shown to them. Folk would cry after the missionary, "There goes the foreigner that eats children," and children would be hurriedly hidden, as if from fear. These taunts were at first disregarded. But there came a time when living children were brought to the mission for sale as food; whereupon the mission made formal complaint in the yamen, and the Fu at once issued a proclamation checking the absurd tales about the foreigners, and ordering the citizens, under many pains and penalties, to treat the foreigners with respect. There has been no trouble since, and, as we walked through the crowded streets, I could see nothing but friendly indifference. Reference to this and other sorrows is made in the missionary's report to *China's Millions*, November, 1893:—

"Soon after this trial had passed away (the rumours of baby eating), still more painful internal sorrow arose. One of the members, who had been baptised three years before and had been useful as a preacher of the Gospel, fell into grievous sin, and had to be excluded from Church fellowship. Then a little later a very promising inquirer, who had been cured of opium-smoking and appeared to be growing in grace, fell again under its power. While still under a cloud he was suddenly removed during the cholera visitation."

The China Inland Mission has pleasant quarters close under the city wall. Their pretty chapel opens into the street, and displays prominently the proclamation of the Emperor concerning the treaty rights of foreign missionaries. Seven children, all of whom are girls, are boarded on the premises, and are being brought up as Christians. They are pretty, bright children, the eldest, a girl of fourteen, particularly so. All are large-footed, and they are to be married to Christian converts. When this fact becomes known it is hoped that more young Chinamen than at present may be emulous to be converted. All seven are foundlings from Chungking where, wrapped in brown paper, they were at different times dropped over the wall into the Mission compound. They have been carefully reared by the Mission.

At the boys' school fifty smart boys, all heathens, were at their lessons. They were learning different subjects, and were teaching their ears the "tones" by reading at the top of their voices. The noise was awful. None but a Chinese boy could study in such a din. In China, when the lesson is finished, the class is silent; noise, therefore, is the indication of work in a Chinese school—not silence.

The schoolmaster was a ragged-looking loafer, dressed in grey. He was in mourning, and had been unshaven for forty-two days in consequence of the death of his father. This was an important day of mourning, because on this day, the forty-second after his death, his dead father became, for the first time, aware of his own decease. A week later, on the forty-ninth day, the funeral rites would cease.

CHAPTER VII.

SUIFU TO CHAOTONG, WITH SOME REMARKS ON THE PROVINCE OF YUNNAN—CHINESE PORTERS, POSTAL ARRANGEMENTS, AND BANKS.

I engaged three new men in Suifu, who undertook to take me to Chaotong, 290 miles, in thirteen days, special inducement being held out to them in the shape of a reward of one shilling each to do the journey in eleven days. Their pay was to be seven shillings and threepence each, apart from the bonus, and of course they had to find themselves. They brought me from the coolie-hong, where they were engaged, an agreement signed by the hong-master, which was to be returned to them in Chaotong, and remitted to their master as a receipt for my safe delivery.

Every condition detailed in the agreement they faithfully carried out, and they took me to Chaotong in ten days and a half, though the ordinary time is fourteen days.

One of the three was a convert, one of the six surviving converts made by the aggregate Inland Mission of Suifu in six years. He was an excellent good fellow, rather dull of wits, but a credit to the Mission. To him was intrusted the paying away of my money—he carried no load. When he wanted money he was to show me his empty hands, and say "*Muta tsien! muta tsien!*" (I have no money! I have no money!).

I knew that perfect confidence could be placed in the convert, apart from the reason of his conversion, because he had a father living in Suifu. Were he to rob me or do me a wrong and run away, we could arrest his father and have him detained in the yamen prison till his son returned. Nothing in China gives one greater protection against fraud and injury than the law which holds a father responsible for the wrongdoing of his son, or, where there is no father, an elder son culpable for the misdeed of the younger.

On the morning of March 22nd we started for Chaotong in Yunnan province. The Inland Missionary and a Brother from the American Baptist Mission kindly came with me for the first thirteen miles. My route lay west on the north bank of the Yangtse, but later, after crossing the Yangtse, would be nearly south to Chaotong.

Shortly before leaving, the *chairen* or yamen-runner—the policeman, that is to say—sent by the Magistrate to shadow me to Tak-wan-hsien, called at the Mission to request that the interpreter would kindly remind the traveller, who did not speak Chinese, that it was customary to give wine-money to the chairen at the end of the journey. The request was reasonable. All the way from Chungking I had been accompanied by yamen-runners without knowing it. The chairen is sent partly for the protection of the traveller, but mainly for the protection of the Magistrate; for, should a traveller provided with a passport receive any injury, the Magistrate of the district would be liable to degradation. It was arranged, therefore, with the convert that, on our arrival in Tak-wan-hsien, I was to give the chairen, if satisfied with his services, 200 cash (five pence); but, if he said "*gowshun! gowshun!*" (a little more! a little more!) with sufficient persistence, I was to increase the reward gradually to sevenpence halfpenny. This was to be the limit; and the chairen, I was assured, would consider this a generous return for accompanying me 227 miles over one of the most mountainous roads in China.

It was a pleasant walk along the river-bank in the fertile alluvial, where the poppy in white flower and tobacco were growing, and where fields of yellow rape-seed alternated with beds of rushes—the rape-seed yielding the oil, and the rushes the rushlights of Chinese lamps. Flocks of wild geese were within easy shot on the sandbanks—the "peaceful geese," whose virtues are extolled by every Chinaman. They live in pairs, and, if one dies, its mate will be for ever faithful to its memory. Such virtue is worthy of being recorded on the arch which here spans the roadway, whose Chinese characters, *Shen* (holy), *Chi* (will), show that it was erected by the holy decree of the Emperor to perpetuate the memory of some widow who never remarried.

As we walked along the missionary gave instructions to my men. "In my grace I had given them very light loads; hurry and they would be richly rewarded"—one shilling extra for doing fourteen stages in eleven days.

At an inn, under the branches of a banyan tree, we sat down and had a cup of tea. While we waited, a hawker came and sat near us. He was peddling live cats. In one of his two baskets was a cat that bore a curious resemblance to a tortoise-shell tabby, that till a week ago had been a pet in the Inland Mission. It had disappeared mysteriously; it had died, the Chinese servant said; and here it was reincarnated.

At the market town the missionaries left me to go on alone with my three men. I had seventeen miles still to go before night.

It was midday, and the sun was hot, so a chair was arranged for to take me the seventeen miles to Anpien. It was to cost 320 cash (eightpence), but, just before leaving, the grasping coolies refused to carry me for less than 340 cash. "Walk on," said the missionary, "and teach them a Christian lesson," so I walked seventeen miles in the sun to rebuke them for their avarice and save one halfpenny. In the evening I am afraid that I was hardly in the frame of mind requisite for conducting an evangelical meeting.

Anpien is a considerable town. It is on the Yangtse River just below where it bifurcates into two rivers, one of which goes north-west, the other south-west. Streets of temporary houses are built down by the river; they form the winter suburb, and disappear in the summer when the river rises in consequence of the melting of the snows in its mountain sources. At an excellent inn, with a noisy restaurant on the first floor, good accommodation was given me. No sooner was I seated than a chairen came from the yamen to ask for my Chinese visiting card; but he did not ask for my passport, though I had brought with me twenty-five copies besides the original.

At daybreak a chair was ready, and I was carried to the River, where a ferry boat was in waiting to take us across below the junction. Then we started on our journey towards the south, along the right bank of the Laowatan branch of the Yangtse. The road was a tracking path cut into the face of the cliff; it was narrow, steep, winding, and slippery. There was only just room for the chair to pass, and at the sudden turns it had often to be canted to one side to permit of its passage. We were high above the river in the mountain gorges. The comfort of the traveller in a chair along this road depends entirely upon the sureness of foot of his two bearers—a false step, and chair and traveller would tumble down the cliff into the foaming river below. Deep and narrow was the mountain river, and it roared like a cataract, yet down the passage a long narrow junk, swarming with passengers, was racing, its oars and bow-sweep worked by a score of sailors singing in chorus. The boat appeared, passed down the reach, and was out of sight in a moment; a single error, the slightest confusion, and it would have been smashed in fragments on the rocks and the river strewn with corpses.

We did a good stage before breakfast. Every few li where the steepness of the valley side permits it, there are straw-thatched, bamboo and plaster inns. Here rice is kept in wooden bins all ready steaming hot for the use of travellers; good tea is brewed in a few minutes; the tables and chopsticks are sufficiently clean.

Leaving the river, we crossed over the mountains by a short cut to the river again, and at a wayside inn, much frequented by Chinese, the chair stage finished. I wished to do some writing, and sat down at one of the tables. A crowd gathered round me, and were much interested. One elderly Chinese with huge glasses, a wag in his own way, seeing that I did not speak Chinese, thought to make me understand and divert the crowd by the loudness of his speech, and, insisting that I was deaf, yelled into my ears in tones that shook the tympanum. I told the foolish fellow, in English, that the less he talked the better I could understand him; but he persisted, and poked his face almost into mine, but withdrew it and hobbled off in umbrage when I drew the attention of the bystanders to the absurd capacity of his mouth, which was larger than any mule's.

I must admit that my knowledge of Chinese was very scanty, so scanty indeed as to be almost non-existent. What few words I knew were rarely intelligible; but, as Mrs. General Baynes, when staying at Boulogne, found Hindostanee to be of great help in speaking French, so did I discover that English was of great assistance to me in conversing in Chinese. Remonstrance was thus made much more effective. Whenever I was in a difficulty, or the crowd too obtrusive, I had only to say a few grave sentences in English, and I was master of the situation. This method of speaking often reminded me of that employed by a Cornish lady of high family whose husband was a colleague of mine in Spain. She had been many years in Andalusia, but had never succeeded in mastering Spanish. At a dinner party given by this lady, at which I was present, she thus addressed her Spanish servant, who did not "possess" a single word of English: "Bring me," she said in an angry aside, "bring me the *cuchillo* with the black-handled heft," adding, as she turned to us and thumped her fist on the table, while the servant stood still mystified, "D—— the language! I wish I had never learnt it."

The inn, where the sedan left me, was built over the pathway, which was here a narrow track, two feet six inches wide. Mountain coolies on the road were passing in single file through the inn, their backs bending under their huge burdens. Pigs and fowls and dogs, and a stray cat, were foraging for crumbs under the table. Through the open doorways you saw the paddy-fields under water and the terraced hills, with every arable yard under cultivation. The air was hot and enervating. "The country of the clouds," as the Chinese term the province of Szechuen, does not belie its name. An elderly woman was in charge of the oven, and toddled about on her deformed feet as if she were walking on her heels. Her husband, the innkeeper, brought us hot water every few minutes to keep our tea basins full. "*Na kaishui lai*" (bring hot water), you heard on all sides. A heap of bedding was in one corner of the room, in another were a number of rolls of straw mattresses; a hollow joint of bamboo was filled with chopsticks for the common use, into another bamboo the innkeeper slipped his takings of copper cash. Hanging from the rafters were strings of straw sandals for the poor, and hemp sandals for moneyed wayfarers like the writer. The people who stood round, and those seated at the tables, were friendly and respectful, and plied my men with questions concerning their master. And I did hope that the convert was not tempted to backslide and swerve from the truth in his answers.

My men were now anxious to push on. Over a mountainous country of surpassing beauty, I continued my journey on foot to Fan-yien-tsen, and rested there for the night, having done two days' journey in one.

On March 24th we were all day toiling over the mountains, climbing and descending wooded steeps, through groves of pine, with an ever-changing landscape before us, beautiful with running water, with cascades and waterfalls tumbling down into the river, with magnificent glens and gorges, and picturesque temples on the mountain tops. At night we were at the village of Tanto, on the river, having crossed, a few li before, over the boundary which separates the province of Szechuen from the province of Yunnan.

From Tanto the path up the gorges leads across a rocky mountain creek in a defile of the mountains. In England this creek would be spanned by a bridge; but the poor heathen, in China, how do they find their way across the stream? By a bridge also. They have spanned the torrent with a powerful iron suspension bridge, 100 feet long by ten feet broad, swung between two massive buttresses and approached under handsome temple-archways.

Mists clothe the mountains—the air is confined between these walls of rock and stone. Population is scanty, but there is cultivation wherever possible. Villages sparsely distributed along the mountain path have water trained to them in bamboo conduits from tarns on the hillside. Each house has its own supply, and there is no attempt to provide for the common good. Besides other reasons, it would interfere with the trade of the water-carriers, who all day long are toiling up from the river.

The mountain slope does not permit a greater width of building space than on each side of the one main street. And on market days this street is almost impassable, being thronged with traffickers, and blocked with stalls and wares. Coal is for sale, both pure and mixed with clay in briquettes, and salt in blocks almost as black as coal, and three times as heavy, and piles of drugs—a medley of bones, horns, roots, leaves, and minerals—and raw cotton and cotton yarn from Wuchang and Bombay, and finished goods from Manchester. At one of the villages there was a chair for hire, and, knowing how difficult was the country, I was willing to pay the amount asked—namely, 7*d.* for nearly seven miles; but my friend the convert, who arranged these things, considered that between the 5*d.* he offered and the 7*d.* they asked the discrepancy was too great, and after some acrimonious bargaining it was decided that I should continue on foot, my man indicating to me by gestures, in a most sarcastic way, that the "*chiaodza*" men had failed to overreach him.

A TEMPLE IN SZECHUEN.

LAOWATAN.

At Sengki-ping it rained all through the night, and I had to sleep under my umbrella because of a solution in the continuity of the roof immediately above my pillow. And it rained all the day following; but my men, eager to earn their reward of one shilling, pushed on through the slush. It was hard work following the slippery path above the river. Few rivers in the world flow between more majestic banks than these, towering as they do a thousand feet above the water. Clad with thick mountain scrub, that has firm foothold, the mountains offer but a poor harvest to the peasant; yet even here high up on the precipitous sides of the cliffs, ledges that seem inaccessible are sown with wheat or peas, and, if the soil be deep enough, with the baneful poppy. As we plodded on through the mud and rain, we overtook a poor lad painfully limping along with the help of a stick. He was a bright lad, who unbound his leg and showed me a large swelling above the knee. He spoke to me, though I did not understand him, but with sturdy independence did not ask for alms, and when I had seen his leg he bound it up again and limped on. Meeting him a little later at an inn, where he was sitting at a table with nothing before him to eat, I gave him a handful of cash which I had put in my pocket for him. He thanked me by raising his clasped hands, and said something, I knew not what, as I hurried on. A little while afterwards I stopped to have my breakfast, when the boy passed. As soon as he saw me he fell down upon his knees and "kotow'd" to me, with every mark of the liveliest gratitude. I felt touched by the poor fellow's gratitude—he could not have been more than fifteen—and mean, to think that the benefaction, which in his eyes appeared so generous, was little more than one penny. There can be no doubt that I gained merit by this action, for this very afternoon as I was on the track a large stone the size of a shell from a 50-ton gun fell from the crag above me, struck the rock within two paces of me, and shot past into the river. A few feet nearer and it would have blotted out the life of one whom the profession could ill spare. We camped at Laowatan.

A chair with three bearers was waiting for me in the morning, so that I left the town of Laowatan in a manner befitting my rank. The town had risen to see me leave, and I went down the street amid serried ranks of spectators. We crossed the river by a wonderful suspension bridge, 250 feet long and 12 feet broad, formed of linked bars of wrought iron. It shows stability, strength, and delicacy of design, and is a remarkable work to have been done by the untutored barbarians of this land of night. We ascended the steep incline opposite, and passed the likin barrier, but at a turn in the road, higher still in the mountain, a woman emerged from her cottage and blocked our path. Nor could the chair pass till my foremost bearer had reluctantly given her a string of cash. "With money you can move the gods," say the Chinese; "without it you can't move a man."

For miles we mounted upwards. We were now in Yunnan, "south of the clouds"—in Szechuen we were always under the clouds—the sun was warm, the air dry and crisp. Ponies passed us in long droves; often there were eighty ponies in a single drove. All were heavily laden with copper and lead, were nozzled to keep them off the grass, and picked their way down the rocky path of steps with the agility and sureness of foot of mountain goats. Time was beaten for them on musical gongs, and the echoes rang among the mountains. Many were decorated with red flags and tufts, and with plumes of the Amherst pheasant. These were official pack animals, which were franked through the likin barriers without examination.

The path, rising to the height of the watershed, where at a great elevation we gain a distant view of water, descends by the counterslope once more to the river Laowatan. A wonderful ravine, a mountain riven perpendicularly in twain, here gives passage to the river, and in full view of this we rested at the little town of Taoshakwan, with the roar of the river hundreds of feet below us. Midway up the face of the precipice opposite there is a sight worth seeing; a mass of coffin boards, caught in a fault in the precipice, have been lying there for untold generations, having been originally carried there by the "ancient flying-men who are now extinct."

A poor little town is Taoshakwan, with a poor little yamen with pretentious tigers painted on its outflanking wall, with a poor little temple, and gods in sad disrepair; but with an admirable inn, with a charming verandah facing a scene of alpine magnificence.

We were entering a district of great poverty. At Tchih-li-pu, where we arrived at midday the next day, the houses are poor, the people poverty-stricken and ill-clad, the hotel dirty, and my room the worst I had yet slept in. The road is a well-worn path flagged in places, uneven, and irregular, following at varying heights the upward course of the tortuous river. The country is bald; it is grand but lonely; vegetation is scanty and houses are few; we have left the prosperity of Szechuen, and are in the midst of the poverty of Yunnan. Farmhouses there are at rare intervals, amid occasional patches of cultivation; there are square white-washed watch towers in groves of sacred trees; there are a few tombstones, and an occasional rudely carved god to guard the way. There are poor mud and bamboo inns with grass roofs, and dirty tables set out with half a dozen bowls of tea, and with ovens for the use of travellers. Food we had now to bring with us, and only at the larger towns where the stages terminate could we expect to find food for sale. The tea is inferior, and we had to be content with maize meal, bean curds, rice roasted in sugar, and sweet gelatinous cakes made from the waste of maize meal. Rice can only be bought in the large towns. It is not kept in roadside inns ready steaming hot for use, as it is in Szechuen. Rarely there are sweet potatoes; there are eggs, however, in abundance, one hundred for a shilling (500 cash), but the coolies cannot eat them because of their dearness. A large bowl of rice costs four cash, an egg five cash, and the Chinaman strikes a balance in his mind and sees more nourishment in one bowl of rice than in three eggs. Of meat there is pork—pork in plenty, and pork only. Pigs and dogs are the scavengers of China. None of the carnivora are more omnivorous than the Chinese. "A Chinaman has the most unscrupulous stomach in the world," says Meadows; "he will eat anything from the root to the leaf, and from the hide to the entrails." He will not even despise the flesh of dog that has died a natural death. During the awful famine in Shansi of 1876-1879 starving men fought to the death for the bodies of dogs that had fattened on the corpses of their dead countrymen. Mutton is sometimes for sale in Mohammedan shops, and beef also, but it must not be imagined that either sheep or ox is killed for its flesh, unless on the point of death from starvation or disease. And the beef is not from the ox but from the water buffalo. Sugar can be bought only in the larger towns; salt can be purchased everywhere.

Beggars there are in numbers, skulking about almost naked, with unkempt hair and no queue, with a small basket for gathering garbage and a staff to keep away dogs. Only beggars carry sticks in China, and it is only the beggars that need beware of dogs. To carry a stick in China for protection against dogs is like carrying a red flag to scare away bulls. Dogs in China are lowly organised; they are not discriminating animals; and, despite the luxurious splendour of my Chinese dress—it cost more than seven shillings—dogs frequently mistook my calling. In Szechuen, as we passed through the towns, there was competition among the inns to obtain our custom. Hotel runners were there to shout to all the world the superior merits of their establishments. But here in Yunnan it is different. There is barely inn accommodation for the road traffic, and the innkeepers are either too apathetic or too shamefaced to call the attention of the traveller to their poor, dirty accommodation houses.

In Szechuen, one of the most flourishing of trades is that of the monumental mason and carver in stone. Huge monoliths are there cut from the boulders which have been dislodged from the mountains, dressed and finished *in situ*, and then removed to the spot where they are to be erected. The Chinese thus pursue a practice different from that of the Westerns, who bring the undressed stone from the quarry and carve it in the studio. With the Chinese the difficulty is one of transport—the finished work is obviously lighter than the unhewn block. In Yunnan, up to the present, I had seen no mason at work, for no masonry was needed. Houses built of stone were falling into ruin, and only thatched, mud-plastered, bamboo and wood houses were being built in their places.

At Laowatan I told my Christian to hire me a chair for thirty or forty li, and he did so, but the chair, instead of carrying me the shorter distance, carried me the whole day. The following day the chair kept company with me, and as I had not ordered it, I naturally walked; but the third day also the chair haunted me, and then I discovered that my admirable guide had engaged the chair not for thirty or forty li, as I had instructed him in my best Chinese, but for three hundred and sixty li, for four days' stages of ninety li each. He had made the agreement "out of consideration for me," and his own pocket; he had made an agreement which gave him wider scope for a little private arrangement of his own with the chair-coolies. For two days I was paying fifteen cash a li for a chair and walking alongside of it charmed by the good humour of the coolies, and unaware that they were laughing in their sleeves at my folly. Trifling mistakes like this are inevitable to one who travels in China without an interpreter.

My two coolies were capital fellows, full of good humour, cheerful, and untiring. The elder was disposed to be argumentative with his countrymen, but he could not quarrel. Nature had given him an uncontrollable stutter, and, if he tried to speak quickly, spasm seized his tongue, and he had to break into a laugh. Few men in China, I think, could be more curiously constructed than this coolie. He was all neck; his chin was simply an upward prolongation of his neck like a second "Adam's apple." Both were very pleasant companions. They were naturally in good humour, for they were well paid, and their loads, as loads are in China, were almost insignificant; I had only asked them to carry sixty-seven pounds each.

We, who live amid the advantages of Western civilisation, can hardly realise how enormous are the weights borne by those human beasts of burthen, our brothers in China. The common fast-travelling coolie of Szechuen contracts to carry eighty catties (107lbs.), forty miles a day over difficult country. But the weight-carrying coolie, travelling shorter distances, carries far heavier loads than that. There are porters, says Du Halde, who will carry 160 of our pounds, ten leagues a day. The coolies, engaged in carrying the compressed cakes of Szechuen tea into Thibet, travel over mountain passes 7000 feet above their starting place; yet there are those among them, says Von Richthofen, who carry 324 catties (432lbs.). A package of tea is called a "*pao*" and varies in weight from eleven to eighteen catties, yet Baber has often seen coolies carrying eighteen of the eighteen-catty *pao* (the "*Yachou pao*") and on one occasion twenty-two, in other words Baber has often seen coolies with more than 400lbs. on their backs. Under these enormous loads they travel from six to seven miles a day. The average load of the Thibetan tea-carrier is, says Gill, from 240lbs. to 264lbs. Gill constantly saw "little boys carrying 120lbs." Bundles of calico weigh fifty-five catties each (73-1/3lbs.), and three bundles are the average load. Salt is solid, hard, metallic, and of high specific gravity, yet I have seen men ambling along the road, under loads that a strong Englishman could with difficulty raise from the ground. The average load of salt, coal, copper, zinc, and tin is 200lbs. Gill met coolies carrying logs, 200lbs. in weight, ten miles a day; and 200lbs., the Consul in Chungking told me, is the average weight carried by the cloth-porters between Wanhsien and Chentu, the capital.

Mountain coolies, such as the tea-carriers, bear the weight of their burden on their shoulders, carrying it as we do a knapsack, not in the ordinary Chinese way, with a pliant carrying pole. They are all provided with a short staff, which has a transverse handle curved like a boomerang, and with this they ease the weight off the back, while standing at rest.

We were still ascending the valley, which became more difficult of passage every day. Hamlets are built where there is scarce foothold in the detritus, below perpendicular escarpments of rock, cut clean like the façades of a Gothic temple. A tributary of the river is crossed by an admirable stone bridge of two arches, with a central pier and cut-water of magnificent boldness and strength, and with two images of lions guarding its abutment. Just below the branch the main stream can be crossed by a traveller, if he be brave enough to venture, in a bamboo loop-cradle, and be drawn across the stream on a powerful bamboo cable slung from bank to bank.

We rested by the bridge and refreshed ourselves, for above us was an ascent whose steepness my stuttering coolie indicated to me by fixing my walking stick in the ground, almost perpendicularly, and running his finger up the side. He did not exaggerate. A zigzag path set with stone steps has been cut in the vertical ascent, and up this we toiled for hours. At the base of the escalade my men sublet their loads to spare coolies who were waiting there in numbers for the purpose, and climbed up with me empty-handed. At every few turns there were rest-houses where one could get tea and shelter from the hot sun. The village of Tak-wan-leo is at the summit; it is a village of some little importance and commands a noble view of mountain, valley, and river. Its largest hong is the coffin-maker's, which is always filled with shells of the thickest timber that money can buy.

Stress is laid in China upon the necessity of a secure resting-place after death. The filial affection of a son can do no more thoughtful act than present a coffin to his father, to prove to him how composedly he will lie after he is dead. And nothing will a father in

China show the stranger with more pride than the coffin-boards presented to him by his dutiful son.

Tak-wan-leo is the highest point on the road between Suifu and Chaotong. For centuries it has been known to the Chinese as the highest point; how, then, with their defective appliances did they arrive at so accurate a determination? Twenty li beyond the village the stage ends at the town of Tawantzu, where I had good quarters in the pavilion of an old temple. The shrine was thick with the dust of years; the three gods were dishevelled and mutilated; no sheaves of joss sticks were smouldering on the altar. The steps led down into manure heaps and a piggery, into a garden rank and waste, which yet commands an outlook over mountain and river worthy of the greatest of temples.

THE OPIUM-SMOKER OF ROMANCE.

On March 30th I reached Tak-wan-hsien, the day's stage having been seventy li (twenty-three and one-third miles). I was carried all the way by three chair-coolies in a heavy chair in steady rain that made the unpaved track as slippery as ice—and this over the dizzy heights of a mountain pathway of extraordinary irregularity. Never slipping, never making a mistake, the three coolies bore the chair with my thirteen stone, easily and without straining. From time to time they rested a minute or two to take a whiff of tobacco; they were always in good humour, and finished the day as strong and fresh as when they began it. Within an hour of their arrival all these three men were lying on their sides in the room opposite to mine, with their opium-pipes and little wooden vials of opium before them, all three engaged in rolling and heating in their opium-lamps treacly pellets of opium. Then they had their daily smoke of opium. "They were ruining themselves body and soul." Two of the men were past middle age; the third was a strapping young fellow of twenty-five. They may have only recently acquired the habit, I had no means of asking them; but those who know Western China will tell you that it is almost certain that the two elder men had used the opium-pipe as a stimulant since they were as young as their companion. All three men were physically well-developed, with large frames, showing unusual muscular strength and endurance, and differed, indeed, from those resurrected corpses whose fleshless figures, drawn by imaginative Chinese artists, we have known for years to be typical of our poor lost brothers—the opium-smoking millions of China. For their work to-day, work that few men out of China would be capable of attempting, the three coolies were paid sevenpence each, out of which they found themselves, and had to pay as well one penny each for the hire of the chair.

On arriving at the inn in Tak-wan-hsien my estimable comrade, one of the six surviving converts of Suifu, indicated to me that his cash belt was empty—up the road he could not produce a single cash for me to give a beggar—and pointing in turn to the bag where I kept my silver, to the ceiling and to his heart, he conveyed to me the pious assurance that if I would give him some silver from the bag he would bring me back the true change, on his honour, so witness Heaven! I gave him two lumps of silver which I made him understand were worth 3420 cash; he went away, and after a suspicious absence returned quite gleefully with 3050 cash, the bank, no doubt, having detained the remainder pending the declaration of a bogus dividend. But he also brought back with him what was better than cash, some nutritious maize-meal cakes, which proved a welcome change from the everlasting rice. They were as large as an English scone, and cost two cash apiece, that is to say, for one shilling I could buy twenty dozen.

Money in Western China consists of solid ingots of silver, and copper cash. The silver is in lumps of one tael or more each, the tael being a Chinese ounce and equivalent roughly to between 1400 and 1500 cash. Speaking generally a tael was worth, during my journey, three shillings, that is to say, forty cash were equivalent to one penny. There are bankers in every town, and the Chinese methods of banking, it is well known, are but little inferior to our own. From Hankow to Chungking my money was remitted by draft through a Chinese bank. West from Chungking the money may be sent by draft, by telegraph, or in bullion, as you choose. I carried some silver with me; the rest I put up in a package and handed to a native post in Chungking, which undertook to deliver it intact to me at Yunnan city, 700 miles away, within a specified time. By my declaring its contents and paying the registration fee, a mere trifle, the post guaranteed its safe delivery, and engaged to make good any loss. Money is thus remitted in Western China with complete confidence and security. My money arrived, I may add, in Yunnan at the time agreed upon, but after I had left for Talifu. As there is a telegraph line between Yunnan and Tali, the money was forwarded by telegraph and awaited my arrival in Tali.

There are no less than four native post-offices between Chungking and Suifu. All the post-offices transmit parcels, as well as letters and bullion, at very moderate charges. The distance is 230 miles, and the charges are fifty cash (1-1/4*d.*) the catty (1-1/3lb.), or any part thereof; thus a single letter pays fifty cash, a catty's weight of letters paying no more than a single letter.

From Chungking to Yunnan city, a distance of 630 miles, letters pay two hundred cash (fivepence) each; packages of one catty, or under, pay three hundred and fifty cash; while for silver bullion there is a special fee of three hundred and fifty cash for every ten taels, equivalent to ninepence for thirty shillings, or two-and-a-half per cent., which includes postage registration, guarantee, and insurance.

Tak-wan-hsien is a town of some importance, and was formerly the seat of the French missionary bishop. It is a walled town, ranking as a Hsien city, with a Hsien magistrate as its chief ruler. There are 10,000 people (more or less), within the walls, but the city is poor, and its poverty is but a reflex of the district. Its mud wall is crumbling; its houses of mud and wood are falling; the streets are ill-paved and the people ill-clad.

CHAPTER VIII.

THE CITY OF CHAOTONG, WITH SOME REMARKS ON ITS POVERTY, INFANTICIDE, SELLING FEMALE CHILDREN INTO SLAVERY, TORTURES, AND THE CHINESE INSENSIBILITY TO PAIN.

By the following day we had crossed the mountains, and were walking along the level upland that leads to the plain of Chaotong. And on Sunday, April 1st, we reached the city. Cedars, held sacred, with shrines in the shelter of their branches, dot the plain; peach-trees and pear-trees were now in full bloom; the harvest was ripening in the fields. There were black-faced sheep in abundance, red cattle with short horns, and the ubiquitous water-buffalo. Over the level roads primitive carts, drawn by red oxen, were rumbling in the dust. There were mud villages, poor and falling into ruins; there were everywhere signs of poverty and famine. Children ran about naked, or in rags. We passed the likin-barrier, known by its white flag, and I was not even asked for my visiting card, nor were my boxes looked into—they were as beggarly as the district—but poor carriers were detained, and a few cash unjustly wrung from them. At a crowded teahouse, a few miles from the city, we waited for the stragglers, while many wayfarers gathered in to see me. Prices were ranging higher. Tea here was 4 cash, and not 2 cash as hitherto. But even this charge was not excessive. In Canton one day, after a weary journey on foot through the crowded streets, I was taken to a five-storied pagoda overlooking the city. At the topmost story tea was brought me, and I drank a dozen cups, and was asked threepence in payment. I thought that the cheapest refreshment I ever had. Yet here I was served as abundantly with better tea at a charge compared with which the Canton charge was twenty-five times greater. Previously in this province the price I had paid for tea in comparison with the price at Canton was as one to fifty.

Early in the afternoon we passed through the south gate into Chaotong, and, picking our way through the streets, were led to the comfortable home of the Bible Christian Mission, where I was kindly received by the Rev. Frank Dymond, and welcomed as a brother missionary of whose arrival he had been advised. Services were ended, but the neighbours dropped in to see the stranger, and ask my exalted age, my honourable name, and my dignified business; they hoped to be able to congratulate me upon being a man of virtue, the father of many sons; asked how many thousands of pieces of silver I had (daughters), and how long I proposed to permit my dignified presence to remain in their mean and contemptible city.

Mr. Dymond is a Devonshire man, and that evening he gave me for tea Devonshire cream and blackberry jam made in Chaotong, and native oatmeal cakes, than which I never tasted any better in Scotland.

Chaotong is a walled Fu city with 40,000 inhabitants. Roman Catholics have been established here for many years, and the Bible Christian Mission, which is affiliated to the China Inland Mission, has been working here since 1887.

There were formerly five missionaries; there are now only two, and one of these was absent. The missionary in charge, Mr. Frank Dymond, is one of the most agreeable men I met in China, broad-minded, sympathetic and earnest—universally honoured and respected by all the district. Since the mission was opened three converts have been baptised, one of whom is in Szechuen, another is in Tongchuan, and the third has been gathered to his fathers. The harvest has not been abundant, but there are now six promising inquirers, and the missionary is not discouraged. The mission premises are built on land which cost two hundred and ninety taels, and are well situated not far from the south gate, the chief yamens, the temples, and the French Mission. People are friendly, but manifest dangerously little interest in their salvation.

At Chaotong I had entered upon a district that had been devastated by recurring seasons of plague and famine. Last year more than 5000 people are believed to have died from starvation in the town and its immediate neighbourhood. The numbers are appalling, but doubt must always be thrown upon statistics derived from Chinese sources. The Chinese and Japanese disregard of accuracy is characteristic of all Orientals. Beggars were so numerous, and became such a menace to the community, that their suppression was called for; they were driven from the streets, and confined within the walls of the temple and grounds beyond the south gate, and fed by common charity. Huddled together in rags and misery, they took famine fever and perished by hundreds. Seventy dead were carried from the temple in one day. Of 5000 poor wretches who crossed the temple threshold, the Chinese say that 2000 never came out alive. For four years past the harvests had been very bad, but there was now hope of a better time coming. Opportune rains had fallen, and the opium crop was good. More than anything else the district depends for its prosperity upon the opium crop—if the crop is good, money is plentiful. Maize-cobs last harvest were four times the size of those of the previous harvest, when they were no larger than one's finger. Wheat and beans were forward; the coming rice crop gave every hope of being a good one. Food was still dear, and all prices were high, because rice was scarce and dear, and it is the price of rice which regulates the market. In a good year one sheng of rice (6-2/3lbs.) costs thirty-five cash (less than one penny), it now costs 110 cash. The normal price of maize is sixteen cash the sheng, it now cost sixty-five cash the sheng. To make things worse, the weight of the sheng had been reduced with the times from twelve catties to five catties, and at the same time the relation of cash to silver had fallen from 1640 to 1250 cash the tael.

The selling of its female children into slavery is the chief sorrow of this famine-stricken district. During last year it is estimated, or rather, it is stated by the Chinese, that no less than three thousand children from this neighbourhood, chiefly female children and a few boys, were sold to dealers and carried like poultry in baskets to the capital. At ordinary times the price for girls is one tael (three shillings) for every year of their age, thus a girl of five costs fifteen shillings, of ten, thirty shillings, but in time of famine children, to speak brutally, become a drug in the market. Female children were now offering at from three shillings and fourpence to six shillings each. You could buy as many as you cared to, you might even obtain them for nothing if you would enter into an agreement with the father, which he had no means of enforcing, to take care of his child, and clothe and feed her, and rear her kindly. Starving mothers would come to the mission beseeching the foreign teachers to take their babies and save them from the fate that was otherwise inevitable.

Girls are bought in Chaotong up to the age of twenty, and there is always a ready market for those above the age of puberty; prices then vary according to the measure of the girl's beauty, an important feature being the smallness of her feet. They are sold in the capital for wives and *yatows*; they are rarely sold into prostitution. Two important factors in the demand for them are the large preponderance in the number of males at the capital, and the prevalence there of goitre or thick neck, a deformity which is absent from the district of Chaotong. Infanticide in a starving city like this is dreadfully common. "For the parents, seeing their children must be doomed to poverty, think it better at once to let the soul escape in search of a more happy asylum than to linger in one condemned to want and wretchedness." The infanticide is, however, exclusively confined to the destruction of female children, the sons being permitted to live in order to continue the ancestral sacrifices.

One mother I met, who was employed by the mission, told the missionary in ordinary conversation that she had suffocated in turn three of her female children within a few days of birth; and, when a fourth was born, so enraged was her husband to discover that it was also a girl that he seized it by the legs and struck it against the wall and killed it.

Dead children, and often living infants, are thrown out on the common among the gravemounds, and may be seen there any morning being gnawed by dogs. Mr. Tremberth of the Bible Christian Mission, leaving by the south gate early one morning, disturbed a dog eating a still living child that had been thrown over the wall during the night. Its little arm was crunched and stript of flesh, and it was whining inarticulately—it died almost immediately. A man came to see me, who for a long time used to heap up merit for himself in heaven by acting as a city scavenger. Early every morning he went round the city picking up dead dogs and dead cats in order to bury them decently—who could tell, perhaps the soul of his grandfather had found habitation in that cat? While he was doing this pious work, never a morning passed that he did not find a dead child, and usually three or four. The dead of the poor people are roughly buried near the surface and eaten by dogs.

An instance of the undoubted truth of the doctrine of transmigration occurred recently in Chaotong and is worth recording. A cow was killed near the south gate on whose intestine—and this fact can be attested by all who saw it—was written plainly and unmistakably the character "*Wong*," which proved, they told me, that the soul of one whose name was Wong had returned to earth in the body of that cow.

I stayed two days in Chaotong, and strolled in pleasant company through the city. Close to the Mission is the yamen of the Chentai or Brigadier-General, the Military Governor of this portion of the province, and a little further is the more crowded yamen of the Fu Magistrate. Here, as in all yamens, the detached wall or fixed screen of stone facing the entrance is painted with the gigantic representation of a mythical monster in red trying to swallow the sun—the Chinese illustration of the French saying "*prendre la lune avec les dents.*" It is the warning against covetousness, the exhortation against squeezing, and is as little likely to be attended to by the magistrate here as it would be by his brother in Chicago. We visited the Confucian Temple among the trees and the examination hall close by, and another yamen, and the Temple of the God of Riches. In the yamen, at the time of our visit, a young official, seated in his four-bearer chair, was waiting in the outer court; he had sent in his visiting card, and attended the pleasure of his superior officer. China may be uncivilised and may yearn for the missionaries, but there was refined etiquette in China, and an interchange of many of the pleasantest courtesies of modern civilisation, when we noble Britons were grubbing in the forest, painted savages with a clout.

As we went out of the west gate, I was shown the spot where a few days before a young woman, taken in adultery, was done to death in a cage amid a crowd of spectators, who witnessed her agony for three days. She had to stand on tiptoe in the cage, her head projecting through a hole in the roof, and here she had to remain until death by exhaustion or strangulation ensued, or till some kind friend, seeking to accumulate merit in heaven, passed into her mouth sufficient opium to poison her, and so end her struggles.

On the gate itself a man not so long ago was nailed with red-hot nails hammered through his wrists above the hands. In this way he was exposed in turn at each of the four gates of the city, so that every man, woman, and child could see his torture. He survived four days, having unsuccessfully attempted to shorten his pain by beating his head against the woodwork, an attempt which was frustrated by padding the woodwork. This man had murdered and robbed two travellers on the high road, and, as things are in China, his punishment was not too severe.

No people are more cruel in their punishments than the Chinese, and obviously the reason is that the sensory nervous system of a Chinaman is either blunted or of arrested development. Can anyone doubt this who witnesses the stoicism with which a Chinaman can endure physical pain when sustaining surgical operation without chloroform, the comfort with which he can thrive amid foul and penetrating smells, the calmness with which he can sleep amid the noise of gunfire and crackers, drums and tomtoms, and the indifference with which he contemplates the sufferings of lower animals, and the infliction of tortures on higher?

Every text-book on China devotes a special chapter to the subject of punishment. Mutilation is extremely common. Often I met men who had been deprived of their ears—they had lost them, they explained, in battle facing the enemy! It is a common punishment to sever the hamstrings or to break the ankle-bones, especially in the case of prisoners who have attempted to escape. And I remember that when I was in Shanghai, Mr. Tsai, the Mixed Court Magistrate, was reproved by the papers because he had from the bench expressed his regret that the foreign law of Shanghai did not permit him to punish in this way a prisoner who had twice succeeded in breaking from gaol. The hand is cut off for theft, as it was in England not so many years ago. I have seen men with the tendon of Achilles cut out, and it is worth noting that the Chinese say that this "acquired deformity" can be cured by the transplantation in the seat of injury of the tendon of a sheep. One embellishment of the Chinese punishment of flogging might with good effect be introduced into England. After a Chinese flagellation, the culprit is compelled to go down on his knees and humbly thank the magistrate for the trouble he has been put to to correct his morals.

There is a branch of the *Missions Étrangères de Paris* in Chaotong. I called at the mission and saw their school of fifteen children, and their tiny little church. One priest lives here solitary and alone; he was reading, when I entered, the famous Chinese story, "The Three Kingdoms." He gave me a kindly welcome, and was pleased to talk in his own tongue. An excellent bottle of rich wine was produced, and over the glass the Father painted with voluble energy the evil qualities of the people whom he has left his beautiful home in the Midi of France to lead to Rome. "No Chinaman can resist temptation; all are thieves. Justice depends on the richness of the accused. Victory in a court of justice is to the richer. Talk to the Chinese of Religion, of a God, of Heaven or Hell, and they yawn; speak to them of business and they are all attention. If you ever hear of a Chinaman who is not a thief and a liar, do not believe it, Monsieur Morrison, do not believe it, they are thieves and liars every one."

For eight years the priest had been in China devoting his best energies to the propagation of his religion. And sorry had been his recompense. The best Christian in the mission had lately broken into the mission house and stolen everything valuable he could lay his impious hands on. Remembrance of this infamy rankled in his bosom and impelled him to this expansive panegyric on Chinese virtue.

Some four months ago the good father was away on a holiday, visiting a missionary brother in an adjoining town. In his absence the mission was entered through a rift made in the wall, and three hundred taels of silver, all the money to the last sou that he possessed, were stolen. Suspicion fell upon a Christian, who was not only an active Catholic himself, but whose fathers before him had been Catholics for generations. It was learned that his wife had some of the money, and that the thief was on his way to Suifu with the remainder. There was great difficulty in inducing the yamen to take action, but at last the wife was arrested. She protested that she knew nothing; but, having been triced up by the wrists joined behind her back, she soon came to reason, and cried out that, if the magistrate would release her hands, she would confess all. Two hundred taels were seized in her house and restored to the priest, and the culprit, her husband, followed to Tak-wan-hsien by the satellites of the yamen, was there arrested, and was now in prison awaiting punishment. The goods he purchased were likewise seized and were now with the poor father.

CHAPTER IX.

Mainly about Chinese Doctors.

Chaotong is an important centre for the distribution of medicines to Szechuen and other parts of the empire. An extraordinary variety of drugs and medicaments is collected in the city. No pharmacop[oe]ia is more comprehensive than the Chinese. No English physician can surpass the Chinese in the easy confidence with which he will diagnose symptoms that he does not understand. The Chinese physician who witnesses the unfortunate effect of placing a drug of which he knows nothing into a body of which he knows less, is no more disconcerted than is his Western brother under similar circumstances; he retires, sententiously observing "there is medicine for sickness but none for fate." "Medicine," says the Chinese proverb, "cures the man who is fated not to die." "When Yenwang (the King of Hell) has decreed a man to die at the third watch, no power will detain him till the fifth."

The professional knowledge of a Chinese doctor largely consists in ability to feel the pulse, or rather the innumerable pulses of his Chinese patient. This is the real criterion of his skill. The pulses of a Chinaman vary in a manner that no English doctor can conceive of. For instance, among the seven kinds of pulse which presage approaching death, occur the five following:—

"1. When the pulse is perceived under the fingers to bubble irregularly like water over a great fire, if it be in the morning, the patient will die in the evening.

"2. Death is no farther off if the pulse seems like a fish whose head is stopped in such a manner that he cannot move, but has a frisking tail without any regularity; the cause of this distemper lies in the kidneys.

"3. If the pulse seems like drops of water that fall into a room through some crack, and when in its return it is scattered and disordered much like the twine of a cord which is unravelled, the bones are dried up even to the very marrow.

"4. Likewise if the motion of the pulse resembles the pace of a frog when he is embarrassed in the weeds, death is certain.

"5. If the motion of the pulse resembles the hasty pecking of the beak of a bird, there is a defect of spirits in the stomach."

Heredity is the most important factor in the evolution of a doctor in China, success in his career as an "hereditary physician" being specially assured to him who has the good fortune to make his first appearance in the world feet foremost. Doctors dispense their own medicines. In their shops you see an amazing variety of drugs; you will occasionally also see tethered a live stag, which on a certain day, to be decided by the priests, will be pounded whole in a pestle and mortar. "Pills manufactured out of a whole stag slaughtered with purity of purpose on a propitious day," is a common announcement in dispensaries in China. The wall of a doctor's shop is usually stuck all over with disused plasters returned by grateful patients with complimentary testimonies to their efficiency; they have done what England is alleged to expect of all her sons—their duty.

Medicines, it is known to all Chinamen, operate variously according to their taste, thus:—"All sour medicines are capable of impeding and retaining; bitter medicines of causing looseness and warmth as well as hardening; sweet possess the qualities of strengthening, of harmonising, and of warming; acids disperse, prove emollient, and go in an athwart direction; salt medicines possess the properties of descending; those substances that are hard and tasteless open the orifices of the body and promote a discharge. This explains the use of the five tastes."

Coming from Szechuen, we frequently met porters carrying baskets of armadillos, leopard skins, leopard and tiger bones. The skins were for wear, but the armadillos and bones were being taken to Suifu to be converted into medicine. From the bones of leopards an admirable tonic may be distilled; while it is well known that the infusion prepared from tiger bones is the greatest of the tonics, conferring something of the courage, agility, and strength of the tiger upon its partaker.

Another excellent specific for courage is a preparation made from the gall bladder of a robber famous for his bravery, who has died at the hands of the executioner. The sale of such a gall bladder is one of the perquisites of a Chinese executioner.

Ague at certain seasons is one of the most common ailments of the district of Chaotong, yet there is an admirable prophylactic at hand against it: write the names of the eight demons of ague on paper, and then eat the paper with a cake; or take out the eyes of the paper door-god (there are door-gods on all your neighbours' doors), and devour them—this remedy never fails.

Unlike the Spaniard, the Chinese disapproves of blood-letting in fevers, "for a fever is like a pot boiling; it is requisite to reduce the fire and not diminish the liquid in the vessel, if we wish to cure the patient."

Unlike the Spaniard, too, the Chinese doctors would not venture to assert, as the medical faculty of Madrid in the middle of last century assured the inhabitants, that "if human excrement was no longer to be suffered to accumulate as usual in the streets, where it might attract the putrescent particles floating in the air, these noxious vapours would find their way into the human body and a pestilential sickness would be the inevitable consequence."

For boils there is a certain cure:—There is a God of Boils. If you have a boil you will plaster the offending excrescence without avail, if that be *all* you plaster; to get relief you must at the same time plaster the corresponding area on the image of the God. Go into his temple in Western China, and you will find this deity dripping with plasters, with scarcely an undesecrated space on his superficies.

At the yamen of the Brigadier-General in Chaotong, the entrance is guarded by the customary stone images of mythical shape and grotesque features. They are believed to represent lions, but their faces are not leonine—they are a reproduction, exaggerated, of the characteristic features of the bulldog of Western China. The images are of undoubted value to the city. One is male and the other female. On the sixteenth day of the first month they are visited by the townspeople, who rub them energetically with their hands, all over from end to end. Every spot so touched confers immunity from pain upon the corresponding region of their own bodies for the ensuing year. And so from year to year these images are visited. Pain accordingly is almost absent from the city, and only that man suffers pain who has the temerity to neglect the opportunity of insuring himself against it.

I was called to a case of opium-poisoning in Chaotong. A son came in casually to seek our aid in saving his father, who had attempted suicide with a large over-dose of opium. He had taken it at ten in the morning and it was now two. We were led to the house and found it a single small unlit room up a narrow alley. In the room two men were unconcernedly eating their rice, and in the darkness they seemed to be the only occupants; but, lying down behind them on a narrow bed, was the dim figure of the dying man, who was breathing stertorously. A crowd quickly gathered round the door and pent up the alley-way. Rousing the man, I caused him to swallow some pints of warm water, and then I gave him a hypodermic injection of apomorphia. The effect was admirable, and pleased the spectators even more than the patient.

Opium is almost exclusively the drug used by suicides. No Chinaman would kill himself by the mutilation of the razor or pistol-shot because awful is the future punishment of him who would so dare to disturb the integrity of the body bequeathed to him by his fathers.

China is the land of suicides. I suppose more people die from suicide in China in proportion to the population than in any other country. Where the struggle for existence is so keen, it is hardly to be wondered at that men are so willing to abandon the struggle. But poverty and misery are not the only causes. For the most trivial reason the Chinaman will take his own life. Suicide with a Chinaman is an act that is recorded in his honour rather than to his opprobrium.

Thus a widow, as we have seen, may obtain much merit by sacrificing herself on the death of her husband. But in a large proportion of cases the motive is revenge, for the spirit of the dead is believed to "haunt and injure the living person who has been the cause of the suicide." In China to ruin your adversary you injure or kill yourself. To vow to commit suicide is the most awful threat with which you can drive terror into the heart of your adversary. If your enemy do you wrong, there is no way in which you can cause him more bitterly to repent his misdeed than by slaying yourself at his doorstep. He will be charged with your murder, and may be executed for the crime; he will be utterly ruined in establishing, if he can establish, his innocence; and he will be haunted ever after by your avenging spirit.

Occasionally two men who have quarrelled will take poison together, and their spirits will fight it out in heaven. Opium is very cheap in Chaotong, costing only fivepence an ounce for the crude article. You see it exposed for sale everywhere, like thick treacle in dirty besmeared jars. It is largely adulterated with ground pigskin, the adulteration being detected by the craving being unsatisfied. Mohammedans have a holy loathing of the pig, and look with contempt on their countrymen whose chief meat-food is pork. But each one in his turn. It is, on the other hand, a source of infinite amusement to the Chinese to see his Mohammedan brother unwittingly smoking the unclean beast in his opium-pipe.

On our way to the opium case we passed a doorway from which pitiful screams were issuing. It was a mother thrashing her little boy with a heavy stick—she had tethered him by the leg and was using the stick with both hands. A Chinese proverb as old as the hills tells you, "if you love your son, give him plenty of the cudgel; if you hate him, cram him with delicacies." He was a young wretch, she said, and she could do nothing with him; and she raised her baton again to strike, but the missionary interposed, whereupon she consented to stay her wrath and did so—till we were round the corner.

"Extreme lenity alternating with rude passion in the treatment of children is the characteristic," says Meadows, "of the lower stages of civilisation." I mention this incident only because of its rarity. In no other country in the world, civilised or "heathen," are children generally treated with more kindness and affection than they are in China. "Children, even amongst seemingly stolid Chinese, have the faculty of calling forth the better feelings so often found latent. Their prattle delights the fond father, whose pride beams through every line of his countenance, and their quaint and winning ways and touches of nature are visible even under the disadvantages of almond eyes and shaven crowns" (Dyer Ball).

A mother in China is given, both by law and custom, extreme power over her sons whatever their age or rank. The Sacred Edict says, "Parents are like heaven. Heaven produces a blade of grass. Spring causes it to germinate. Autumn kills it with frost. Both are by the will of heaven. In like manner the power of life and death over the body which they have begotten is with the parents."

And it is this law giving such power to a mother in China which tends, it is believed, to nullify that other law whereby a husband in China is given extreme power over his wife, even to the power in some cases of life and death.

The Mohammedans are still numerous in Chaotong, and there are some 3000 families—the figures are Chinese—in the city and district. Their numbers were much reduced during the suppression of the rebellion of 1857-1873, when they suffered the most awful cruelties. Again, thirteen years ago, there was an uprising which was suppressed by the Government with merciless severity. One street is exclusively occupied by Moslems, who have in their hands the skin trade of the city. Their houses are known by a conspicuous absence from door and window of the coloured paper door-gods that are seen grotesquely glaring from the doors of the unbelievers. Their mosque is well cared for and unusually clean. In the centre, within the main doorway, as in every mosque in the empire, is a gilt tablet of loyalty to the living Emperor. "May the Emperor reign ten thousand years!" it says, a token of subjection which the mosques of Yunnan have especially been compelled to display since the insurrection. At the time of my visit an aged mollah was teaching Arabic and the Koran to a ragged handful of boys. He spoke to me through an interpreter, and gave me the impression of having some little knowledge of things outside the four seas that surround China. I told him that I had lived under the shelter of two of the greatest mosques, but he seemed to question my contention that the mosque in Cordova and the Karouin mosque in Fez are even more noble in their proportions than his mosque in Chaotong. In some of the skin-hongs that I entered, the walls were ornamented with coloured plans of Mecca and Medinah, bought in Chentu, the capital city of the province of Szechuen.

CHAPTER X.

THE JOURNEY FROM CHAOTONG TO TONGCHUAN.

In Chaotong I engaged three new men to go with me to Tongchuan, a distance of 110 miles, and I rewarded liberally the three excellent fellows who had accompanied me from Suifu. My new men were all active Chinamen. The headman Laohwan was most anxious to come with me. Recognising that he possessed characteristics which his posterity would rejoice to have transmitted to them, he had lately taken to himself a wife and now, a fortnight later, he sought rest. He would come with me to Burma, the further away the better; he wished to prove the truth of the adage about distance and enchantment. The two coolies who were to carry the loads were country lads from the district. My men were to receive 4*s*. 6*d*. each for the 110 miles, an excessive wage, but all food was unusually dear, and people were eating maize instead of rice; they were to find themselves on the way, in other words, they were "to eat their own rice," and, in return for a small reward, they were to endeavour to do the five days' stages in three days. I bought a few stores, including some excellent oatmeal and an annular cake of that compressed tea, the "Puerh-cha," which is grown in the Shan States and is distributed as a luxury all over China. It is in favour in the palace of the Emperor in Peking itself; it is one of the finest teas in China, yet, to show how jealous the rivalry now is between China tea and Indian, when I submitted the remainder of this very cake to a well-known tea-taster in Mangoe Lane, Calcutta, and asked his expert opinion, he reported that the sample was "of undoubted value and of great interest, as showing what *muck can be called tea*."

We left on the 3rd, and passed by the main-street through the crowded city, past the rich wholesale warehouses, and out by the west gate to the plain of Chaotong. The country spread before us was smiling and rich, with many farmsteads, and orchards of pears and peaches—a pretty sight, for the trees were now in full blossom. Many carts were lumbering along the road on their uneven wheels. Just beyond the city there was a noisy altercation in the road for the possession apparently of a blunt adze. Carts stopped to see the row, and all the bystanders joined in with their voices, with much earnestness. It is rare for the disputants to be injured in these questions. Their language on these occasions is, I am told, extremely rich in allusions. It would often make a *gendarme* blush. Their oaths are more ornate than the Italians'; the art of vituperation is far advanced in China. A strong wind was blowing in our faces. We rested at some mud hovels where poverty was stalking about with a stick in rags and nakedness. Full dress of many of these beggars would disgrace a Polynesian. Even the better dressed were hung with garments in rags, tattered, and dirty as a Paisley ragpicker's. The children were mostly stark-naked. In the middle of the day we reached a Mohammedan village named Taouen, twenty miles from Chaotong, and my man prepared me an *al fresco* lunch. The entire village gathered into the square to see me eat; they struggled for the orange peel I threw under the table.

From here the road rises quickly to the village of Tashuitsing (7380 feet above sea level), where my men wished to remain, and apparently came to an understanding with the innkeeper; but I would not understand and went on alone, and they perforce had to follow me. There are only half-a-dozen rude inns in the village, all Mohammedan; but just outside the village the road passes under a magnificent triple archway in four tiers made of beautifully cut stone, embossed with flowers and images, and richly gilt—a striking monument in so forlorn a situation. It was built two years ago, in obedience to the will of the Emperor, by the richest merchant of Chaotong, and is dedicated to the memory of his virtuous mother, who died at the age of eighty, having thus experienced the joy of old age, which in China is the foremost of the five measures of felicity. It was erected and carved on the spot by masons from Chungking. Long after dark we reached an outlying inn of the village of Kiangti, a thatched mud barn, with a sleeping room surrounded on three sides by a raised ledge of mud bricks upon which were stretched the mattresses. The room was dimly lit by an oil-lamp; the floor was earth; the grating under the rafters was stored with maize-cobs. Outside the door cooking was done in the usual square earthen stove, in which are sunk two iron basins, one for rice, the other for hot water; maize stalks were being burnt in the flues. The room, when we entered, was occupied by a dozen Chinese, with their loads and the packsaddles of a caravan of mules; yet what did the good-natured fellows do? They must all have been more tired than I; but, without complaining, they all got up when they saw me, and packed their things and went out of the room, one after the other, to make way for myself and my companions. And, while we were comfortable, they crowded into another room that was already crowded.

Next day a tremendously steep descent took us down to Kiangti, a mountain village on the right bank of a swift stream, here spanned in its rocky pass by a beautiful suspension bridge, which swings gracefully high above the torrent. The bridge is 150 feet long by 12 feet broad, and there is no engineer in England who might not be proud to have been its builder. At its far end the parapets are guarded by two sculptured monkeys, hewn with rough tools out of granite, and the more remarkable for their fidelity of form, seeing that the artist must have carved them from memory. The inevitable likin-barrier is at the bridge to squeeze a few more cash out of the poor carriers. That the Inland Customs dues of China are vexatious there can be no doubt; yet it is open to question if the combined duties of all the likin-barriers on any one main road extending from frontier to frontier of any single province in China are greater than the *ad valorem* duties imposed by our colony of Victoria upon the protected goods crossing her border from an adjoining colony.

PAGODA BY THE WAYSIDE, WESTERN CHINA.

Leaving the bridge, the road leads again up the hills. Poppy was now in full flower, and everywhere in the fields women were collecting opium. They were scoring the poppy capsules with vertical scratches and scraping off the exuded juice which had bled from the incisions they made yesterday. Hundreds of pack horses carrying Puerh tea met us on the road; while all day long we were passing files of coolies toiling patiently along under heavy loads of crockery. They were going in the same direction as ourselves to the confines of the empire, distributing those teacups, saucers, and cuplids, china spoons, and rice-bowls that one sees in every inn in China. Most of the crockery is brought across China from the province of Kiangsi, whose natural resources seems to give it almost the monopoly of this industry. The trade is an immense one. In the neighbourhood of King-teh-chin, in Kiangsi, at the outbreak of the Taiping rebellion, more than one million workmen were employed in the porcelain manufactories. Cups and saucers by the time they reach so far distant a part of China as this, carried as they are so many hundreds of miles on the backs of coolies, are sold for three or four times their original cost. Great care is taken of them, and no piece can be so badly broken as not to be mended. Crockery-repairing is a recognised trade, and the workmen are unusually skilful even for Chinese. They rivet the pieces together with minute copper clamps. To have a specimen of their handiwork I purposely in Yunnan broke a cup and saucer into fragments, only to find when I had done so that there was not a mender in the district. Rice bowls and teacups are neatly made, tough, and well finished; even the humblest are not inelegantly coloured, while the high-class china, especially where the imperial yellow is used, often shows the richest beauty of ornamentation.

Inns on this road were few and at wide distances; they were scarcely sufficient for the numbers who used them. The country was red sandstone, open, and devoid of all timber, till, descending again into a valley, the path crossed an obstructing ridge, and led us with pleasant surprise into a beautiful park. It was all green and refreshing. A pretty stream was humming past the willows, its banks covered with the poppy in full flower, a blaze of colour, magenta, white, scarlet, pink and blue picked out with hedges of roses. The birds were as tame as in the Garden of Eden; magpies came almost to our feet; the sparrows took no notice of us; the falcons knew we would not molest them; the pigeons seemed to think we could not. All was peaceful, and the peasants who sat with us under the cedars on the borders of the park were friendly and unobtrusive. Long after sundown we reached, far from the regular stage, a lonely pair of houses, at one of which we found uncomfortable accommodation. Fire had to be kindled in the room in a hollow in the ground; there was no ventilation, the wood was green, the smoke almost suffocating. My men talked on far into the night until I lost patience and yelled at them in English. They thought that I was swearing, and desisted for fear that I should injure their ancestors. There was a shrine in this room for private devotions, the corresponding spot in the adjoining room being a rough opium-couch already occupied by two lusty thickset "slaves to this thrice-accursed drug." My men ate the most frugal of suppers. Food was so much in advance of its ordinary price that my men, in common with thousands of other coolies, were doing their hard work on starvation rations.

On the 5th we did a long day's stage and spent the night at a bleak hamlet 8500 feet above sea level, in a position so exposed that the roofs of the houses were weighted with stones to prevent their being carried away by the wind. This was the "Temple of the Dragon King," and it was only twenty li from Tongchuan.

Next day we were astir early and soon after daylight we came suddenly to the brow of the tableland overlooking the valley of Tongchuan. The compact little walled city, with its whitewashed buildings glistening in the morning sun, lay beyond the gleaming plats of the irrigated plain, snugly ensconced under rolling masses of hills, which rose at the far end of the valley to lofty mountains covered with snow. All the plain is watered with springs; large patches of it are under water all the year round, and, rendered thus useless for cultivation, are employed by the Chinese for the artificial rearing of fish and as breeding grounds for the wild duck and the "faithful bird," the wild goose. A narrow dyke serpentining across the plain leads into the pretty city, where, at the north-east angle of the wall, I was charmed to find the cheerful home of the Bible Christian Mission, consisting of Mr. and Mrs. Sam Pollard and two lady assistants, one of whom is a countrywoman of my own. This is, I believe, the most charming spot for a mission station in all China. Mr. Pollard is quite a young man, full of enthusiasm, modest, and clever. Everywhere he is received kindly; he is on friendly terms with the officials, and there is not a Chinese home within ten miles of the city where he and his pretty wife are not gladly welcomed. His knowledge of Chinese is exceptional; he is the best Chinese scholar in Western China, and is examiner in Chinese for the distant branches of the Inland Mission.

The mission in Tongchuan was opened in 1891, and the results are not discouraging, seeing that the Chinaman is as difficult to lead into the true path as any Jew. No native has been baptized up to date. The convert employed by the mission as a native helper is one of the three converts of Chaotong. He is a bright-faced lad of seventeen, as ardent an evangelist as heart of missionary could desire, but a native preacher can never be so successful as the foreign missionary. The Chinese listen to him with complacency, "You eat Jesus's rice and of course you speak his words," they say.

The attitude of the Chinese in Tongchuan towards the Christian missionary is one of perfect friendliness towards the missionary, combined with perfect apathy towards his religion. Like any other trader, the missionary has a perfect right to offer his goods, but he must not be surprised, the Chinese thinks, if he finds difficulty in securing a purchaser for wares as much inferior to the home production as is the foreign barbarian to the subject of the Son of Heaven.

There is a Catholic Mission in Tongchuan, but the priest does not associate with the Protestant. How indeed can the two associate when they worship different Gods!

The difficulty is one which cannot be easily overcome while there exists in China that bone of contention among missionaries which is known as the "Term Question."

The Chinese recognise a supreme God, or are believed by some to recognise a supreme God—"High Heaven's ruler" (*Shangtien hou*), who is "probably intended," says Williams, "for the true God." The Mohammedans, when they entered China, could not recognise this god as identical with the only one God, to whom they accordingly gave the Chinese name of "true Lord" (*Chên Chu*). The Jesuits, when they entered China, could not recognise either of these gods as identical with the God of the Hebrews, whom they accordingly represented in Chinese first by the characters for "Supreme Ruler" (*Shang ti*), and subsequently by the characters for "Lord of Heaven" (*Tien Chu*). The Protestants naturally could not be identified with the Catholics, and invented another Chinese name, or other Chinese names, for the true God; while the Americans, superior to all other considerations, discovered a different name still for the true God to whom they assigned the Chinese characters for "the true Spirit" (*Chên Shên*), thereby suggesting by implication, as Little observes, that the other spirits were false. But, as if such divergent terms were not sufficiently confusing for the Chinese, the Protestants themselves have still more varied the Chinese characters for God. Thus, in the first translation of the Bible, the term for God used is the Chinese character for "Spirit" (*Shên*); in the second translation this term is rejected and "Supreme Ruler" (*Shang ti*), substituted; the third translation reverts to the "Spirit"; the fourth returns to the "Supreme Ruler"; and the fifth, by Bishop Burdon of Hong Kong, and Dr. Blodget of Peking, in 1884, rejects the title that was first accepted by the Jesuits, and accepts the title "Lord of Heaven" (*Tien Chu*), that was first rejected by the Jesuits.

"Many editions," says the Rev. J. Wherry, of Peking, "with other terms have since been published." "Bible work in particular," says the Rev. Mr. Muirhead, of Shanghai, "is carried on under no small disadvantage in view of this state of things." "It is true, however," adds Mr. Muirhead, "that God has blest all terms in spite of our incongruity." But obviously the Chinese are a little puzzled to know which of the contending gods is most worthy of their allegiance.

But apart from the "Term Question" there must be irreconcilable antagonism between the two great missionary churches in China, for it cannot be forgotten that "in the development of the missionary idea three great tasks await the (Protestant) Church.... The second task is *to check the schemes of the Jesuit*. In the great work of the world's evangelisation the Church has no foe at all comparable with the Jesuit.... Swayed ever by the vicious maxim that the end justifies the means, he would fain put back the shadow of the dial of human progress by half a dozen centuries. Other forms of superstition and error are dangerous, but Jesuitism overtops them all, and stands forth an organised conspiracy against the liberties of mankind. This foe is not likely to be overcome by a divided Protestantism. If we would conquer in this war we must move together, and in our movements must manifest a patience, a heroism, a devotion equal to anything the Jesuit can claim." (The Rev. A. Sutherland, D.D., Delegate from Canada to the Missionary Conference, 1888, *Records*, i., 145.)

And, on the other hand, the distracted Chinese reads that:— "Protestantism is not only a veritable Babel, but a horrible theory, and an immoral practice which blasphemes God, degrades man, and endangers society." (Cardinal Cuesta's Catechism cited in "China and Christianity," by Michie, p. 8.)

CHAPTER XI.

THE CITY OF TONGCHUAN, WITH SOME REMARKS UPON INFANTICIDE.

When I entered Tongchuan the town was in commotion; kettledrums and tomtoms were beating, and crackers and guns firing; the din and clatter was continuous and deafening. An eclipse of the sun was commencing—it was the 6th of April—"the sun was being swallowed by the Dog of Heaven," and the noise was to compel the monster to disgorge its prey. Five months ago the Prefect of the city had been advised of the impending disaster, and it was known that at a certain hour he would publicly intervene with Heaven to avert from the city the calamity of darkness. I myself saw with my own eyes the wonderful power of this man. The sun was darkened when I went to the Prefect's yamen. A crowd was already gathered in the court. At the foot of the steps in the open air, a loosely built framework of wood ten feet high was standing, displaying on its vertex a yellow disc of paper inscribed with the characters for "voracity."

As we waited the sun became gradually clearer, when, just as the moon was disappearing across its edge, the Prefect in full dress, stepped from his yamen into the court, accompanied by the city magistrate and a dozen city fathers. Every instrument of discord was still clanging over the city. Then all these men of weight walked solemnly three times round the scaffold, and halted three times, while the Prefect went down on his knees, and did obeisance with nine kotows to the rickety frame and its disc of yellow paper. There was almost immediate answer to his prayer. With a sigh of relief we saw the lingering remnant of darkness disappear, and the midday sun shone full and bright. Then the Prefect retired, his suite dividing to let him pass, and we all went home blessing the good man whose intercession had saved the town from darkness. For there can be little doubt, I hope, that it is due to the action of this Prefect that the sun is shining to-day in Tongchuan. The Chinese might well ask if any barbarian missionary could do as he did.

Eclipses in China are foretold by the Government almanac published annually in Peking by a bureau of astrology attached to the Board of Rites. The almanac is a Government monopoly, and any infraction of its copyright is a penal offence. "It monopolises the management of the superstitions of the people, in regard to the fortunate or unlucky conjunctions of each day and hour. No one ventures to be without it, lest he be liable to the greatest misfortunes and run the imminent hazard of undertaking important events on blackballed days."

The Chinese almanac is much more comprehensive than ours, for even eclipses are foretold that never happen. Should an error take place in their almanac, and an expected eclipse not occur, the royal astronomers are not disconcerted—far from it; they discover in their error reason for rejoicing; they then congratulate the Emperor that "the heavens have dispensed with this omen of ill-luck in his favour." For eclipses forebode disaster, and every thoughtful Chinaman who has heard of the present rebellion of the Japanese must attribute the reverses caused by the revolt to the eclipse of April 6th, occurring immediately before the insurrection.

Tongchuan is one of the most charming towns I have ever visited; it is probably the cleanest city in China, and the best governed. Its prefect is a man of singular enlightenment, who rules with a justice that is rarely known in China. His people regard him as something more than mortal. Like Confucius "his ear is an obedient organ for the reception of truth." Like the Confucian Superior Man "his dignity separates him from the crowd; being reverent he is beloved; being loyal he is submitted to; and being faithful he is trusted. By his word he directs men, and by his conduct he warns them."

For several years he was attached to the Embassy in Japan, and he boasts that he has made Tongchuan as clean a city as any to be found in the empire of the Mikado. The yamen is a model of neatness. Painted on the outflanking wall there is the usual huge representation of the fabulous monster attempting to swallow the sun—the admonition against extortion—and probably the only magistrate in China who does not stand in need of the warning is the Prefect of Tongchuan.

Prices in Tongchuan at the time of my visit were high and food was scarce. It was difficult to realise that men at that moment were dying of starvation in the pretty town. Rice cost 400 cash for the same quantity that in a good season can be bought for 60 cash;

maize was 300 cash the sheng, whereas the normal price is only 40 cash. Sugar was 15 cash the cake instead of 6 cash the cake, and so on in all things. Poppy is not grown in the valley to the same extent as hitherto, because poppy displaces wheat and beans, and the people have need of all the land they can spare to grow breadstuffs. In the other half of the year, rice, maize, and tobacco are grown together on the plain, and at the same season potatoes, oats, and buckwheat are grown in the hills.

Part of the plain is permanently under water, but it was the drought in the winter and the rains in the summer of successive years that caused the famine. There are no Mohammedans in the town—there have been none since the rebellion—but there are many small Mohammedan villages across the hills. No district in China is now more peaceful than the Valley of Tongchuan. The Yangtse River—"The River of Golden Sand"—is only two days distant, but it is not navigable even by Chinese boatmen. Sugarcane grows in the Yangtse Valley in little pockets, and it is from there that the compressed cakes of brown sugar seen in all the markets of Western Yunnan are brought. Coal comes from a mine two or three days inland; white-wax trees provide an important industry; the hills to the west contain the most celebrated copper mines in the empire.

The cash of Tongchuan are very small and inferior, 2000 being equivalent to one tael, whereas in Chaotong, 110 miles away, the cash vary from 1260 to 1640 the tael. Before the present Prefect took office the cash were more debased still, no less than 4000 being then counted as one tael, but the Prefect caused all these cash to be withdrawn from circulation.

Unlike Chaotong, no children are permitted to be sold in the city, but during last year no fewer than 3000 children (the figures are again Chinese) were carried through the town on their way from Chaotong to the capital. The edict of the Prefect which forbids the selling of children increases the cases of infanticide, and in time of famine there are few mothers among the starving poor who can truthfully assert that they have never abandoned any of their offspring.

The subject of infanticide in China has been discussed by a legion of writers and observers; and the opinion they come to seems to be generally that the prevalence of the crime, except in seasons of famine, has been enormously overstated. The prevalent idea with us Westerns appears to be, that the murder of their children, especially of their female children, is a kind of national pastime with the Chinese, or, at the best, a national peculiarity. Yet it is open to question whether the crime, excepting in seasons of famine, is, in proportion to the population, more common in China than it is in England. H. A. Giles of H.B.M. Chinese Consular Service, one of the greatest living authorities on China, says "I am unable to believe that infanticide prevails to any great extent in China.... In times of famine or rebellion, under stress of exceptional circumstances, infanticide may possibly cast its shadow over the empire, but as a general rule I believe it to be no more practised in China than in England, France, the United States and elsewhere." (*Journal, China Branch R.A.S.*, 1885, p. 28.)

G. Eugène Simon, formerly French Consul in China, declares that "infanticide is a good deal less frequent in China than in Europe generally, and particularly in France." A statement that inferentially receives the support of Dr. E. J. Eitel. (*China Review*, xvi., 189.)

The prevailing impression as to the frequency of infanticide in China is derived from the statements of missionaries, who, no doubt unintentionally, exaggerate the prevalence of the crime in order to bring home to us Westerns the deplorable condition of the heathen among whom they are labouring. But, even among the missionaries, the statements are as divergent as they are on almost every other subject relating to China. Thus the Rev. Griffith John argues "from his own experience that infanticide is common all over the Empire," the Rev. Dr. Edkins on the other hand says that "infanticide is a thing almost unknown in Peking." And the well known medical missionary, Dr. Dudgeon of Peking (who has left the London Mission), agrees with another medical missionary, Dr. Lockhart, "that infanticide is almost as rare in China as in England."

The Rev. A. H. Smith ("Chinese Characteristics," p. 207) speaks "of the enormous infanticide which is known to exist in China." The Rev. Justus Doolittle ("Social Life of the Chinese," ii. p. 203) asserts that "there are most indubitable reasons for believing that infanticide is tolerated by the Government, and that the subject is treated with indifference and with shocking levity by the mass." ...

But Bishop Moule "has good reason to conclude that the prevalence of the crime has been largely exaggerated." (*Journal, China Branch R.A.S., ut supra.*)

One of the best known Consuls in China, who lately retired from the Service, told the writer that in all his thirty years' experience of China he had only had personal knowledge of one authentic case of infanticide.

"Exaggerated estimates respecting the frequency of infanticide," says the Rev. Dr. D. J. MacGowan, "are formed owing to the withholding interment from children who die in infancy." And he adds that "opinions of careful observers will be found to vary with fields of observation." (*China Review*, xiv., 206.)

Whatever the relative frequency of infanticide in China and Europe may be, it cannot, I think, admit of question that the crime of infanticide is less common among the barbarian Chinese than is the crime of f[oe]ticide among the highly civilised races of Europe and America.

There are several temples in Tongchuan, and two beyond the walls which are of more than ordinary interest. There is a Temple to the Goddess of Mercy, where deep reverence is shown to the images of the Trinity of Sisters. They are seated close into the wall, the nimbus of glory which plays round their impassive features being represented by a golden aureola painted on the wall. The Goddess of Mercy is called by the Chinese "*Sheng-mu*," or Holy Mother, and it is this name which has been adopted by the Roman Catholic Church as the Chinese name of the Virgin Mary.

There is a fine City Temple which controls the spirits of the dead of the city as the yamens of the magistrates control the living of the city. The Prefect and the City Magistrate are here shown in their celestial abodes administering justice—or its Chinese equivalent—to the spirits who, when living, were under their jurisdiction on earth. They hold the same position in Heaven and have the same authority as they had on earth; and may, as spirits, be bribed to deal gently with the spirits of departed friends just as, when living, they were open to offers to deal leniently with any living prisoner in whose welfare the friends were prepared to express practical sympathy.

In the Buddhist Temple are to be seen, in the long side pavilions, the chambers of horrors with their realistic representations of the torments of a soul in its passage through the eight Buddhist hells. I looked on these scenes with the calmness of an unbeliever; not so a poor woman to whom the horrors were very vivid truths. She was on her knees before the grating, sobbing piteously at a ghastly scene where a man, while still alive, was being cast by monsters from a hill-top on to red-hot spikes, there to be torn in pieces by serpents. This was the torture her dead husband was now enduring; it was this stage he had reached in his onward passage through hell—the priest had told her so, and only money paid to the priests could lighten his torment.

Beyond the south gate, amid groves of lofty pine trees, are the temple and grounds, the pond and senior wrangler bridge, of the Confucian Temple—the most beautifully-finished temple I have seen in China. We have accustomed ourselves to speak in ecstacies of the wood-carving in the temples of Japan, but not even in the Shōgun chapels of the Shiba temples in Tokyo have I seen wood-carving superior to the exquisite delicacy of workmanship displayed in the carving of the Imperial dragons that frame with their fantastic coils the large Confucian tablet of this temple. Money has been lavished on this building. The inclined marble slabs that divide the terrace steps are covered with fanciful tracery; the parapets of the bridge are chiselled in marble; sculptured images of elephants with howdahs crown the pillars of the marble balustrades; the lattice work under the wide eaves is everywhere beautifully carved. Lofty pillars of wood support the temple roofs. They are preserved by a coating of hemp and protected against fire by an outer coating of plaster stained the colour of the original wood. Gilding is used as freely in the decoration of the grand altar and tablets of this temple, as it is in a temple in Burma.

On a hill overlooking the city and valley is the Temple to the God of Literature. The missionary and I climbed to the temple and saw its pretty court, its ancient bronze censer, and its many beautiful flowers, and then sat on the terrace in the sun and watched the picturesque valley spread out before us.

As we descended the hill again, a lad, who had attached himself to us, offered to show us the two common pits in which are cast the dead bodies of paupers and criminals. The pits are at the foot of the hill, open-mouthed in the uncut grass. With famine in the city, with people dying at that very hour of starvation, there was no lack of dead, and both pits were filled to within a few feet of the surface. Bodies are thrown in here without any covering, and hawks and crows strip them of their flesh, a mode of treating the dead grateful to the Parsee, but inexpressibly hateful to the Chinese, whose poverty must be overwhelming when he can be found to permit it. Pigtails were lying carelessly about and skulls separated from the trunk. Human bones gnawed by dogs were to be picked up in numbers in the long grass all round the hill; they were the bones of the dead who had been loosely buried close to the surface, through which dogs—the domestic dogs one met afterwards in the street—had scraped their way. Many, too, were the bones of dead children; for poor children are not buried, but are thrown outside the wall, sometimes before they are dead, to be eaten perhaps by the very dog that was their playmate since birth.

I called upon the French priest, Père Maire, and he came with much cordiality to the door of the mission to receive me. His is a pretty mission, built in the Chinese style, with a modest little church and a nice garden and summer-house. The father has been four years in Tongchuan and ten in China. Like most of the French priests in China he has succeeded in growing a prodigious beard whose imposing length adds to his influence among the Chinese, who are apt to estimate age by the length of the beard. Only three weeks ago he returned from the capital. Signs of famine were everywhere apparent. The weather was very cold, and the road in many places deeply covered with snow. Riding on his mule he passed at different places on the wayside eight bodies, all recently dead from hunger and cold. No school is attached to the mission, but there is an *orphèlinat* of little girls, *ramassées dans les rues*, who had been cast away by their parents; they are in charge of Chinese Catholic nuns, and will be reared as nuns. As we sat in the pavilion in the garden and drank wine sent to him by his brother in Bordeaux—true French wine—the priest had many things to tell me of interest, of the native rebellion on the frontier of Tonquin, of the mission of Monsieur Haas to Chungking, and the Thibetan trade in tea. "The Chinese? ah! yes. He loves the Chinese because he loves all God's creatures, but they are liars and thieves. Many families are converted, but even the Christians are never Christian till the third generation." These were his words.

CHAPTER XII.

TONGCHUAN TO YUNNAN CITY.

From Tongchuan to Yunnan city, the provincial seat of Government and official residence of the Viceroy, whither I was now bound, is a distance of two hundred miles. My two carriers from Chaotong had been engaged to go with me only as far as Tongchuan, but they now re-engaged to go with Laohwan, my third man, as far as the capital. The conditions were that they were to receive 6*s*. 9*d*. each (2.25 taels), one tael (3*s*.) to be paid in advance and the balance on arrival, and they were to do the distance in seven days. The two taels they asked the missionary to remit to their parents in Chaotong, and he promised to receive the money from me and do so. There was no written agreement of any kind—none of the three men could read; they did not even see the money that the missionary was to get for them; but they had absolute confidence in our good faith.

I had a mule with me from Tongchuan to Yunnan, which saved me many miles of walking, and increased my importance in the eyes of the heathen. I was taking it to the capital for sale. It was a big-boned rough-hewn animal, of superior intelligence, and I was authorised to sell it, together with its saddle and bridle, for four pounds. Like most Chinese mules it had two corns on the forelegs, and thus could see at night. Every Chinaman knows that the corns are adventitious eyes which give the mule this remarkable power.

We were on our way early in the afternoon of the 7th, going up the valley. Below the curiously draped pagoda which commands Tongchuan we met two pairs of prisoners, who were being led into the city under escort. They were coupled by the neck; they were suffering cruelly, for their wrists were so tightly manacled that their hands were strangulated, a mode of torture to which, it will be remembered, the Chinese Government in 1860 subjected Bowlby, the *Times* correspondent, and the other prisoners seized with him "in treacherous violation of a flag of truce," till death ended their sufferings. These men were roadside robbers caught red-handed. Their punishment would be swift and certain. Found guilty on their own confession, either tendered voluntarily to escape torture, or under the compulsion of torture, "self-accusation wrested from their agony," they would be sentenced to death, carried in baskets without delay—if they had not previously "died in prison"—died, that is, from the torture having been pushed too far—to the execution ground, and there beheaded.

We stopped at an inn that was not the ordinary stage, where in consequence we had few comforts. In the morning my men lay in bed till late, and when I called them they opened the door and pointed to the road, clearly indicating that rain had fallen, and that the roads were too slippery for traffic. But what was my surprise on looking myself to find the whole country deeply under snow, and that it was still snowing. All day, indeed, it snowed. The track was very slippery, but my mule, though obstinate, was sure-footed, and we kept going. We passed a huge coffin—borne by a dozen men with every gentleness, not to disturb the dead one's rest—preceded, not followed, by mourners, two of whom were carrying a paper sedan chair, which would be burnt, and so, rendered invisible, would be sent to the invisible world to bear the dead man's spirit with becoming dignity. All day we were in the mountains travelling up the bed of a creek with mountains on both sides of us. We passed Chehki, ninety li from Tongchuan, and thirty li further were glad to escape from the cold and snow to the shelter of a poor thatched mud inn, where we rested for the night.

A hump-back was in charge. The only bedroom was half open to the sky, but the main room was still whole, though it had seen better days. There was a shrine in this room with ancestral tablets, and a sheet of many-featured gods, conspicuous amongst them being the God of Riches, who had been little attentive to the prayers offered him in this poor hamlet. In a stall adjoining our bedroom the mule was housed, and jingled his bell discontentedly all through the night. A poor man, nearly blind with acute inflammation of the eyes, was shivering over the scanty embers of an open fire which was burning in a square hole scooped in the earthern floor near the doorway. He ate the humblest dishful of maize husks and meal strainings. That night I wondered did he sleep out in the open under a hedge, or did the inn people give him shelter with my mule in the next room. My men and I had to sleep in the same room. They were still on short rations. They ate only twice a day, and then sparingly, of maize and vegetables; they took but little rice, and no tea, and only a very small allowance of pork once in two days. Food was very dear, and, though they were receiving nearly double wages to carry half-loads, they must needs be careful. What admirable fellows they were! In all my wanderings I have never travelled with more good-natured companions. The attendant Laohwan was a powerful Chinese, solid and determined, but courteous in manner, voluble of speech, but with an amusing stammer; he had a wide experience of travel in Western China. He seemed to enjoy his journey—he never appeared lovesick; but, of course, I had no means of asking if he felt keenly the long separation from his bride.

At the inn there was no bedding for my men; they had to cover themselves, as best they could, with some pieces of felt brought them by the hunchback, and sleep all huddled together from the cold. They had a few hardships to put up with, but their lot was a thousand times better than that of hundreds of their countrymen who were dying from hunger as well as from cold.

On the 9th, as I was riding on my mule up the mountain road, with the bleak, bare mountain tops on every side, I was watching an eagle circling overhead, when my men called out to me excitedly and pointed to a large wolf that leisurely crossed the path in front of us and slunk over the brow. It had in its mouth a haunch of flesh torn from some poor wretch who had perished during the night. This was the only wolf I saw on my journey, though they are numerous in the province. Last year, not twenty li from Chaotong, a little girl of four, the only child of the mission cook, was killed by a wolf in broad daylight before its mother's eyes, while playing at the cabin door.

Again, to-day, I passed a humpbacked dwarf on the hills, making his solitary way towards Tongchuan, and I afterwards saw others, an indication of the prosperity that had left the district, for in time of famine no child who was badly deformed at birth would be suffered to live.

We stopped the night at Leitoupo, and next day from the bleak tableland high among the mountains, where the wind whistled in our faces, we gradually descended into a country of trees and cultivation and fertility. We left the bare red hills behind us, and came down into a beautiful glade, with pretty streams running in pebbly beds past terraced banks. At a village among the trees, where the houses made some pretension to comfort, and where poppies with brilliantly coloured flowers, encroached upon the street itself, we rested under a sunshade in front of a teahouse. A pretty rill of mountain water ran at our feet. Good tea was brought us in new clean cups, and a sweetmeat of peanuts, set in sugar-like almond toffee. The teahouse was filled. In the midst of the tea drinkers a man was lying curled on a mat, a bent elbow his pillow, and fast asleep, with the opium pipe still beside him, and the lamp still lit. A pretty little girl from the adjoining cottage came shyly out to see me. I called her to me and gave her some sweetmeat. I wished to put it in her mouth but she would not let me, and ran off indoors. I looked into the room after her and saw her father take the lolly from her and give it to her fat little baby brother, who seemed the best fed urchin in the town. But I stood by and saw justice done, and saw the little maid of four enjoy the first luxury of her life-time. Girls in China early learn that they are, at best, only necessary evils, to be endured, as tradition says Confucius taught, only as the possible mothers of men. Yet the condition of women in China is far superior to that in any other heathen country. Monogamy is the rule in China, polygamy is the exception, being confined to the three classes, the rich, the officials, and those who can by effort afford to take a secondary wife, their first wife having failed to give birth to a son.

It is impossible to read the combined experiences of many missionaries and travellers in China without forming the opinion that the condition of women in China is as nearly satisfactory as could be hoped for, in a kingdom of "civilised and organised heathenism," as the Rev. C. W. Mateer terms it. The lot of the average Chinese woman is certainly not one that a Western woman need envy. She cannot enjoy the happiness which a Western woman does, but she is happy in her own way nevertheless. "Happiness does not always consist in absolute enjoyment—but in the idea which we have formed of it."

There was no impertinent curiosity to see the stranger. The people in Yunnan seem cowed and crushed. That arrogance which characterises the Chinese elsewhere is entirely wanting here. They have seen the horrors of rebellion and civil war, of battle, murder and sudden death, of devastation by the sword, famine, ruin, and misery. They are resigned and spiritless. But their friendliness is charming; their courtesy and kindliness is a constant delight to the traveller. At meal time you are always pressed to join the table in the same manner, and with the identical phrases still used by the Spaniards, but the request is one of politeness only, and like the "*quiere Vd. gustar?*" is not meant to be accepted.

We continued on our way. Comparatively few coolies now met us, and the majority of those who did were travelling empty-handed; but there were many ponies and mules coming from the capital, laden with tea and with blocks of white salt like marble. Every here and there a rude shelter was erected by the wayside, where a dish of cabbage and herbs could be obtained, which you ate out of cracked dishes at an improvised bench made from a coffin board resting on two stones. Towards sundown we entered the village of Kong-shan, a pretty place on the hill slope, with views across a fertile hollow that was pleasant to see. Here we found an excellent inn with good quarters. Our day's journey was thirty-seven miles, of which I walked fifteen miles and rode twenty-two miles. We were travelling quickly. Distances in China are, at first, very confusing. They differ from ours in a very important particular: they are not fixed quantities; they vary in length according to the nature of the ground passed over. Inequalities increase the distance; thus it by no means follows that the distance from A to B is equal to the distance from B to A—it may be fifty per cent. or one hundred per cent. longer. The explanation is simple. Distance is estimated by time, and, speaking roughly, ten li (3-1/3 miles) is the unit of distance equivalent to an hour's journey. "Sixty li still to go" means six hours' journey before you; it may be uphill all the way. If you are returning downhill you need not be surprised to learn that the distance by the same road is only thirty li.

To-night before turning in I looked in to see how my mule was faring. He was standing in a crib at the foot of some underground stairs, with a huge horse trough before him, the size and shape of a Chinese coffin. He was peaceful and meditative. When he saw me he looked reproachfully at the cut straw heaped untidily in the trough, and then at me, and asked as clearly as he could if that was a reasonable ration for a high-spirited mule, who had carried my honourable person up hill and down dale over steep rocks and by tortuous paths, a long spring day in a warm sun. Alas, I had nothing else to offer him, unless I gave him the uncut straw that was stitched into our paillasses. What straw was before him was Chinese chaff, cut into three-inch lengths, by a long knife worked on a pivot and board, like the tobacco knife of civilisation. And he had to be content with that or nothing.

Next day we had an early start soon after sunrise. It was a lovely day with a gentle breeze blowing and a cloudless sky. The village of Kong-shan was a very pretty place. It was built chiefly on two sides of a main road which was as rugged as the dry bed of a mountain creek. The houses were better and the inns were again provided with heaps of bedding at the doorways. Advertisement bills in blue and red were displayed on the lintels and doorposts, while fierce door-gods guarded against the admission of evil spirits. Brave indeed must be the spirits who venture within reach of such fierce bearded monsters, armed with such desperate weapons, as were here represented. I stood on the edge of the town overlooking the valley while my mule was being saddled. Patches of wheat and beans were scattered among fields of white-flowered poppy. Coolies carrying double buckets of water were winding up the sinuous path from the border of the garden where "a pebbled brook laughs upon its way." Boys were shouting to frighten away the sparrows from the newly-sown rice beds; while women were moving on their little feet among the poppies, scoring anew the capsules and gathering the juice that had exuded since yesterday. Down the road coolies were filing laden with their heavy burdens—a long day's toil before them; rude carts were lumbering past me drawn by oxen and jolting on wheels that were solid but not circular. Then the mule was brought to me, and we went on through an avenue of trees that were half hidden in showers of white roses, by hedges of roses in full bloom and wayside flowers, daisies and violets, dandelions and forget-me-nots, a pretty sight all fresh and sparkling in the morning sun.

We went on in single file, my two coolies first with their light loads that swung easily from their shoulders, then myself on the mule, and last my stalwart attendant Laohwan with his superior dress, his huge sun hat, his long pipe, and umbrella. A man of unusual endurance was Laohwan. The day's journey done—he always arrived the freshest of the party—he had to get ready my supper, make my bed, and look after my mule. He was always the last to bed and the first to rise. Long before daybreak he was about again, attending to the mule and preparing my porridge and eggs for breakfast. He thought I liked my eggs hard, and each morning construed my look of remonstrance into one of approbation. It is very true of the Chinaman that precedent determines his action. The first morning Laohwan boiled the eggs hard and I could not reprove him. Afterwards of course he made a point of serving me the eggs every morning in the same way. I could say in Chinese "I don't like them," but the morning I said so Laohwan applied my dislike to the eggs not to their condition of cooking, and saying in Chinese "good, good," he obligingly ate them for me.

Leaving the valley we ascended the red incline to an open tableland, where the soil is arid, and yields but a reluctant and scanty harvest. Nothing obstructs the view, and you can see long distances over the downs, which are bereft of all timber except an occasional clump of pines that the axe has spared because of the beneficial influence the geomancers declare they exercise over the neighbourhood. The roadway in places is cut deeply into the ground; for the path worn by the attrition of countless feet soon becomes a waterchannel, and the roadway in the rains is often the bed of a rapid stream. At short intervals are vast numbers of grave mounds with tablets and arched gables of well dressed stone. No habitations of the living are within miles of them, a forcible illustration of the devastation that has ravaged the district. This was still the famine district. In the open uncultivated fields women were searching for weeds and herbs to save them from starvation till the ingathering of the winter harvest. Their children it was pitiful to see. It is rare for Australians to see children dying of hunger. These poor creatures, with their pinched faces and fleshless bones, were like the patient with typhoid fever who has long been hovering between life and death. There were no beggars. All the beggars were dead long ago. All through the famine district we were not once solicited for either food or money, but those who were still living were crying for alms with silent voices a hundred times more appealing. When we rested to have tea the poor children gathered round to see us, skeletons dressed in skins and rags, yet meekly independent and friendly. Their parents were covered with ragged garments that hardly held together. Many wore over their shoulders rude grass cloths made from pine fibre that appear to be identical with the native petticoats worn by the women of New Guinea.

Leaving the poor upland behind us, we descended to a broad and fertile plain where the travelling was easy, and passed the night in a large Moslem inn in the town of Iangkai.

All next day we pursued our way through fertile fields flanked by pretty hills, which it was hard to realise were the peaks of mountains 10,000 to 11,000 feet above sea-level. Before sundown we reached the prosperous market town of Yanglin, where I had a clean upstairs room in an excellent inn. The wall of my bedroom was scrawled over in Chinese characters with what I was told were facetious remarks by Chinese tourists on the quality of the fare.

In the evening my mule was sick, Laohwan said, and a veterinary surgeon had to be sent for. He came with unbecoming expedition. Then in the same way that I have seen the Chinese doctors in Australia diagnose the ailments of their human patients of the same great family, he examined the poor mule with the inscrutable air of one to whom are unveiled the mysteries of futurity, and he retired with his fee. The medicine came later in a large basket, and consisted of an assortment of herbs so varied that one at least might be expected to hit the mark. My Laohwan paid the mule doctor, so he said, for advice and medicine 360 cash (ninepence), an exorbitant charge as prices are in China.

On Friday, April 13th, we had another pleasant day in open country, leading to the low rim of hills that border the plain and lake of Yunnan city. Ruins everywhere testify to the march of the rebellion of thirty years ago—triumphal arches in fragments, broken temples, battered idols destroyed by Mohammedan iconoclasts. Districts destitute of habitations, where a thriving population once lived, attest that suppression of a rebellion in China spells extermination to the rebels.

On the road I met a case of goitre, and by-and-by others, till I counted twenty or more, and then remembered that I was now entering on a district of Asia extending over Western Yunnan into Thibet, Burma, the Shan States, and Siam, the prevailing deformity of whose people is goitre.

THE BIG EAST GATE OF YUNNAN CITY.

Ten miles before Yunnan my men led me off the road to a fine building among the poplars, which a large monogram on the gateway told me was the Catholic College of the *Missions Étrangères de Paris*, known throughout the Province as Jinmaasuh. Situated on rising ground, the plain of Yunnan widening before it, the College commands a distant view of the walls and turretted gateways, the pagodas and lofty temples of the famous city. Chinese students are trained here for the priesthood. At the time of my visit there were thirty students in residence, who, after their ordination, will be scattered as evangelists throughout the Province. Père Excoffier was at home, and received me with characteristic courtesy. His news was many weeks later than mine. M. Gladstone had retired from the Premiership, and M. Rosebery was his successor. England had determined to renew the payment of the tribute which China formerly exacted by right of suzerainty from Burma. The Chinese were daily expecting the arrival of two white elephants from Burma, which were coming in charge of the British Resident in Singai (Bhamo), M. Warry, as a present to the Emperor, and were the official recognition by England that Burma is still a tributary of the Middle Kingdom. I may here say that I often heard of this tribute in Western China. The Chinese had been long waiting for the arrival of the elephants, with their yellow flags floating from the howdahs, announcing, as did the flags of Lord Macartney's Mission to Peking, "Tribute from the English to the Emperor of China," and I suppose that there are governments idiotic enough to thus pander to Chinese arrogance. No doubt what has given rise to the report is the knowledge that the Government of India is bound, under the Convention of 1886, to send, every ten years, a complimentary mission from the Chief Commissioner of Burma to the Viceroy of Yunnan.

It was late when I left Jinmaasuh, and long after sundown before I reached the city. The flagged causeway across the plain was slippery to walk on, and my mule would not agree with me that there was any need to hurry. He knew the Chinese character better than I did. Gunfire, the signal for the closing of the gates, had sounded when we were two miles from the wall; but sentries are negligent in China and the gates were still open. Had we been earlier we should have entered by the south gate, which is always the most important of the gates of a Chinese city, and the one through which all officials make their official entry; but, unable to do this, we entered by the big east gate. Turning sharply to the right along the city wall we were conducted in a few minutes to the Telegraph Offices, where I received a cordial welcome from Mr. Christian Jensen, the superintendent of telegraphs in the two great provinces of Yunnan and Kweichow. These are his headquarters, and here I was to rest a delightful week. It was a pleasant change from silence to speech, from Chinese discomfort to European civilisation. Chinese fare one evening, pork, rice, tea, and beans; and the next, chicken and the famed Shuenwei ham, mutton and green peas and red currant jelly, pancakes and aboriginal Yunnan cheese, claret, champagne, port, and cordial Medoc.

CHAPTER XIII.

AT YUNNAN CITY.

Yunnan City is one of the great cities of China, not so much in size as in importance. It is within easy access at all seasons of the year of the French colony of Tonquin, whereas the trade route from here to British Burma is long, arduous, and mountainous, and in its Western portions is closed to traffic during the rains. From Yunnan City to Mungtze on the borders of Tonquin, where there is a branch of the Imperial Maritime Customs of China, is a journey of eight days over an easy road. Four days from Mungtze is Laokai on the Red River, a river which is navigable by boat or steamer to Hanoi, the chief river port of Tonquin. In the middle of 1889 the French river steamer, *Le Laokai*, made the voyage from Hanoi to Laokai in sixty hours.

From Yunnan City to Bhamo on the Irrawaddy, in British Burma, is a difficult journey of thirty-three stages over a mountainous road which can never by any human possibility be made available for other traffic than caravans of horses or coolies on foot. The natural highway of Central and Southern Yunnan is by Tonquin, and no artificial means can ever alter it. At present Eastern Yunnan sends her trade through the provinces of Kweichow and Hunan to the Yangtse above Hankow, or viâ the two Kuangs to Canton. Shortness of distance, combined with facility of transport, must soon tap this trade or divert it into the highways of Tonquin. Northern Yunnan must send her produce and receive her imports, viâ Szechuen and the Yangtse. As for the trade of Szechuen, the richest of the provinces of China, no man can venture to assert that any other trade route exists, or can ever be made to exist, than the River Yangtse; and all the French Commissioners in the world can no more alter the natural course of this trade than they can change the channel of the Yangtse itself.

I am not, of course, the first distinguished visitor who has been in Yunnan City. Marco Polo was here in 1283, and has left on record a description of the city, which, in his time, was known by the name of Yachi. Jesuit missionaries have been propagating the faith in the province since the seventeenth century. But the distinction of being the first European traveller, not a missionary priest, to visit the city since the time of Marco Polo rests with Captain Doudart de la Grée of the French Navy, who was here in 1867.

Margary, the British Consul, who met a cruel death at Manwyne, passed through Yunnan in 1875 on his famous journey from Hankow; and two years later the tardy mission under Grosvenor, with the brilliant Baber as interpreter, and Li Han Chang, the brother of Li Hung Chang, as delegate for the Chinese, arrived here in the barren hope of bringing his murderers to justice.

Hosie, formerly H.B.M. Consul in Chungking, and well known as a traveller in Western China, was in Yunnan City in 1882.

In September, 1890, Bonvalot and Prince Henri d'Orleans stopped here at the French Mission on their way to Mungtze in Tonquin. It was on the completion of their journey along the eastern edge of *Tibet Inconnu*—"Unknown Thibet!" as they term it, although the whole route had been traversed time and again by missionary priests, a journey whose success was due—though few have ever heard his name—to its true leader, interpreter, and guide, the brave Dutch priest from Kuldja, Père Dedeken.

Another famous missionary traveller, Père Vial, who led Colquhoun out of his difficulty in that journey "Across Chryse," which Colquhoun describes as a "Journey of Exploration" (though it was through a country that had been explored and accurately mapped a century and a half before by Jesuit missionaries), and conducted him in safety to Bhamo in Burma, has often been in Yunnan City, and is a possible successor to the Bishopric.

M. Boell, who left the Secretaryship of the French Legation in Peking to become the special correspondent of *Le Temps*, was here in 1892 on his way from Kweiyang, in Kweichow, to Tonquin, and a few months later Captain d'Amade, the Military Secretary of the French Legation, completed a similar journey from Chungking. In May, 1892, the Commissioner from the French Government opium farm in Hanoi, M. Tommé, arrived in Yunnan City from Mungtze, sent by his Government in search of improved methods of poppy cultivation—the Yunnan opium, with the exception of the Shansi opium, being probably the finest in China. Finally, in May, 1893, Lenz, the American bicyclist, to the profound amazement of the populace, rode on his "living wheel" to the *Yesutang*. This was the most remarkable journey of all. Lenz practically walked across China, surmounting hardships and dangers that few men would venture to face. I often heard of him. He stayed at the mission stations. All the missionaries praise his courage and endurance, and the admirable good humour with which he endured every discomfort. But one missionary lamented to me that Lenz did not possess that close acquaintance with the Bible which was to be expected of a man of his hardihood. It seems that at family prayers at this good missionary's, the chapter for reading was given out when poor Lenz was discovered feverishly seeking the Epistle to the Galatians in the Old Testament. When his mistake was gently pointed out to him he was not discouraged, far from it; it was the missionary who was dismayed to hear that in the United States this particular Epistle is always reckoned a part of the Pentateuch.

I paid an early visit of courtesy to my nominal host, Li Pi Chang, the Chinese manager of the Telegraphs. He received me in his private office, gave me the best seat on the left, and handed me tea with his own fat hands. A mandarin whose rank is above that of an expectant Taotai, Li is to be the next Taotai of Mungtze, where, from an official salary of 400 taels per annum, he hopes to save from 10,000 to 20,000 taels per annum.

"Squeezing," as this method of enrichment is termed, is, you see, not confined to America. Few arts, indeed, seem to be more widely distributed than the art of squeezing. "Dives, the tax-dodger," is as common in China as he is in the United States. Compare, however, any city in China, in the midst of the most ancient civilisation in the world, with a city like Chicago, which claims to have reached the highest development of modern civilisation, and it would be difficult to assert that the condition of public morals in the heathen city was even comparable with the corruption and sin of the American city, a city "nominally Christian, which is studded with churches and littered with Bibles," but still a city "where perjury is a protected industry." No community is more ardent in its evangelisation of the "perishing Chinese" than Chicago, but where in all China is there "such a supreme embodiment of fraud, falsehood, and injustice," as prevails in Chicago? An alderman in Chicago, Mr. Stead tells us (p. 172 *et seq.*) receives only 156 dollars a year salary; but, in addition to his salary, he enjoys "practically unrestricted liberty to fill his pockets by bartering away the property of the city." "It is expected of the alderman, as a fundamental principle, that he will steal," and, in a fruitful year, says the *Record*, the average crooked alderman makes 15,000 to 20,000 dollars. An assessorship in Chicago is worth nominally 1500 dollars per annum, but "everyone knows that in Chicago an assessorship is the shortest cut to fortune."

Squeezing in China may be common, but it is a humble industry compared with the monumental swindling which Mr. Stead describes as existing in Chicago.

Besides being manager in Yunnan City, Li is the chief telegraph director of the two provinces of Yunnan and Kweichow. That he is entirely innocent of all knowledge of telegraphy, or of the management of telegraphs, is no bar to such an appointment. He is a mandarin, and is, therefore, presumably fitted to take any position whatever, whether it be that of Magistrate or Admiral of the Fleet, Collector of Customs, or General commanding in the field. Of the mandarin in China it is truly said that "there is nothing he isn't."

Li is also Chief Secretary of the *Shan-hao-Tsung-Kuh*, "The Supreme Board of Reorganisation" of the province, the members of which are the four highest provincial officials next below the Governor (*Futai*)—viz., the Treasurer (*Fantai*), Provincial Judge (*Niehtai*), the Salt Comptroller, and the Grain Intendant.

Li, it may be said at once, is a man of no common virtue. He is the father of seven sons and four daughters; he can die in peace; in his family there is no fear of the early extinction of male descendants, for the succession is as well provided against as it is in the most fertile Royal family in Europe. His family is far spreading, and it is worth noting as an instance of the patriarchal nature of the family in China, that Li is regarded as the father of a family, whose members dependent upon him for entire or partial support number eighty persons. He has had three wives. His number one wife still lives at the family seat in Changsha; another secondary wife is dead; his present number two wife lives with him in Yunnan. This is his favourite wife, and her story is worth a passing note. She was not a "funded houri," but a poor *yatow*, a "forked head" or slave girl, whom he purchased on a lucky day, and, smitten with her charms, made her his wife. It was a case of love at first sight. Her conduct since marriage has more than justified the choice of her master. Still a young woman, she has already presented her lord with nine children, on the last occasion surpassing herself by giving birth to twins. She has a most pleasant face, and really charming children; but the chief attraction of a Chinese lady is absent in her case. Her feet are of natural size, and not even in the exaggerated murmurings of love could her husband describe them as "three-inch gold lilies."

That this was a marriage of inclination there can be no doubt whatever. It is idle to argue that the Chinese are an unemotional people, incapable of feeling the same passions that move us. We ridicule the image of a Chinaman languishing in love, just as the Chinaman derides the possibility of experiencing the feelings of love for the average foreign woman he has seen in China. Their poetry abounds in love episodes. Students of Chinese civilisation seem to agree that a *mariage de convenance* in China is more likely even than on the Continent to become instantly a marriage of affection. The pleasures of female society are almost denied the Chinaman; he cannot fall in love before marriage because of the absence of an object for his love. "The faculty of love produces a subjective ideal; and craves for a corresponding objective reality. And the longer the absence of the objective reality, the higher the ideal becomes; as in the mind of the hungry man ideal foods get more and more exquisite."

In Meadows' "Essay on Civilisation in China," there is a charming story, translated from the Chinese, of love at first sight, given in illustration of the author's contention that "it is the men to whom women's society is almost unknown that are most apt to fall violently in love at first sight. Violent love at first sight is a general characteristic of nations where the sexes have no intercourse before marriage.... The starved cravings of love devour the first object":—

"A Chinese who had suffered bitter disenchantments in marriage retired with his infant son to the solitude of a mountain inaccessible for little-footed Chinese women. He trained up the youth to worship the gods and stand in awe and abhorrence of devils, but he never mentioned even the name of woman to him. He always descended to market alone, but when he grew old and feeble he was at length compelled to take the young man with him to carry the heavy bag of rice. He very reasonably argued, 'I shall always accompany my son, and take care that if he does see a woman by chance, he shall never speak to one; he is very obedient; he has never heard of woman; he does not know what they are; and as he has lived in that way for twenty years already, he is, of course, now pretty safe.'

"As they were on the first occasion leaving the market town together, the son suddenly stopped short, and, pointing to three approaching objects, inquired: 'Father, what are these things? Look! look! what are they?' The father hastily answered: 'Turn away your head. They are devils.' The son, in some alarm, instantly turned away from things so bad, and which were gazing at his motions with surprise from under their fans. He walked to the mountain top in silence, ate no supper, and from that day lost his appetite and was afflicted with melancholy. For some time his anxious and puzzled parent could get no satisfactory answer to his inquiries; but at length the poor young man burst out, almost crying from an inexplicable pain: 'Oh, father, that tallest devil! that tallest devil, father!'"

Girls for Yunnan City are bought at two chief centres—at Chaotong, as we have seen, and at Bichih. They are carried to the city in baskets. They are rarely sold into prostitution, but are bought as slave girls for domestic service, as concubines, and occasionally as wives. Their great merit is the absence of the "thickneck," goitre.

The morning after my visit, Li sent me his card, together with a leg of mutton and a pile of sweet cakes. I returned my card, and gave the bearer 200 cash (fivepence), not as a return gift to the mandarin, but as a private act of generosity to his servant—all this being in accordance with Chinese etiquette.

My host in Yunnan, and the actual manager and superintendent of the telegraphs of the two provinces, is a clever Danish gentleman, Mr. Christian Jensen, an accomplished linguist, to whom every European resident and traveller in the province is indebted for a thousand acts of kindness and attention. He has a rare knowledge of travel in China. Mr. Jensen arrived in China in 1880 in the service of the Great Northern Telegraph Company—a Danish company. From December, 1881, when the first Chinese telegraph line was opened (that from Shanghai to Tientsin), till the spring of 1883, he was one of eight operatives and engineers lent by the Company to the Chinese Government. In December 1883, having returned in the meantime to the Great Northern he accepted an engagement under the Imperial Government and he has been in their employ ever since. During this time he has superintended the construction of 7000 li (2350 miles) of telegraph lines, and it was he who, on the 20th May, 1890, effected the junction of the Chinese system with the French lines at Laokai. Among the more important lines constructed by him are those joining the two capital cities of the provinces of Yunnan and Kweichow; that from Yunnan City to Mungtze, on the frontier of Tonquin; that from Canton to the boundary of Fuhkien province; and that from Yunnan City through Tali to Tengyueh (Momien), this last line being the one which will eventually unite with the marvellous Indian telegraph system at the Burmese frontier. In the course of his many journeys through China, Mr. Jensen has been invariably well treated by the Chinese, and it is pleasant to hear one who has seen so much of the inner life of the country speak as he does of the universal courtesy and hospitality, attention, and kindness that has been shown him by all classes of Chinese from the highest officials to the humblest coolies.

VIEW IN YUNNAN CITY.

Many interesting episodes have marked his stay in China. Once, when repairing the line from Pase, in Kwangsi, to Mungtze, during the rainy season of 1889, fifty-six out of sixty men employed by him died of what there can be little doubt was the same plague that has lately devastated Hong Kong. On this occasion, of twelve men who at different times were employed as his chair-bearers, all died.

In October, 1886, he came to Yunnan City, and made this his headquarters. He has always enjoyed good health.

One of the chief difficulties that formerly impeded the extension of the telegraph in China was the belief that the telegraph poles spoil the "*fungshui*"—in other words, that they divert good luck from the districts they pass through. This objection has been everywhere overcome. It last revealed itself in the extreme west of the line from Yunnan. Villagers who saw in the telegraph a menace to the good fortune of their district would cut down the poles—and sell the wire in compensation for their trouble. The annoyance had to be put a stop to. An energetic magistrate took the matter in hand. He issued a warning to the villagers, but his warning was unheeded. Then he took more vigorous measures. The very next case that occurred he had two men arrested, and charged with the offence. They were probably innocent, but under the persuasion of the bamboo they were induced to acquiesce in the magistrate's opinion as to their guilt. They were sentenced to be deprived of their ears, and then they were sent on foot, that all might see them, under escort along the line from Yunnan City to Tengyueh and back again. No poles have been cut down since.

CHAPTER XIV.

GOLD, BANKS, AND TELEGRAPHS IN YUNNAN.

Yunnan City is the great gold emporium of China, for most of the gold found in China comes from the province of which it is the capital. When a rich Chinaman returns from Yunnan to another province, or is summoned on a visit to the Emperor at Peking, he carries his money in gold not silver. Gold leaf sent from Yunnan gilds the gods of Thibet and the temples and pagodas of Indo-China. No caravan returns to Burma from Western China whose spare silver has not been changed into gold leaf. In the Arracan Temple in Mandalay, as in the Shway-dagon Pagoda in Rangoon, you see the gold leaf that Yunnan produces, and in the future will produce in infinitely greater quantities.

Gold comes chiefly from the mines of Talang, eighteen days journey by land S.W. from Yunnan City, on the confines of the district which produces the famous Puerh tea. The yield must be a rich one despite the ineffective appliances that are employed in its extraction. Gold has always been abundant in this province; at the time of Marco Polo's visit it was so abundant that its value in relation to silver was only as one to six.

When gold is worth in Shanghai 35 times its weight in silver, it may be bought in Yunnan City or Talifu for from 25 to 27.5 times its weight in silver, and in quantities up to hundreds of ounces. To remit silver by telegraphic transfer from Shanghai or Hong Kong to Yunnan city costs six per cent., and either of the two leading banks in the city will negotiate the transfer from their agents at the seaports of any amount up to 10,000 ounces of silver in a single transaction. The gold can always be readily sold in Shanghai or Hong Kong, and the only risk is in the carriage of the gold from the inland city to the seaport. So far as I could learn, no gold thus sent has gone astray. It is carried overland by the fastest trade route—that through Mungtze to Laokai—and thence by a boat down stream to Hanoi in Tonquin, from which port it is sent by registered post to Saigon and Hong Kong. Here then is a venture open to all, with excitement sufficient for the most *blasé* speculator. Ample profits are made by the dealer. For instance, a large quantity of gold was purchased in Yunnan city on the 21st January, 1894, at

23.2, its value in Shanghai on the same date being 30.9; but on the date that the gold arrived in Shanghai its value had risen to 35, at which price it was sold. At the time of my visit gold was 25.5 to 27 in Yunnan, and 35 in Shanghai, and I have since learnt that, while gold has become cheaper in the province, it has become dearer at the seaport.

The gold is brought to the buyer in the form of jewellery of really exquisite workmanship, of rings and bracelets, earrings and head ornaments, of those tiny images worn by rich children in a half circlet over the forehead, and bridal charms that would make covetous the heart of a nun. Ornaments of gold such as these are 98 per cent. fine and are sold, weighed on the same scales, for so many times their weight in silver. They are sold not because of the poverty of their owners, but because their owners make a very large profit on their original cost by so disposing of them. If, however, the purchaser prefer it, gold will be brought him in the leaf 99 per cent. fine, and this is undoubtedly the best form into which to convert your silver. The gold beaters of Yunnan are a recognised class, and are so numerous that they have a powerful guild or trade's union of their own.

Gold-testing is also a recognised profession, but the methods are primitive and require the skill of an expert, consisting, as they do, of a comparison of the rubbing on a stone of the unknown gold, with a similar rubbing of gold whose standard has been accurately determined. One of the best gold-testers in the city has been taught electric gilding by Mr. Jensen and does some skilful work.

The principle of self-protection restrains the Chinaman from the ostentatious exhibition of his wealth—he fears being squeezed by the officials who are apt to regard wealth as an aggravation of crime, to be the more severely punished the better able is the accused to purchase exemption from punishment. I have seen a stranger come into the room where Mr. Jensen and I were sitting, who from his appearance seemed to be worth perhaps a five-dollar bill, and after a preliminary interchange of compliments, I have seen his hand disappear up his long sleeve and produce a package of gold leaf worth perhaps 2000 taels of silver. This he would offer for sale; there was some quiet bargaining; when, should they agree, the gold was weighed, the purchaser handed a cheque on his Chinese banker for the amount in silver, and the transaction was finished as quickly and neatly as if it had taken place in Bond Street, and not in the most inland capital of an "uncivilised country"; whose civilisation has nevertheless kept it intact and mighty since the dawn of history, and whose banking methods are the same now as they were in the days of Solomon.

The silver of Yunnan is of the same standard as the silver of Shanghai, namely 98 per cent. pure, and differs to the eye from the absolutely unalloyed silver of Szechuen.

The cash of Yunnan vary in a way that is more than usually bewildering. Let me explain, in a few sentences, the "cash" currency of the Middle Kingdom. The current coin of China as everyone knows is the brass cash, which is perforated so that it may be carried on a string. Now, theoretically, a "string of cash" contains 100 coins, and in the Eastern provinces ten strings are the theoretical equivalent of one Mexican dollar. But there are eighteen provinces in China, and the number of brass cash passing for a string varies in each province from the full 100, which I have never seen, to 83 in Taiyuen, and down to 33 in the Eastern part of the province of Chihli. In Peking I found the system charmingly simple. One thousand cash are there represented by 100 coins, whereas 1000 "old cash" consist of 1000 coins, though 1000 "capital cash" are only 500 coins. The big cash are marked as 10 capital cash, but count the same as 5 old cash. Nowhere does a Chinaman mean 1000 cash when he speaks of 1000 cash. In Tientsin 1000 cash means 500 cash—that is to say 5 times 100 cash, the 100 there being any number you can pass except 100, though by agreement the 100 is usually estimated at 98. In Nanking I found a different system to prevail. There cash are 1075 the 1000, but of the 10 strings of 100 cash, 7 contain only 98 cash each, and 3 only 95, yet the surplus 75 cash—that is to say the number which for the time being is the Nanking equivalent of 75—are added all the same. At Lanchow in Chihli on the Imperial Chinese Railway near Shanhai-kwan, 16 old cash count as 100 cash, yet 33 are required to make up 200; in Tientsin from which point the railway starts, 1000 cash are really 500 cash and 98 count there as 100. Now 2000 Chihli cash are represented by 325 coins, and 1000 by 162 coins, and 6000 by 975 coins, which again count as 1000 large cash and equal on an average one Mexican dollar. Therefore to convert Lanchow cash into Tientsin cash you must divide the

Lanchow cash by 3, count 975 as 1000, and consider this equal to a certain percentage of a theoretical amount of silver known as a tael, which is always varying of itself as well as by the fluctuations in the market value of silver, and which is not alike in any two places, and may widely vary in different portions of the same place.

Could anything be simpler? And yet there are those who say that the system of money exchange in China is both cumbrous and exasperating. Take as a further instance the cash in Yunnan. Everyone knows that theoretically there are 2000 cash in the tael, each tael containing 20 "strings," and each "string" 100 cash, but in Yunnan 2000 cash are not 2000 cash—they are only 1880 cash. This does not mean that 1880 cash are represented by 1880 coins, not at all; because 62 cash in Yunnan are counted as 100. Eighteen hundred and eighty cash are therefore represented by only 1240 cash coins and all prices must be paid in this proportion. Immediately outside the city, however, a string of cash is a "full string" and contains 100 cash or rather it contains as few cash as possibly can be passed for 100, a fair average number being 98.

Silver is weighed in the City banks and at the wholesale houses on the "capital scale," but in the retail stores on scales that are heavier by 14 per cent. (one mace and 4 candareens in the tael). Outside the city on the road to Tali there is a loss on exchange varying according to your astuteness from 3 to 6 per cent. on the capital scale.

There are two chief banks in Yunnan city. Wong's whose bank, the signboard tells us, is "Beneficent, Rich, United," and Mong's "Bank of the Hundred Streams," which is said to be still richer.

With Mr. Jensen I called one evening upon Wong, and found him with his sons and chief dependents at the evening meal. All rose as we entered and pressed us to take a seat with them, and when we would not, the father and grown-up son showed us into the guest-room and seated us on the opium-dais under the canopy. The opium-lamps were already lit; on a beautiful tray inlaid with mother-of-pearl there were pipes for visitors, and phials of prepared opium. Here we insisted on their leaving us and returning to their supper; they finished speedily and returned to their visitors. We were given good tea and afterwards a single cigar was handed to each of us. In offering you a cigar it is not the Chinese custom to offer you your choice from the cigar box; the courtesy is too costly, for there are few Chinamen in these circumstances who could refrain from helping themselves to a handful. "When one is eating one's own" says the Chinese proverb, "one does not eat to repletion; when one is eating another's, one eats till the tears run."

Wong is one of the leading citizens of Yunnan, and is held in high honour by his townsmen. His house is a handsome Chinese mansion; it has a dignified entrance and the garden court is richly filled with plants in porcelain vases. It may thus be said of him, as of the Confucian Superior Man, "riches adorn his house and virtue his person, his heart is expanded, and his body is at ease."

A Szechuen man, a native of Chungking, fifty-nine years of age, Wong is a man of immense wealth, his bank being known all over China, and having branches in capital cities so far distant from each other as Peking, Canton, Kweiyang, Shanghai, Hankow, Nanchang, Soochow, Hangchow, and Chungking. I may add that he has smoked opium for many years.

I formed a high opinion of the intelligence of Wong. He questioned me like an insurance doctor as to my family history, and professed himself charmed with the amazing richness in sons of my most honourable family. He had heard of my native country, which he called *Hsin Chin Shan*, the "New Gold Mountain," to distinguish it from the *Lao Chin Shan*, the "Old Gold Mountain," as the Chinese term California. I was the more pleased to find that Wong had some knowledge of Australia and its gold, because a few months before I had been pained by an incident bearing on this very subject, which occurred to me in the highly civilised city of Manila, in the Philippine Islands. On an afternoon in August, 1893, I stood in the Augustine Church, in Old Manila, to witness the funeral service of the Padre Provincial of the Augustines. It was the first occasion for one hundred and twenty-three years that the Provincial of the Order had died while in the actual exercise of his office, and it was known that the ceremony would be one of the most imposing ever seen in the Islands. The fine old church, built by the son of the architect of the Escorial—the only building in Manila left standing by the earthquake of 1645—was crowded with mourners, and almost every notability of the province was said to be present. During the service two young Spaniards, students from the University close by, pushed their way in beside me. Wishing to learn who were the more distinguished of the mourners, I asked the students to kindly point out to me the Governor-General (Blanco), and other prominent officials, and they did so with agreeable courtesy. When the service was finished I thanked them for the trouble they had taken and was coming away, when one of them stopped me.

"Pardon me, Caballero," he said, "but will you do me the favour to tell me where you come from?"

"I am from Australia."

"From Austria! so then you come from Austria?"

"No, sir, from Australia."

"But 'Australia'—where is it?"

"It is a rich colony of England of immense importance."

"But where is it?" he persisted.

"*Dios mio!*" I exclaimed aghast, "it is in China."

But his friend interposed. "The gentleman is talking in fun," he said. "Thou knowest, Pepe, where is Australia, where is Seednay, and Melboornay, where all the banks have broken one after the other in a bankruptcy colossal."

"*Ya me figuraba donde era,*" Pepe replied, as I edged uncomfortably away.

During my journey across China it was not often that I was called upon to make use of my profession. But I was pleased to be of some service to this rich banker. He wished to consult me professionally, because he had heard from the truthful lips of rumour of the wonderful powers of divination given to the foreign medical man. What was his probable tenure of life? That was the problem. I gravely examined two of his pulses—every properly organised Chinaman has four hundred—and finding his heart where it should be in the centre of his body, with the other organs ranged round it like the satellites round the sun—every Chinaman is thus constructed—I was glad to be able to assure him that he will certainly live forty years longer—if Heaven permit him.

Wong has a grown-up son of twenty who will succeed to the bank; he is at present the managing proprietor of a small general store purchased for him by his father. The son has been taught photography by Mr. Jensen, and has an excellent camera obtained from Paris. He is quite an enthusiast. In his shop a crowd is always gathered round the counter looking at the work of this Chinese amateur. There are a variety of stores for sale on the shelves, and I was interested to notice the cheerful promiscuity with which bottles of cyanide of potassium and perchloride of mercury were scattered among bottles of carbonate of soda, of alum, of Moët and Chandon (spurious), of pickles, and Howard's quinine. The first time that cyanide of potassium is sold for alum, or corrosive sublimate for bicarbonate of soda there will be an *éclat* given to the dealings of this shop which will be very gratifying to its owner.

The telegraph in Yunnan is very largely used by the Chinese, especially by the bankers and officials. By telegraph you can remit, as I have said, through the Chinese banks, telegraphic transfers to the value of thousands of taels in single transactions. It is principally the banks and the Government who make use of the telegraph, and their communications are sent by private code. When the Tsungli Yamen in Peking sends a telegram to the Viceroy in Yunnan it is in code that the message comes; and it is by private code also that a Chinese bank in Shanghai telegraphs to its far inland agents. Messages are sent in China by the Morse system. The method of telegraphing Chinese characters, whose discovery enabled the Chinese to make use of the telegraph, was the ingenious invention of a forgotten genius in the Imperial Maritime Customs of China. The method is simplicity itself. The telegraph code consists of ten thousand numbers of four numerals each, and each group so constituted represents a Chinese character. Any operator, however ignorant of Chinese, can thus telegraph or receive a message in Chinese. He receives, for instance, a message containing a series of numbers such as 0018, 0297, 5396, 8424. He has before him a series of ten thousand wood blocks on which the number is cut at one end and the corresponding Chinese character at the other, he takes out the number, touches the inkpad with the other end, and stamps opposite each group its Chinese character. The system permits, moreover, of the easy arrangement of indecipherable private codes, because by adding or subtracting a certain number from each group of figures, other characters than those telegraphed can be indicated.

I need hardly add that the system of wood blocks is not in practical use, for the numbers and their characters are now printed in code-books. And here we have an instance of the marvellous faculty of memorising characteristic of the Chinese. A Chinaman's memory is something prodigious. From time immemorial the memory of the Chinese has been developed above all the other faculties. Memory is the secret of success in China, not originality. Among a people taught to associate innovation with impiety, and with whom precedent determines all action, it is inevitable that the faculty of recollection should be the most highly developed of all the mental faculties. Necessity compels the Chinaman to have a good memory. No race has ever been known where the power of memory has been developed even in rare individual cases to the degree that is common to all classes of the Chinese, especially to the literati.

The Chinese telegraph clerk quickly learns all the essential portion of the code-book by heart. The book then lies in the drawer a superfluity. It is claimed for Chiang, the second Chinese clerk in Yunnan, that he knows all the 10,000 numbers and their corresponding characters.

Telegrams from Yunnan to Shanghai cost twenty-two tael cents (at the present value of the tael this is equal to sixpence) for each Chinese character; but each word in any other language is charged double, that is, forty-four cents.

SOLDIERS ON THE WALL OF YUNNAN CITY.

From Yunnan to Talifu is a distance of 307 miles. The native banker in the capital will remit for you by wire to his agent in Tali the sum of 1000 taels, for a charge of eight taels, exclusive of the cost of the telegram, and, as the value of silver in Tali is one per cent. higher than it is in Yunnan, the traveller can send his money by wire with perfect safety, and lose nothing in the remittance, not even the cost of the telegram.

The telegraph offices are separated from the city wall by a small common, which is quite level, and which the Chinaman of the future will convert into a bowling green and lawn-tennis ground. There is a handsome entrance. The large portal is painted with horrific gods armed with monstrous weapons. The Chinese still seem to adhere to the belief that the deadliness of a weapon must be in proportion to the savageness of its aspect. Inside, there are spacious courts and well-furnished guest rooms, roomy apartments, and offices for the mandarin, as well as comfortable quarters for Mr. Jensen and his body of Chinese clerks and operators. There is a pretty garden all bright and sunny, with a pond of gold fish and ornamental parapet. Wandering freely in the enclosure are peacocks and native companions, while a constant play-mate of the children is a little laughing monkey of a kind that is found in the woods beyond Tali. At night a watchman passes round the courts every two hours, striking a dismal gong under the windows, and waking the foreigner from his slumbers; but the noise he makes does not disturb the sleep of the Chinese—indeed, it is open to question if there is any discord known which, as mere noise, *could* disturb a Chinaman.

The walls that flank the entrance are covered with official posters giving the names of the men of Yunnan City who contributed to the relief of the sufferers by a recent famine in Shansi, together with the amounts of their contributions and the rewards to which their gifts entitled them. The Chinese are firm believers in the doctrine of justification by works, and on these posters one could read the exact return made in this world for an act of merit, apart, of course, from the reward that will be reaped in Heaven. In a case like this it is usually arranged that for "gifts amounting to a certain percentage of the sums ordinarily authorised, subscribers may obtain brevet titles, posthumous titles, decorations, buttons up to the second class, the grade of licentiate, and brevet rank up to the rank of Colonel. Disgraced officials may apply to have their rank restored. Nominal donations of clothes, if the money value of the articles be presented instead, will entitle the givers to similar honours."—*The Peking Gazette*, August 22, 1892.

In the centre of the green stands the hollow pillar in which Chinese printed waste-paper is reverently burnt. "When letters were invented," the Chinese say, "Heaven rejoiced and Hell trembled." "Reverence the characters," is an injunction of Confucius which no Chinaman neglects to follow. He remembers that "he who uses lettered paper to kindle the fire has ten demerits, and will have itchy sores"; he remembers that "he who tosses lettered paper into dirty water, or burns it in a filthy place, has twenty demerits and will frequently have sore eyes or become blind," whereas "he who goes about and collects, washes, and burns lettered paper, has 5000 merits, adds twelve years to his life, will become honoured and wealthy, and his children and grandchildren will be virtuous and filial." But his reverence has strict limits, and while he reverences the piece of paper upon which a moral precept is written, he often thinks himself absolved from reverencing the moral precept itself, just as a deacon in England need not necessarily be one who never over-reached his neighbours or swindled his creditors.

CHAPTER XV.

THE FRENCH MISSION AND THE ARSENAL IN YUNNAN CITY.

The most prominent structure within the city walls is the Heavenly Lord Hall (*Tien-chu-tang*), the pile of buildings which form the headquarters of the French Mission in the province of Yunnan. It was a master-stroke to secure possession of so important a site. The palace is on a higher level even than the yamen of the Viceroy, and must intercept much of the good fortune that would otherwise flow into the city. The façade of the central hall has been ornamented with a superb cross of porcelain mosaic, which is a conspicuous object from the city wall. A large garden, where the eucalyptus has been wisely planted, surrounds the buildings. In residence in the Heavenly Hall are the venerable Vicaire Apostolique of the province, Monseigneur Fenouil, the Provicaire, and four missionary priests, all four of whom are from Alsace. In the province altogether there are twenty-two French priests and eight ordained Chinese priests—thirty in all; their converts number 15,000. Monseigneur Fenouil is a landmark of Western China; he first set foot in the province in 1847, and is the oldest foreign resident in the interior of China. No Chinaman speaks purer Chinese than he; he thinks in Chinese. Present in the province throughout the Mohammedan insurrection, he was an eye-witness of the horrors of religious warfare. Few men have had their path in life marked by more thrilling episodes. He was elected Bishop, in 1880, by the unanimous vote of all the priests in the province, a vote confirmed by Rome; which is, I am told, the mode of election by which Catholic Missionary Bishops in China are always chosen.

The grand old Bishop seemed much amused at my journey. "I suppose you are riding a mule," he said, "for you English have large bones, and the Chinese ponies are very small." I said that I had come so far most of the way on foot. "You speak Chinese, of course?"

"Hardly at all; I speak only a dozen words of Chinese."

"Then you have a Chinese interpreter? No! An English companion who can speak Chinese? No! A Chinese servant who can speak English? No, and no escort! But without doubt you are armed?

No! No escort, no revolver, no companion, and you can live on Chinese food. Ah! you have a brave heart, Monsieur."

At the time of my visit to Yunnan, Père de Gorostarza, the accomplished Provicaire, was absent at Mungtze deciding a question of discipline. Four months before one of the most trusted converts of the mission had been sent to Mungtze to purchase a property for the use of the mission. He was given the purchase-money of 400 taels, but, when he arrived in Mungtze, and the eye of the mission was no longer upon him, he invested the money, not in premises for the mission, but in a coolie-hong for himself. His backsliding had availed him little. And he was now defending his conduct as best he could before the Bishop's deputy.

Converts of the French mission in China, it is well to remember, are no longer French subjects or *protégés*; the objection is no longer tenable that the mission shields bad characters who only become converted in order to escape from the consequences of their guilt.

How wonderful has been the pioneer work done by the Jesuit Missionaries in China! It may almost be said that the foundation of all that we know about China we owe to the Jesuit Missionaries. All maps on China are founded upon the maps of the Jesuit Missionaries employed for the purpose by the Emperor Kanghi (1663-1723), "the greatest prince who ever graced the throne of China." Their accuracy has been the wonder of all geographers for a century past. "Now that the 'Great River' (the Yangtse) has been surveyed," says Captain Blakiston, "for nearly 1600 miles from the ocean, and with instruments and appliances such as were unknown in the days of those energetic and persevering men, no small praise is due to the first Christian explorers for the extraordinary correctness of their maps and records." The reports of the early Jesuit Missionaries even Voltaire describes as the "productions of the most intelligent travellers that have extended and embellished the fields of science and philosophy."

Yet we, as Protestants, are warned by a great missionary that we must not be deluded by these insidious compliments; we must not forget that the work of the Jesuits in China "overtops all other forms of superstition and error in danger, and stands forth an organised conspiracy against the liberties of mankind. The schemes of the Jesuits must be checked."

One Sunday morning Mr. Jensen and I rode round the city wall. This is one of the most massive walls in a country of walled cities. It is built of brick and stone over a body of earth thirty feet thick; it is of imposing height, and wide enough for a carriage drive. When I was mounted on my mule the upper edge of the parapet was on a level with my forehead. There are six city gates. The great north gate is closely barred all through the rains to prevent the entrance of the "Flood God," who, fortunately, his intelligence being limited, knows no other way to enter the city than by this gate. The great turreted south gate is the most important of all, as it is in all Chinese cities. Near this gate the Viceroy's Yamen is situated, and the Yamen of the Futai (Governor of the Province); both buildings, of course, looking to the south, as did the Temple of Solomon and the tombs of the Mings, and as Chinese custom requires that every building of importance shall do, whether temple or yamen, private residence or royal palace. But why should they look south? Because from the south the sun comes, bringing with it "genial and animating influence," and putting new life into plant and animal after the winter.

The south gate is a double gate in a semi-circular bastion. Beyond it is a splendid triumphal arch erected by a grateful community to the memory of the late viceroy. A thickly-populated suburb extends from here to the wide common, where stands the lofty guardian pagoda of the city, 250 feet high, a conspicuous sight from every part of the great Yunnan plain. Rich temples are all around it, their eaves hung with sweet-toned bells, which tinkle with every breath of wind, giving forth what the Chinese poetically describe as "the tribute of praise from inanimate nature to the greatness of Buddha."

THE PAGODA OF YUNNAN CITY, 250 FEET HIGH.

In the early morning the traveller is awakened by the steam whistle of the arsenal, a strange sound to be heard in so far inland a city in China. The factory is under Chinese management, a fact patent to any visitor. Its two foremen were trained partly in the arsenal in Nanking under Dr. Macartney (now Sir Halliday Macartney), and partly in the splendid Shanghai arsenal under Mr. Cornish. I went to the arsenal, and was received as usual in the opium-room. There was nothing to conceal, and I was freely shown everything. The arsenal turns out Krupp guns of 7-1/2 centimetres calibre, but the iron is inferior, and the workmen are in need of better training. Cartridges are also made here. And in one room I saw two men finishing with much neatness a pure silver opium-tray intended for the Fantai (provincial treasurer), but why made in the arsenal only a Chinaman could tell you. Work in the furnace is done at a disadvantage owing to the shortness of the furnace chimney, which is only 25 feet high. All attempts to increase its height are now forbidden by the authorities. There was agitation in the city when the chimney was being heightened. Geomancers were consulted, who saw the feeling of the majority, and therefore gave it as their unprejudiced opinion that, if the chimney were not stunted, the *fungshui* (good luck) of the Futai's yamen (provincial governor), and of that portion of the city under its protection, would depart for ever. All the machinery of the arsenal is stamped with the name of Greenwood, Battley and Co., Leeds. Rust and dirt are everywhere, and the 100 workmen for whom pay is drawn never number on the rare pay days more than sixty persons, a phenomenon observed in most establishments in China worked by government. Yet with a foreigner in charge excellent work could be turned out from the factory. The buildings are spacious, the grounds are ample.

The powder factory is outside the city, near the north-eastern angle of the wall, but the powder magazine is on some rising ground inside the city. No guns are stationed anywhere on the walls, though they may be in concealment in the turrets; but near the small west gate I saw some small cannon of ancient casting, built on the model of the guns cast by the Jesuit missionaries in China two centuries ago, if they were not the actual originals. They were all marked in relief with a cross and the device I.H.S.—a motto that you would think none but a Chinaman could select for a weapon designed to destroy men, yet characteristic of this country of contradictions. "The Chinese statesman," says Wingrove Cooke, the famous *Times* correspondent, "cuts off 10,000 heads, and cites a passage from Mencius about the sanctity of human life. He pockets the money given him to repair an embankment and thus inundates a province, and he deplores the land lost to the cultivator of the soil."

Du Halde tells us that "the first Chinese cannon were cast under the directions of Père Verbiest in 1682, who blest the cannon, and gave to each the name of a saint." "A female saint!" says Huc.

Near the arsenal and drill ground there is a large intramural swamp or reedy lake, the reeds of which have an economic value as wicks for Chinese candles. Dykes cross the swamp in various directions, and in the centre there is a well known Taoist Temple, a richly endowed edifice, with superior gods and censers of great beauty.

Where the swamp deepens into a pond at the margin of the temple, a pretty pavilion has been built, which is a favourite resort of the Yunnan gentry. The most *chic* dinner parties in the province are given here. The pond itself swarms with sacred fish; they are so numerous that when the masses move the whole pond vibrates. Many merits are gained by feeding the fish, and, as it happened at the time of my visit that I had no money, I was constrained to borrow fifteen cash from my chair coolies, with which I purchased some of the artificial food that women were vending and threw it to the fish, so that I might add another thousand to the innumerable merits I have already hoarded in Heaven.

Upon a pretty wooded hill near the centre of the city is the Confucian Temple, and on the lower slope of the hill, in an admirable position, are the quarters of the China Inland Mission, conducted by Mr. and Mrs. X., assisted by Mr. Graham, who at the time of my visit was absent in Tali, and by two exceedingly nice young girls, one of whom comes from Melbourne. The single ladies live in quarters of their own on the edge of a swamp, and suffer inevitably from malarial fever. Mr. X. "finds the people very hard to reach," he told me, and his success has only been relatively cheering. After labouring here nearly six years—the mission was first opened in 1882—he has no male converts, though there are two promising nibblers, who are waiting for the first vacancy to become adherents. There *was* a convert, baptised before Mr. X. came here, a poor manure-coolie, who was employed by the mission as an evangelist in a small way; but "Satan tempted him, he fell from grace, and had to be expelled for stealing the children's buttons." It was a sad trial to the mission. The men refuse to be saved, recalcitrant sinners! but the women happily are more tractable. Mr. X. has up to date (May, 1894), baptised his children's nurse girl, the "native helper" of the single ladies, and his wife's cook. Mr. X. works hard, far too hard. He is of the type that never can be successful in China. He was converted when nearing middle age, is narrow and uncompromising in his views, and is as stern as a Cameronian. It is a farce sending such men to China. At his services there is never any lack of listeners, who marvel greatly at the new method of speaking Chinese which this enterprising emissary—in London he was in the oil trade—is endeavouring to introduce into the province. Of "tones" instead of the five used by the Chinese, he does not recognise more than two, and these he uses indifferently. He hopes, however, to be understood by loud speaking, and he bellows at the placid coolies like a bull of Bashan.

I paid an early visit to my countrymen at the *Yesu-tang* (Jesus Hall), the mission home, as I thought that my medical knowledge might be of some service. I wished to learn a little about their work, but to my great sorrow I was no sooner seated than they began plying me with questions about the welfare of my soul. I am a "poor lost sinner," they told me. They flung texts at my head, and then sang a terrifying ballad, by which I learnt for the first time the awful fate that is to be mine. It is something too dreadful to contemplate. And the cheerful equanimity with which they announced it to me! I left the *Yesu-tang* in a cold sweat, and never returned there.

Missionary work is being pursued in the province with increasing vigour. Among its population of from five to seven millions, spread over an area of 107,969 square miles, there are eighteen Protestant missionaries, nine men and nine ladies (this is the number at present, but the usual strength is twenty-three). Stations are open at Chaotong (1887), Tongchuan (1891), Yunnan City (1882), Tali (1881), and Kuhtsing (1889). The converts number— the work, however, must not be judged by statistics—two at Chaotong, one at Tongchuan, three at Yunnan City, three at Tali, and two at Kuhtsing.

That the Chinese are capable of very rapid conversion can be proved by numberless instances quoted in missionary reports on China. The Rev. S. F. Woodin (in the *Records* of the Missionary Conference, 1877, p. 91) states that he converted a "grossly immoral Chinaman, who had smoked opium for more than twenty years," simply by saying to him "in a spirit of earnest love, elder brother Six, as far as I can see, you must perish; you are Hell's child."

Mr. Stanley P. Smith, B.A., who was formerly stroke of the Cambridge eight, had been only seven months in China when he performed that wonderful conversion, so applauded at the Missionary Conference of 1888, of "a young Chinaman, a learned man, a B.A. of his University," who heard Mr. Smith speak in the Chinese that can be acquired in seven months, and "accepted Him there and then." (*Records* of the Missionary Conference, 1888, i.,

46). Indeed, the earlier the new missionaries in China begin to preach the more rapid are the conversions they make.

Now, in this province of Yunnan, conversions will have to be infinitely more rapid before we can say that there is any reasonable hope of the proximate conversion of the province. The problem is this: In a population of from five to seven millions of friendly and peaceable people, eighteen missionaries in eight years (the average time during which the mission stations have been opened), have converted eleven Chinese; how long, then, will it take to convert the remainder?

"I believe," said a late member of the House of Commons, who was once Lord Mayor of London, speaking at the anniversary meeting of the China Inland Mission in 1884, "I believe God intends to accomplish great things in China," and, undoubtedly, the opinion of an ex-Lord Mayor on such a subject is entitled to great weight.

"The Gospel," he said, "is making rapid progress in China,.... We are amazed at the great things God hath wrought" (in the conversion of the Chinese).

Let us examine for a moment an instance of the rapid progress which excited the amazement of this good man. No missionary body in China is working with greater energy than the China Inland Mission. Their missionaries go far afield in their work, and they are, what their mission intends them to be, pioneer Protestant missionaries in Inland China. At the present time, the beginning of 1894, the Inland Mission numbers 611 male and female missionaries. They are assisted by 261 paid native helpers, and the combined body of 872 Evangelists baptised during the year just passed (1893) 821 Chinese. These figures, taken from *China's Millions*, 1894, p. 122, attest a rather lower rate of progress than the other missions can boast of; but a considerable part of the inland work, it must be remembered, is the most difficult work of all—the preaching of the Gospel for the first time in newly-opened districts.

THE VICEROY OF THE TWO PROVINCES OF YUNNAN AND KWEICHOW.

The Viceroy of the two provinces of Yunnan and Kweichow, Wong-wen-shao, is one of the most enlightened rulers in China. No stranger could fail to be impressed with his keen intellectual face and courtly grace of manner. His career has been a distinguished one. Good fortune attended him even at his birth. He is a native of Hangchow, in Chehkiang, a city famous in China for its coffins. Every Chinaman will tell you that true felicity consists in three things: to be born in Peking (under the shadow of the Son of Heaven); to live in Soochow (where the girls are prettiest); and to die in Hangchow (where the coffins are grandest). Twelve years ago he was Governor of the province of Hunan. Called then to Peking as one of the Ministers of State of the "Tsungli Yamen," or Foreign Office, he remained there four years, his retirement being then due to the inexorable law which requires an official to resign office and go into mourning for three years on the death of one of his parents. In this case it was his mother. (A Chinese mother suckles her child two and a half years, and, as the age of the child is dated from a time anterior by some months to birth, the child is three years old before it leaves its mother's breast. Three years, therefore, has been defined as the proper period for mourning.) At the termination of the three years, Wong was reappointed Governor of Hunan, and a year and a half later, in May, 1890, he was appointed to his present important satrapy, where he has the supreme control of a district larger than Spain and Portugal, and with a population larger than that of Canada and Australia combined. In May, 1893, he made application to the throne to be allowed to return to his ancestral home to die, but the privilege was refused him.

Before leaving Yunnan city the Mandarin Li kindly provided me with a letter of introduction to his friend Brigadier-General Chang-chen Nien, in Tengyueh. Since it contained a communication between persons of rank, the envelope was about the size of an ordinary pillow-slip. The General was presumably of higher rank than the traveller; I had, therefore, in accordance with Chinese etiquette, to provide myself with a suitable visiting card of a size appropriate to his importance. Now Chinese visiting cards differ from ours in differing in size according to the importance of the person to whom they are to be presented. My ordinary card is eight inches by three, red in colour—the colour of happiness—and inscribed in black with the three characters of my Chinese name. But the card that I was expected to present to the General was very much larger than this. Folded it was of the same size, but unfolded it was ten times the size of the other (eight by thirty inches), and the last page, politely inscribed in Chinese, contained this humiliating indication of its purport: "Your addlepated nephew Mo-li-son bows his stupid head, and pays his humble respects to your exalted Excellency."

莫理循   MO LI SON.

I still have this card in my possession; and I should be extremely reluctant to present it to any official in the Empire of lower rank than the Emperor.

CHAPTER XVI.

THE JOURNEY FROM YUNNAN CITY TO TALIFU.

I sold the mule in Yunnan City, and bought instead a little white pony at a cost, including saddle, bridle, and bells, of £3 6s. In doing this I reversed the exchange that would have been made by a Chinaman. A mule is a more aristocratic animal than a pony; it thrives better on a journey, and is more sure-footed. If a pony, the Chinese tell you, lets slip one foot, the other three follow; whereas a mule, if three feet slip from under him, will hold on with the fourth.

My men, who had come with me from Chaotong, were paid off in Yunnan; but it was pleasant to find all three accept an offer to go on with me to Talifu. Coolies to do this journey are usually supplied by the coolie agents for the wage of two *chien* a day each (7d.), each man to carry seventy catties (93lbs.), find himself by the way, and spend thirteen days on the journey. But no coolies, owing to the increase in the price of food, were now willing to go for so little. Accordingly I offered my two coolies three taels each (9s.), instead of the hong price of 7s. 9d., and loads of fifty catties instead of seventy catties. I offered to refund them 100 cash each (2-1/2d.) a day for every day that they had been delayed in Yunnan, and, in addition, I promised them a reward of five mace each (1s. 6d.) if they would take me to Tali in nine days, instead of thirteen, the first evening not to count. To Laohwan, who had no load to carry, but had to attend to me and the pony and pay away the cash, I made a similar offer. These terms, involving me in an outlay of 36s. for hiring three men to go with me on foot 915 li, and return empty-handed, were considered liberal, and were agreed to at once.

The afternoon, then, of the 19th April saw us again *en route*, bound to the west to Talifu, the most famous city in western China, the headquarters of the Mohammedan "Sultan" during the great rebellion of 1857-1873.

By the courtesy of the Mandarin Li, two men were detailed to "sung" me—to accompany me, that is—and take the responsibility for my safe delivery at the next hsien. One was a "wen," a chairen, or yamen runner; the other was a "wu," a soldier, with a sightless right eye, who was dressed in the ragged vestiges of a uniform that reflected both the poverty of his environment and, inversely, the richness of his commanding officer. For in China the officer enriches himself by the twofold expedient of drawing pay for soldiers who have no existence, except in his statement of claim, and by diverting the pay of his soldiers who do exist from their pockets into his own.

THE GIANT OF YUNNAN.

As I was leaving, a colossal Chinaman, sent by the Fantai to speed the foreign gentleman on his way, strode into the court. He was dressed in military jacket and official hat and foxtails. He was the Yunnan giant, Chang Yan Miun, a kindly-featured monster, whom it is a pity to see buried in China when he might be holding *levées* of thousands in a Western side-show. For the information of those in search of novelties, I may say that the giant is thirty years of age, a native of Tongchuan, born of parents of ordinary stature; he is 7ft.

1in. in his bare feet, and weighs, when in condition, 27st. 6lb. With that ingenious arrangement for increasing height known to all showmen, this giant might be worth investing in as a possible successor to his unrivalled namesake. There is surely money in it. Chang's present earnings are rather less than 7s. a month, without board and lodging; he is unmarried, and has no incumbrance; and he is slightly taller and much more massively built than a well-known American giant whom I once had permission to measure, who has been shown half over the world as the "tallest man on earth," his height being attested as "7ft. 11in. in his stockings' soles," and who commands the salary of an English admiral.

We made only a short march the first evening, but after that we travelled by long stages. The country was very pretty, open glades with clumps of pine, and here and there a magnificent sacred tree like the banyan, under whose far-reaching branches small villages are often half concealed. Despite the fertility of the country, poverty and starvation met us at every step; the poor were lingering miserably through the year. Goitre, too, was increasing in frequency. It was rarely that a group gathered to see us some of whose members were not suffering from this horrible deformity. And everywhere in the pretty country were signs of the ruthless devastation of religious war. That was a war of extermination. "A storm of universal fire blasted every field, consumed every house, destroyed every temple."

Crumbling walls are at long distances from the towns they used to guard; there are pastures and waste lands where there were streets of buildings; walls of houses have returned whence they came to the mother earth; others are roofless. In the open country, far from habitation, the traveller comes across groups of bare walls with foundations still uncovered, and dismantled arches, and broken images in the long grass, that were formerly yamens and temples in the midst of thriving communities. Yet there are signs of a renaissance; many new houses are being built along the main road; walls are being repaired, and bridges reconstructed. When an exodus takes place from Szechuen to this province, there is little reason why Yunnan should not become one of the richest provinces in China. It has every advantage of climate, great fertility of soil, and immense mineral resources hardly yet developed. It needs population. It needs the population that dwelt in the province before the rebellion involved the death of millions. It can absorb an immense proportion of the surplus population of China. During, and subsequent to, the Taiping rebellion the province of Szechuen increased by 45,000,000 in forty years (1842-82); given the necessity, there seems no reason why the population of Yunnan should not increase in an almost equal proportion.

On the 22nd we passed Lu-feng-hsien, another ruined town. The finest stone bridge I have seen in Western China, and one that would arrest attention in any country in the world, is at this town. It crosses the wide bed of a stream that in winter is insignificant, but which grows in volume in the rains of summer to a broad and powerful river. It is a bridge of seven beautiful arches; it is 12 yards broad and 150 yards long, of perfect simplicity and symmetry, with massive piers, all built of dressed masonry and destined to survive the lapse of centuries. Triumphal archways with memorial tablets and pedestals of carved lions are befitting portals to a really noble work.

On the 23rd we reached the important city of Chuhsing-fu, a walled city, still half-in-ruins, that was long occupied by the Mohammedans, and suffered terrible reprisals on its recapture by the Imperialists. For four days we had travelled at an average rate of one hundred and five li (thirty-five miles) a day. I must, however, note that these distances as estimated by Mr. Jensen, the constructor of the telegraph line, do not agree with the distances in Mr. Baber's itinerary. The Chinese distances in li agree in both estimates; but, whereas Mr. Jensen allows three li for a mile, Mr. Baber allows four and a-half, a wide difference indeed. For convenience sake I have made use of the telegraph figures, but Mr. Baber was so scrupulously accurate in all that he wrote that I have no doubt the telegraph distances are over-estimated.

We were again in a district almost exclusively devoted to the poppy; the valley-plains sparkled with poppy flowers of a multiplicity of tints. The days were pleasant, and the sun shone brightly; every plant was in flower; doves cooed in the trees, and the bushes in blossom were bright with butterflies. Lanes led between hedges of wild roses white with flower, and, wherever a creek trickled across the plain, its willow-lined borders were blue with forget-me-nots. And everywhere a peaceful people, who never spoke a word to the foreigner that was not friendly.

On the evening of the 24th, at a ruined town thirty li from Luho, we received our first check. It was at a walled town, with gateways and a pagoda that gave some indication of its former prosperity, prettily situated among the trees on the confines of a plain of remarkable fertility. Near sundown we passed down the one long street, all battered and dismantled, which is all that is left of the old town. News of the foreigner quickly spread, and the people gathered into the street to see me—no reception could be more flattering. We did not wait, but, pushing on, we passed out by the west gate and hastened on across the plain. But I noticed that Laohwan kept looking back at the impoverished town, shaking his head and stuttering "*pu-pu-pu-pu-hao! pu-pu-pu-hao!*" (bad! bad!) We had thus gone half a mile or so, when we were arrested by cries behind us, and our last chairen was seen running, panting, after us. We waited for him; he was absurdly excited, and could hardly speak. He made an address to me, speaking with great energy and gesticulation; but what was its purport, *Dios sabe*. When he had finished, not to be outdone in politeness, I thanked him in English for the kindly phrases in which he had spoken to me, assured him of my continued sympathy, and undertook to say that, if ever he came to Geelong, he would find there a house at his disposition, and a friend who would be ever ready to do him a service. He seemed completely mystified, and began to speak again, more excitedly than before. It was getting late, and a crowd was collecting, so I checked him by waving my left hand before my face and bawling at him with all my voice: "*Putung*, you stupid ass, *putung* (I don't understand)! Can't you see I don't understand a word you say, you benighted heathen you? *Putung*, man, *putung*! Advance Australia, *dzo* (go)!" And, swinging open my umbrella, I walked on. His excitement increased—we must go back to the town; he seized me by the wrists, and urged me to go back. We had a slight discussion; his feet gave from under him and he fell down, and I was going on cheerfully when he burst out crying. This I interpreted to mean that he would get into trouble if I did not return, so, of course, I turned back at once, for the tears of a Chinaman are sadly affecting. Back, then, we were taken to an excellent inn in the main street, where a respectful *levée* of the townsfolk had assembled to welcome me. A polite official called upon me, to whom I showed, with simulated indignation, my official card and my Chinese passport, and I hinted to him in

English that this interference with my rights as a traveller from England, protected by the favour of the Emperor, would—let him mark my word—be made an international question. While saying this, I inadvertently left on my box, so that all might see it, the letter of introduction to the Brigadier-General in Tengyueh, which was calculated to give the natives an indication of the class of Chinese who had the privilege to be admitted to my friendship. The official was very polite and apologetic. I freely forgave him, and we had tea together.

He had done it all for the best. A moneyed foreigner was passing through his town near sundown without stopping to spend a single cash there. Was it not his duty, as a public-spirited man, to interfere and avert this loss, and compel the stranger to spend at least one night within his gates?

This was what I wrote at the time. I subsequently found that I had been sent for to come back because the road was believed to be dangerous, there was no secure resting-place, and the authorities could not guarantee my safety. Imagine a Chinese in a Western country acting with the bluster that I did, although in good humour; I wonder whether he would be treated with the courtesy that those Chinamen showed to me!

On the 25th an elderly chairen was ready to accompany us in the morning, and he remained with us all day. All day he was engrossed in deep thought. He spoke to no one, but he kept a watchful eye over his charge, never leaving me a moment, but dogging my very footsteps all the hundred li we travelled together. Poorly clad, he was better provided than his brother of yesterday in that he wore sandals, whereas the chairen of yesterday was in rags and barefoot. He was, of course, unprovided with weapon of any kind—it was moral force that he relied on. Over his shoulder was slung a bag from which projected his opium-pipe; a tobacco pipe and tobacco box hung at his girdle; a green glass bottle of crude opium he carried round his neck.

The chairen is the policeman of China, the lictor of the magistrate, the satellite of the official; the soldier is the representative of military authority. Now, China, in the person of her greatest statesman, Li Hung Chang, has, through the secretary of the Anti-Opium Society, called upon England "to aid her in the efforts she is now making to suppress opium." If, then, China is sincere in her alleged efforts to abolish opium, it is the chairen and the soldier who must be employed by the authorities to suppress the evil; yet I have never been accompanied by either a chairen or a soldier who did not smoke opium, nor have I to my knowledge ever met a chairen or a soldier who was not an opium-smoker. Through all districts of Yunnan, wherever the soil permits it, the poppy is grown for miles, as far as the sight can reach, on every available acre, on both sides of the road.

But why does China grow this poppy? Have not the *literati* and elders of Canton written to support the schemes of the Anti-Opium Society in these thrilling words: "If Englishmen wish to know the sentiments of China, here they are:—If we are told to let things go on as they are going, then there is no remedy and no salvation for China. Oh! it makes the blood run cold, and we want in this our extremity to ask the question of High Heaven, what unknown crimes or atrocity have the Chinese people committed beyond all others that they are doomed to suffer thus?" (Cited by Mr. S. S. Mander, *China's Millions*, iv., 156.)

And the women of Canton, have they not written to the missionaries "that there is no tear that they shed that is not red with blood because of this opium?" ("China," by M. Reed, p. 63). Why, then, does China, while she protests against the importation of a drug which a Governor of Canton, himself an opium-smoker, described as a "vile excrementitious substance" ("Barrow's Travels," p. 153), sanction, if not foster, with all the weight of the authorities in the ever-extending opium-districts the growth of the poppy? To the Rev. G. Piercy (formerly of the W.M.S., Canton), we are indebted for the following explanation of this anomaly: China, it appears, is growing opium in order to put a stop to opium-smoking.

"Moreover, China has not done with the evils of opium, even if our hands were washed of this traffic to-day. China in her desperation has invoked Satan to cast out Satan. She now grows her own opium, vainly dreaming that, if the Indian supply lapse, she can then deal with this rapidly growing evil. But Satan is not divided against himself; he means his kingdom to stand. Opium-growing will not destroy opium-smoking." (Missionary Conference of 1888, *Records*, ii., 546.)

"Yet the awful guilt remains," said the Ven. Archdeacon Farrar on a recent occasion in Westminster Abbey, "that we, 'wherever winds blow and waters roll,' have girdled the world with a zone of drunkenness, until I seem to shudder as I think of the curses, not loud but deep, muttered against our name by races which our fire-water has decimated and our vice degraded." (*National Righteousness*, December 1892, p. 4.)

And this patriotic utterance of a distinguished Englishman the Chinese will quote in unexpected support of the memorial "On the Restriction of Christianity" addressed to the Throne of China in 1884 by the High Commissioner Pêng Yü-lin, which memorial stated in severe language that "*since the treaties have permitted foreigners from the West to spread their doctrines, the morals of the people have been greatly injured.*" ("The Causes of the Anti-Foreign Disturbances in China." Rev. Gilbert Reid, M.A., p. 9.)

Forty li from our sleeping place we came to the pretty town of Shachiaokai, on some undulating high ground well sheltered with trees. Justice had lately been here with her headsman and brought death to a gang of malefactors. Their heads, swinging in wooden cages, hung from the tower near the gateway. They could be seen by all persons passing along the road, and, with due consideration for the feelings of the bereaved relatives, they were hung near enough for the features to be recognised by their friends. Each head was in a cage of its own, and was suspended by the pigtail to the rim, so that it might not lie upside down but could by-and-by rattle in its box as dead men's bones should do. To each cage a white ticket was attached giving the name of the criminal and his confession of the offence for which he was executed. They were the heads of highway robbers who had murdered two travellers on the road near Chennan-chow, and it was this circumstance which accounted for the solicitude of the officials near Luho to prevent our being benighted in a district where such things were possible.

THE "EAGLE NEST BARRIER," ON THE ROAD BETWEEN YUNNAN AND TALIFU.

Midway between Shachiaokai and Pupêng there was steep climbing to be done till we reached Ying-wu-kwan, the "Eagle Nest Barrier," which is more than 8000 feet above the sea. Then by very hilly and poor country we came to Pupêng, and, pursuing our way over a thickly-peopled plateau, we reached a break in the high land from which we descended into a wide and deep valley, skirted with villages and gleaming with sheets of water—the submerged rice-fields. At the foot of the steep was a poor mud town, but, standing back from it in the fields, was a splendid Taoist temple fit for a capital. In this village we were delayed for nearly an hour while my three men bargained against half the village for the possession of a hen that was all unconscious of the comments, flattering and deprecatory, that were being passed on its fatness. It was secured eventually for 260 cash, the vendors having declared that the hen was a family pet, hatched on a lucky day, that it had been carefully and tenderly reared, and that nothing in the world could induce them to part with it for a cash less than 350. My men with equal confidence, based upon long experience in the purchase of poultry, asserted that the real value of the hen was 200 cash, and that not a single cash more of the foreign gentleman's money could they conscientiously invest in such a travesty of a hen as *that*. But little by little each party gave way till they were able to *tomber d'accord*.

A pleasant walk across the busy plain brought us to Yunnan Yeh, where we passed the night.

On the 27th we had an unsatisfactory day's journey. We travelled only seventy li over an even road, yet with four good hours of daylight before us my men elected to stop when we came to the village of Yenwanshan. We had left the main road for some unknown reason, and were taking a short cut over the mountains to Tali. But a short-cut in China often means the longest distance, and I was sure that this short-cut would bring us to Tali a day later than if we had gone by the main road—in ten days, that is, from Yunnan, instead of the nine which my men had promised me. Laohwan, who, like most Chinaman I met, persisted in thinking that I was deaf, yelled to me in the presence of the village that the next stopping place was twenty miles distant, that "*mitte liao! mitte liao!*" ("there were no beans") on the way for the pony, and that assuredly we would reach Tali to-morrow, having given the pony the admirable rest that here offered. As he stammered these sentences the people supported what he said. Obviously their statements were *ex parte*, and were promoted solely by the desire to see the distinguished foreign mandarin sojourn for one night in their hungry midst. So here I was detained in a tumble-down inn that had formerly been a temple. All of us, men and master, were housed in the old guest-room. Beds were formed of disused coffin boards, laid between steps made of clods of dry clay; the floor was earth, the windows paper. The pony was feeding from a trough in the temple hall itself, an armful of excellent grass before it, while a bucket of beans was soaking for him in our corner. Other mules and ponies were stationed in the side pavilions where formerly were displayed the scenes of torture in the Buddhist Hells.

As I wrote at a table by the window, a crowd collected, stretching across the street and quarrelling to catch a glimpse of the foreign teacher and his strange method of writing, so different from the Chinese. Poor sickly people were these—of the ten in the first row three were suffering from goitre, one from strabismus, and two from ophthalmia. All were poorly clad and poorly nourished; all were very dirty, and their heads were unshaven of the growth of days. But, despite their poverty, nearly all the women, the children as well as the grandmothers, wore silver earrings of pretty filigree.

Now, even among these poor people, I noticed that there was a disposition rather to laugh at me than to open the eyes of wonder; and this is a peculiarity of the Chinese which every traveller will be struck with. It often grieved me. During my journey, although I was treated with undeniable friendliness, I found that the Chinese, instead of being impressed by my appearance, would furtively giggle when they saw me. But they were never openly rude like the coloured folk were in Jamaica, when, stranded in their beautiful island, I did them the honour to go as a "walk-foot buccra" round the sugar plantations from Ewarton to Montego Bay. Even poor ragged fellows, living in utter misery, would laugh and snigger at me when not observed, and crack jokes at the foreigner who was well-fed, well-clad, and well-mounted in a way you would think to excite envy rather than derision. But Chinese laughter seems to be moved by different springs from ours. The Chinaman makes merry in the presence of death. A Chinaman, come to announce to you the death of a beloved parent or brother, laughs heartily as he tells you—you might think he was overflowing with joy, but he is really sick and sore at heart, and is only laughing to deceive the spirits. So it may be that the poor beggars who laughed at that noble presence which has been the admiration of my friends in four continents, were moved to do so by the hope to deceive the evil spirits who had punished them with poverty, and so by their apparent gaiety induce them to relax the severity of their punishment.

To within two or three miles of this village the road was singularly level; I do not think that it either rose or fell 100 feet in twenty miles. Forty li from where we slept the night before, having previously left the main road, we came to the large walled town of Yunnan-hsien. The streets were crowded, for it was market day, and both sides of the main thoroughfares, especially in the vicinity of the Confucian Temple, were thronged with peasant women selling garden produce, turnips, beans and peas, and live fish caught in the lake beyond Tali. Articles of Western trade were also for sale—stacks of calico, braid, and thread, "new impermeable matches made in Trieste," and "toilet soap of the finest quality." I had a royal reception as I rode through the crowd, and the street where was situated the inn to which we went for lunch speedily became impassable. There was keen competition to see me. Two thieves were among the foremost, with huge iron crowbars chained to their necks and ankles, while a third prisoner, with his head pilloried in a *cangue*, obstructed the gaze of many. There was the most admirable courtesy shown me; it was the "foreign teacher" they wished to see, not the "foreign devil." When I rose from the table, half a dozen guests sitting at the other tables rose also and bowed to me as I passed out. Of all people I have ever met, the Chinese are, I think, the politest. My illiterate Laohwan, who could neither read nor write, had a courtesy of demeanour, a well-bred ease of manner, a graceful deference that never approached servility, which it was a constant pleasure to me to witness.

As regards the educated classes, there can be little doubt, I think, that there are no people in the world so scrupulously polite as the Chinese. Their smallest actions on all occasions of ceremony are governed by the most minute rules. Let me give, as an example, the method of cross-examination to which the stranger is subjected, and which is a familiar instance of true politeness in China.

When a well-bred Chinaman, of whatever station, meets you for the first time, he thus addresses you, first asking you how old you are:

"What is your honourable age?"

"I have been dragged up a fool so many years," you politely reply.

"What is your noble and exalted occupation?"

"My mean and contemptible calling is that of a doctor."

"What is your noble patronymic?"

"My poverty-struck family name is Mô."

"How many honourable and distinguished sons have you?"

"Alas! Fate has been niggardly; I have not even one little bug."

But, if you can truthfully say that you are the honourable father of sons, your interlocutor will raise his clasped hands and say gravely, "Sir, you are a man of virtue; I congratulate you." He continues—

"How many tens of thousands of pieces of silver have you?" meaning how many daughters have you?

"My yatows" (forked heads or slave children), "my daughters," you answer with a deprecatory shrug, "number so many."

So the conversation continues, and the more minute are the inquiries the more polite is the questioner.

Unlike most of the Western nations, the Chinese have an overmastering desire to have children. More than death itself the Chinaman fears to die without leaving male progeny to worship at his shrine; for, if he should die childless, he leaves behind him no provision for his support in heaven, but wanders there a hungry ghost, forlorn and forsaken—an "orphan" because he has no children. "If one has plenty of money," says the Chinese proverb, "but no children, he cannot be reckoned rich; if one has children, but no money, he cannot be considered poor." To have sons is a foremost virtue in China; "the greatest of the three unfilial things," says Mencius, "is to have no children." (Mencius, iv., pt. i., 26).

In China longevity is the highest of the five grades of felicity. Triumphal arches are erected all over the kingdom in honour of those who have attained the patriarchal age which among us seems only to be assured to those who partake in sufficient quantity of certain fruit-salts and pills. Age when not known is guessed by the length of the beard, which is never allowed to grow till the thirty-second year. Now it happens that I am clean-shaven, and, as it is a well-known fact that the face of the European is an enigma to the Oriental, just as the face of the Chinaman is an inscrutable mystery to most of us, I have often been amused by the varying estimates of my age advanced by curious bystanders. It has been estimated as low as twelve—"look at the foreigner," they said, "there's a fine fat boy!"—and never higher than twenty-two. But it is not only in China that a youthful appearance has hampered me in my walk through life.

I remember that on one occasion, some years ago, I obliged a medical friend by taking his practice while he went away for a few days to be married. It was in a semi-barbarian village named Portree, in a forgotten remnant of Scotland called the Isle of Skye. The time was winter. The first case I was called to was that of a bashful matron, the baker's wife, who had lately given birth to her tenth child. I entered the room cheerfully. She looked me over critically, and then greatly disconcerted me by remarking that: "She was gey thankfu' to the Lord that it was a' by afore I cam', as she had nae wush to be meddled wi' by a laddie of nineteen." Yet I was two years older than the doctor who had attended her.

If in China you are so fortunate as to be graced with a beard, the Chinaman will add many years to your true age. In the agreeable company of one of the finest men in China, I once made a journey to the Nankow Pass in the Great Wall, north of Peking. My friend had a beard like a Welsh bard's, and, though a younger man than his years, forty-four, there was not a native who saw him, who did not gaze upon him with awe, as a possible Buddha, and not one who attributed to him an age less than eighty.

Next day, the 28th of April, despite my misgivings, my men fulfilled their promise, and led me into Tali on the ninth day out from Yunnan. We had come 307 miles in nine days. They walked all the way, living frugally on scanty rations. I walked only 210 miles; I was better fed than they, and I had a pony at my hand ready to carry me whenever I was tired.

My men thus earned a reward of eighteen pence each for doing thirteen stages in nine days. Long before daylight we were on our way. For miles and miles in the early morning we were climbing up the mountains, till we reached a plateau where the wind blew piercingly keen, and my fingers ached with the cold, and the rarefaction in the atmosphere made breathing uneasy. The road was lonely and unfrequented. We were accompanied by a muleteer who knew the way, by his sturdy son of twelve, and his two pack horses. By midday we had left the bare plateau, had passed the three pagoda peaks, and were standing on the brow of a steep hill overlooking the valleys of Chaochow and Tali. The plains were studded with thriving villages, in rich fields, and intersected with roadways lined with hedges. There on the left was the walled city of Chaochow, beyond, to the right, was the great lake of Tali, hemmed in by mountains, those beyond the lake thickly covered with snow, and rising 7000 feet above the lake, which itself is 7000 feet above the sea.

We descended into the valley, and, as we picked our way down the steep path, I could count in the lap of the first valley eighteen villages besides the walled city. Crossing the fields we struck the main road, and mingled with the stream of people who were bending their steps towards Hsiakwan. Many varieties of feature were among them, a diversity of type unlooked for by the traveller in China who had become habituated to the uniformity of type of the Chinese face. There were faces plainly European, others as unmistakably Hindoo, Indigenes of Yunnan province, Thibetans, Cantonese pedlars, and Szechuen coolies. A broad flagged road brought us to the important market town of Hsiakwan, which guards the southern pass to the Valley of Tali. It is on the main road going west to the frontier of Burma, and is the junction where the road turns north to Tali. It is a busy town. It is one of the most famous halting places on the main road to Burma. The two largest caravanserais in Western China are in Hsiakwan, and I do not exaggerate when I say that a regiment of British cavalry could be quartered in either of them. At a restaurant near the cross-road we had rice and a cup of tea, and a bowl of the vermicelli soup known as *mien*, the muleteer and his son sitting down with my men. When the time came to go, the muleteer, unrolling a string of cash from his waistband, was about to pay his share, when Laohwan with much civility refused to permit him. He insisted, but Laohwan was firm; had they been Frenchmen, they could not have been more polite and complimentary. The muleteer gave way with good grace, and Laohwan paid with my cash, and gained merit by his courtesy.

CHAPTER XVII.

THE CITY OF TALI—PRISONS—POISONING—PLAGUES AND MISSIONS.

Three hours later we were in Tali. A broad paved road, smooth from the passage of countless feet, leads to the city. Rocky creeks drain the mountain range into the lake; they are spanned by numerous bridges of dressed stone, many of the slabs of which are well cut granite blocks eighteen feet in length. At a stall by the roadside excellent ices were for sale, genuine ices, made of concave tablets of pressed snow sweetened with treacle, costing one cash each—equal to one penny for three dozen. We passed the Temple to the Goddess of Mercy, and entered Tali by the south gate. Then by the yamen of the Titai and the Great Five Glory Gate, the northern entrance of what was for seventeen years the palace of the Mohammedan king during the rebellion, we turned down the East street to the *Yesu-tang*, the Inland Mission, where Mr. and Mrs. John Smith gave me a cordial greeting.

Tali has always been an important city. It was the capital of an independent kingdom in the time of Kublai Khan and Marco Polo. It was the headquarters of the Mohammedan Sultan or Dictator, Tu Wen Hsiu, during the rebellion, and seemed at one time destined to become the capital of an independent Moslem Empire in Western China.

The city surrendered to the Mohammedans in 1857. It was recaptured by the Imperialists under General Yang Yu-ko on January 15th, 1873, the Chinese troops being aided by artillery cast by Frenchmen in the arsenal of Yunnan and manned by French gunners. At its recapture the carnage was appalling; the streets were ankle-deep in blood. Of 50,000 inhabitants 30,000 were butchered. After the massacre twenty-four panniers of human ears were sent to Yunnan city to convince the people of the capital that they had nothing more to fear from the rebellion.

In March, 1873, Yang was appointed *Titai* or Commander-in-chief of Yunnan Province, with his headquarters in Tali, not in the capital, and Tali has ever since been the seat of the most important military command in the province.

The subsequent history of Yang may be told in a few words. He assumed despotic power over the country he had conquered, and grew in power till his authority became a menace to the Imperial Government. They feared that he aspired to found a kingdom of his own in Western China, and recalled him to Peking—to do him honour. He was not to be permitted to return to Yunnan. At the time of his recall another rebellion had broken out against China—the rebellion of the French—and, like another Uriah, the powerful general was sent to the forefront in Formosa, where he was opportunely slain by a French bullet, or by a misdirected Chinese one.

After his death it was found that Yang had made a noble bequest to the City of Tali. During his residence he had built for himself a splendid yamen of granite and marble. This he had richly endowed and left as a free gift to the city as a college for students. It is one of the finest residences in China, and, though only seventy undergraduates were living there at the time of my visit, the rooms could accommodate in comfort many hundreds.

SNOW-CLAD MOUNTAINS BEHIND TALIFU.

Tali is situated on the undulating ground that shelves gently from the base of snow-clad mountains down to the lake. The lower slopes of the mountain, above the town, are covered with myriads of grave-mounds, which in the distance are scarcely distinguishable from the granite blocks around them. Creeks and rills of running water spring from the melting of the snows far up the mountain, run among the grave-mounds, and are then trained into the town. The Chinese residents thus enjoy the privilege of drinking a diluted solution of their ancestors. Half-way to the lake, there is a huge tumulus of earth and stone over-grown with grass, in which are buried the bones of 10,000 Mohammedans who fell during the massacre. There is no more fertile valley in the world than the valley of Tali. It is studded with villages. Between the two passes, Hsiakwan on the south, and Shang-kwan on the north, which are distant from each other a long day's walk, there are 360 villages, each in its own plantation of trees, with a pretty white temple in the centre with curved roof and upturned gables. The sunny reaches of the lake are busy with fleets of fishing boats. The poppy, grown in small pockets by the margin of the lake, is probably unequalled in the world; the flowers, as I walked through the fields, were on a level with my forehead.

Tali is not a large city; its wall is only three and a half miles in circumference. Before the rebellion populous suburbs extended half-way to Hsiakwan, but they are now only heaps of rubble. In the town itself there are market-gardens and large open spaces where formerly there were narrow streets of Chinese houses. The wall is in fairly good repair, but there are no guns in the town, except a few old-fashioned cannon lying half buried in the ground near the north gate.

One afternoon we climbed up the mountain intending to reach a famous cave, "The Ph[oe]nix-eyed Cave" (*Fung-yen-tung*) which overlooks a precipice, of some fame in years gone by as a favourite spot for suicides. We did not reach the cave. My energy gave out when we were only half-way, so we sat down in the grass and, to use a phrase that I fancy I have heard before, we feasted our eyes on the scene before us. And here we gathered many bunches of edelweiss.

As we were coming back down the hill, picking our way among the graves, a pensive Chinaman stopped us to ask our assistance in finding him a lucky spot in which to bury his father, who died a year ago but was still above ground. He was sorry to hear that we could not pretend to any knowledge of such things. He was of an inquiring mind, for he then asked us if we had seen any precious stones in the hillside—every Chinaman knows that the foreigner with his blue eyes can see four feet underground—but he was again disappointed with our reply, or did not believe us.

At the poor old shrine to the God of Riches, half a dozen Chinamen in need of the god's good offices were holding a small feast in his honour. They had prepared many dishes, and, having "dedicated to the god the spiritual essence, were now about to partake of the insipid remains." "*Ching fan*," they courteously said to us when we approached down the path. "We invite (you to take) rice." We raised our clasped hands: "*Ching, ching*," we replied, "we invite (you to go on), we invite," and passed on. They were bent upon enjoyment. They were taking as an *apéritif* a preliminary cup of that awful spirit *tsiu*, which is almost pure alcohol and can be burnt in lamps like methylated spirit.

On the level sward, between this poor temple and the city, the annual Thibetan Fair is held on the 17th, 18th, and 19th of April, when caravans of Thibetans, with herds of ponies, make a pilgrimage from their mountain villages to the ancient home of their forefathers. But the fair is falling into disfavour owing to the increasing number of likin-barriers on the northern trade routes.

There are many temples in Tali. The finest is the Confucian Temple, with its splendid halls and pavilions, in a beautiful garden. Kwanti, the God of War, has also a temple worthy of a god whose services to China in the past can never be forgotten. Every Chinaman knows, that if it had not been for the personal aid of this god, General Gordon could never have succeeded in suppressing the Taiping rebellion. In the present rebellion of the Japanese, the god appears to have maintained an attitude of strict neutrality.

The City Temple is near the drill-ground. As the Temple of a Fu city it contains the images of both Fu magistrate and Hsien magistrate, with their attendants. In its precincts the *Kwan* of the beggars, (the beggar king or headman), is domiciled, who eats the

Emperor's rice and is officially responsible for the good conduct of the guild of beggars.

In the main street there is a Memorial Temple to General Yang, who won the city back from the Mohammedans. But the temple where prayer is offered most earnestly, is the small temple near the *Yesu-tang*, erected to the goddess who has in her power the dispensation of the pleasures of maternity. Rarely did I pass here without seeing two or three childless wives on their knees, praying to the goddess to remove from them the sin of barrenness.

Some of the largest caravanserais I have seen in China are in Tali. One of the largest belongs to the city, and is managed by the authorities for the benefit of the poor, all profits being devoted to a poor-relief fund. There are many storerooms here, filled with foreign goods and stores imported from Burma, and useful wares and ornamental nick-nacks brought from the West by Cantonese pedlars. Prices are curiously low. I bought condensed milk, "Milkmaid brand," for the equivalent of 7*d.* a tin. In the inn there is stabling accommodation for more than a hundred mules and horses, and there are rooms for as many drivers. The tariff cannot be called immoderate. The charges are: For a mule or horse per night, fodder included, one farthing; for a man per night, a supper of rice included, one penny.

Even larger than the city inn is the caravanserai where my pony was stabled; it is more like a barracks than an inn. One afternoon the landlord invited the missionary and me into his guest-room, and as I was the chief guest, he insisted, of course, that I should occupy the seat of honour on the left hand. But I was modest and refused to; he persisted and I was reluctant; he pushed me forward and I held back, protesting against the honour he wished to show me. But he would take no refusal and pressed me forward into the seat. I showed becoming reluctance of course, but I would not have occupied any other. By-and-by he introduced to me with much pride his aged father, to whom, when he came into the room, I insisted upon giving my seat, and humbly sat on an inferior seat by his side, showing him all the consideration due to his eighty years. The old man bore an extraordinary resemblance to Moltke. He had smoked opium, he told Mr. Smith, the missionary, for fifty years, but always in moderation. His daily allowance was two *chien* of raw opium, rather more than one-fifth of an ounce, but he knew many Chinese, he told the missionary, who smoked daily five times as much opium as he did without apparent injury.

In Tali there are four chief officials: the Prefect or Fu Magistrate, the Hsien or City Magistrate, the Intendant or Taotai, and the Titai. The yamen of the Taotai is a humble residence for so important an official; but the yamen of the Titai, between the South Gate and the Five Glory Tower, is one of the finest in the province. The Titai is not only the chief military commander of the province of Yunnan, but he is a very much married man. An Imperialist, he has yet obeyed the Mohammedan injunction and taken to himself four wives in order to be sure of obtaining one good one. He has been abundantly blessed with children. In offices at the back of the Titai's yamen and within its walls, is the local branch of the Imperial Chinese telegraphs, conducted by two Chinese operators, who can read and write English a little, and can speak crudely a few sentences.

The City Magistrate is an advanced opium-smoker, a slave to the pipe, who neglects his duties. In his yamen I saw the wooden cage in which prisoners convicted of certain serious crimes are slowly done to death by starvation and exhaustion, as well as the wooden cages of different shape in which criminals of another class condemned to death are carried to and from the capital.

The City prison is in the Hsien's yamen, but permission to enter was refused me, though the missionary has frequently been admitted. "The prison," explained the Chinese clerk, "is private, and strangers cannot be admitted." I was sorry not to be allowed to see the prison, all the more because I had heard from the missionary nothing but praise of the humanity and justice of its management.

The gaols of China, or, as the Chinese term them, the "hells," just as the prison hulks in England forty years ago were known as "floating hells," have been universally condemned for the cruelties and deprivations practised in them. They are probably as bad as were the prisons of England in the early years of the present century.

The gaolers purchase their appointments, as they did in England in the time of John Howard, and, as was the case in England, they receive no other pay than what they can squeeze from the prisoners or the prisoners' friends. Poor and friendless, the prisoners fare badly. But I question if the cruelties practised in the Chinese gaols, allowing for the blunted nerve sensibility of the Chinaman, are less endurable than the condition of things existing in English prisons so recently as when Charles Reade wrote "It is Never Too Late to Mend." The cruelties of Hawes, the "punishment jacket," the crank, the dark cell, and starvation, "the living tortured, the dying abandoned, the dead kicked out of the way"; when boys of fifteen, like Josephs, were driven to self-slaughter by cruelty. These are statements published in 1856, "every detail of which was verified, every fact obtained, by research and observation." ("Life of Charles Reade," ii., 33.)

And it cannot admit, I think, of question that there are no cruelties practised in the Chinese gaols greater, even if there are any equal to the awful and degraded brutality with which the England of our fathers treated her convicts in the penal settlements of Norfolk Island, Fort Arthur, Macquarie Harbour, and the prison hulks of Williamstown. "The convict settlements were terrible cesspools of iniquity, so bad that it seemed, to use the words of one who knew them well, 'the heart of man who went to them was taken from him, and there was given to him the heart of a beast.'"

Can the mind conceive of anything more dreadful in China than the incident narrated by the Chaplain of Norfolk Island, the Rev. W. Ullathorne, D.D., afterwards Roman Catholic Bishop of Birmingham, in his evidence before the Commission of the House of Commons in 1838: "As I mentioned the names of those men who were to die, they one after another, as their names were pronounced, dropped on their knees and thanked God that they were to be delivered from that horrible place, whilst the others remained standing mute, weeping. It was the most horrible scene I have ever witnessed."

Those who have read Marcus Clarke's "For the Term of His Natural Life," remember the powerfully-drawn character of Maurice Frere, the Governor of Norfolk Island. It is well known, of course, that the story is founded upon fact, and is a perfectly true picture of the convict days. The original of Maurice Frere is known to have been the late Colonel ----, who was killed by the convicts in the prison hulk "Success," at Williamstown, in 1853. To this day there is no old lag that was ever exposed to his cruelty but reviles his memory. I once knew the convict who gave the signal for his murder. He was sentenced to death, but was reprieved and served a long term of imprisonment. The murder happened forty-one years ago, yet to this day the old convict commends the murder as a just act of retribution, and when he narrates the story he tells you with bitter passion that the "Colonel's dead, and, if there's a hell, he's frizzling there yet."

Captain Foster Fyans, a former Governor of Norfolk Island Convict Settlement, spent the last years of his life in the town I belong to, Geelong, in Victoria. The cruelties imposed on the convicts under his charge were justified, he declared, by the brutalised character of the prisoners. On one occasion, he used to tell, a band of convicts attempted to escape from the Island; but their attempt was frustrated by the guard. The twelve convicts implicated in the outbreak were put on their trial, found guilty, and sentenced to death by strangulation, as hanging really was in those days. Word was sent to headquarters in Sydney, and instructions were asked for to carry the sentence into effect. The laconic order was sent back from Sydney to "hang half of them." The Captain acknowledged the humour of the despatch, though it placed him in a difficulty. Which half should he hang, when all were equally guilty? In his pleasant way the Captain used to tell how he acted in the dilemma. He went round to the twelve condemned wretches, and asked each man separately if, being under sentence of death, he desired a reprieve or wished for death. As luck would have it, of the twelve men, six pleaded for life and six as earnestly prayed that they might be sent to the scaffold. So the Captain hanged the six men who wished to live, and spared the six men who prayed for death to release them from their awful misery. This is an absolutely true story, which I have heard from men to whom the Captain himself told it. Besides, it bears on its face the impress of truth. And yet we are accustomed to speak of the Chinese as centuries behind us in civilisation and humanity.

I went to two opium-poisoning cases in Tali, both being cases of attempted suicide. The first was that of an old man living not *at* the South Gate as the messenger assured us, who feared to discourage us if he told the truth, but more than a mile beyond it. On our way we bought in the street some sulphate of copper, and a large dose made the old man so sick that he said he would never take opium again, and, if he did, he would not send for the foreign gentleman.

The other was that of a young bride, a girl of unusual personal attraction, only ten days married, who thus early had become weary of the pock-marked husband her parents had sold her to. She was dressed still in her bridal attire, which had not been removed since marriage; she was dressed in red—the colour of happiness. "She was dressed in her best, all ready for the journey," and was determined to die, because dead she could repay fourfold the injuries which she had received while living. In this case many neighbours were present, and, as all were anxious to prevent the liberation of the girl's evil spirit, I proved to them how skilful are the barbarian doctors. The bride was induced to drink hot water till it was, she declared, on a level with her neck, then I gave her a hypodermic injection of that wonderful emetic apomorphia. The effect was very gratifying to all but the patient.

Small-pox, or, as the Chinese respectfully term it, "Heavenly Flowers," is a terrible scourge in Western China. It is estimated that two thousand deaths—there is a charming vagueness about all Chinese figures—from this disease alone occur in the course of a year in the valley of Tali. Inoculation is practised, as it has been for many centuries, by the primitive method of introducing a dried pock-scab, on a lucky day, into one of the nostrils. The people have heard of the results of Western methods of inoculation, and immense benefit could be conferred upon a very large community by sending to the Inland Mission in Talifu a few hundred tubes of vaccine lymph. Vaccination introduced into Western China would be a means, the most effective that could be imagined, to check the death rate over that large area of country which was ravaged by the civil war, and whose reduced population is only a small percentage of the population which so fertile a country needs for its development. Infanticide is hardly known in that section of Yunnan of which Tali may be considered the capital. Small-pox kills the children. There is no need for a mother to sacrifice her superfluous children, for she has none.

Another disease endemic in Yunnan is the bubonic plague, which is, no doubt, identical with the plague that has lately played havoc in Hong Kong and Canton. Cantonese peddlers returning to the coast probably carried the germs with them.

The China Inland Mission in Tali was the last of the mission stations which I was to see on my journey. This is the furthest inland of the stations of the Inland Mission in China. It was opened in 1881 by Mr. George W. Clarke, the most widely-travelled, with the single exception of the late Dr. Cameron, of all the pioneer missionaries of this brave society; I think Mr. Clarke told me that he has been in fourteen out of the eighteen provinces. His work here was not encouraging; he was treated with kindness by the Chinese, but they refused to accept the truth when he placed it before them.

"For the Bible and the Light of Truth," says Miss Guinness, in her charming but hysterical "Letters from the Far East"—a book that has deluded many poor girls to China—"For the Bible and the Light of Truth the Chinese cry with outstretched, empty, longing hands" (p. 173). But this allegation unhappily conflicts with facts when applied to Tali.

For the first eleven years the mission laboured here without any success whatever; but now a happier time seems coming, and no less [fewer] than three converts have been baptised in the last two years.

There are now three missionaries in Tali—there are usually four; they are universally respected by the Chinese; they have made their little mission home one of the most charming in China. Mr. John Smith, who succeeded Mr. Clarke, has been ten years in Tali. He is welcomed everywhere, and in every case of serious sickness or opium-poisoning he is sent for. During all the time he has been in Tali he has never refused to attend a summons to the sick, whether by day or night. In the course of the year he attends, on an average, between fifty and sixty cases of attempted suicide by opium in the town or its environs, and, if called in time, he is rarely unsuccessful. Should he be called to a case outside the city wall and be detained after dark, the city gate will be kept open for him till he returns. The city magistrate has himself publicly praised the benevolence of this missionary, and said, "there is no man in Tali like Mr. Smith—would that there were others!" He is a Christian in word and deed, brave and simple, unaffected and sympathetic—the type of missionary needed in China—an honour to his mission. I saw the courageous man working here almost alone, far distant from all Western comforts, cut off from the world, and almost unknown, and I contrasted him with those other missionaries—the majority—who live in luxurious mission-houses in absolute safety in the treaty ports, yet whose courage and self-denial we have accustomed ourselves to praise in England and America, when with humble voices they parade the dangers they undergo and the hardships they endure in preaching, dear friends, to the "perishing heathen in China, God's lost ones!"

In addition to the three converts who have been baptised in Tali in the last two years, there are two inquirers—one the mission cook—who are nearly ready for acceptance. At the Sunday service I met the three converts. One is the paid teacher in the mission school; another is a humble pedlar; the third is a courageous native belonging to one of the indigenous tribes of Western China, a Minchia man, whose conversion, judged by all tests, is one of those genuine cases which bring real joy to the missionary. He has only recently been baptised. Every Sunday he comes in fifteen li from the small patch of ground he tills to the mission services. His son is at the mission school, and is boarded on the premises. There is a small school in connection with the mission under the baptised teacher, where eight boys and eight girls are being taught. They are learning quickly, their wonderful gifts of memory being a chief factor in their progress. At the service there was another worshipper, a sturdy boy of fourteen, who slept composedly all through the exhortation. If any boy should feel gratitude towards the kind missionaries it is he. They have reared him from the most degraded poverty, have taught him to read and write, and are now on the eve of apprenticing him to a carpenter. He was a beggar boy, the son of a professional beggar, who, with unkempt hair and in rags and filth, used to shamble through the streets gathering reluctant alms. The father died, and some friends would have sold his son to pay the expenses of his burial; but the missionaries intervened and, to save the son from slavery, buried his father. This action gave them some claim to help the boy, and the boy has accordingly been with them since in a comfortable, kindly home, instead of grovelling round the streets in squalor and nakedness.

The mission-house, formerly occupied by Mr. George Clarke is near the City Temple. We went to see it a day or two after my arrival. It is now in the possession of a family of Mohammedans, one of the very few Moslem families still living in the valley of Tali. "When we were in possession of the valley," said the father sorrowfully, "we numbered '12,000 tens' (120,000 souls), now we are '100 fives' (500 souls). Our men were slain, our women were taken in prey, only a remnant escaped the destroyer." Several members of the family were in the court when we entered, and among the men were three with marked Anglo-Saxon features, a peculiarity frequently seen in Western China, where every traveller has given a different explanation of the phenomenon. One especially moved my curiosity, for he possessed to an absurd degree the closest likeness to myself. Could I give him any higher praise than that?

That the Mohammedan Chinese is physically superior to his Buddhist countryman is acknowledged by all observers; there is a fearlessness and independence of bearing in the Mohammedan, a militant carriage that distinguishes him from the Chinese unbeliever. His religion is but a thinly diluted Mohammedanism, and excites the scorn of the true believers from India who witness his devotion, or rather his want of devotion.

One of the men talking to us in the old mission-house was a comical-looking fellow, whose head-dress differed from that of the other Chinese, in that, in addition to his queue, lappets of hair were drawn down his cheeks in the fashion affected by old ladies in England. I raised these strange locks—impudent curiosity is often polite attention in China—whereupon the reason for them was apparent. The body bequeathed to him by his fathers had been mutilated—he had suffered the removal of both ears. He explained to us how he came to lose them, but we knew even before he told us; "he had lost them in battle facing the enemy"—and of course we believed him. The less credulous would associate the mutilation with a case of theft and its detection and punishment by the magistrate; but "a bottle-nosed man," says the Chinese proverb, "may be a teetotaller and yet no one will think so."

Our milkman at the mission was a follower of the Prophet, and the milk he gave us was usually as reduced in quality as are his co-religionists in number. In the milk he supplied there was what a chemist describes as a remarkable absence of butter fat. Yet, when he was reproached for his deceit, he used piously to say, even when met coming from the well, "I could not put a drop of water in the milk, for there is a God up there"—and he would jerk his chin towards the sky—"who would see me if I did."

CHAPTER XVIII.

THE JOURNEY FROM TALI, WITH SOME REMARKS ON THE CHARACTER OF THE CANTONESE, CHINESE EMIGRANTS, CRETINS, AND WIFE-BEATING IN CHINA.

The three men who had come with me the six hundred and seventeen miles from Chaotong left me at Tali to return all that long way home on foot with their well-earned savings. I was sorry to say good-bye to them; but they had come many miles further than they intended, and their friends, they said, would be anxious: besides Laohwan, you remember, was newly married.

I engaged three new men in their places. They were to take me right through to Singai (Bhamo). Every day was of importance now with four hundred and fifty miles to travel and the rainy season closing in. Laotseng was the name of the Chinaman whom I engaged in place of Laohwan. He was a fine young fellow, active as a deer, strong, and high-spirited. I agreed to pay him the fancy wage of 24*s.* for the journey. He was to carry no load, but undertook, in the event of either of my coolies falling sick, to carry his load until a new coolie could be engaged. The two coolies I engaged through a coolie-hong. One was a strongly-built man, a "chop dollar," good-humoured, but of rare ugliness. The other was the thinnest man I ever saw outside a Bowery dime-show. He had the opium habit. He was an opium-eater rather than an opium-smoker; and he ate the ash from the opium-pipe, instead of the opium itself—the most vicious of the methods of taking opium. He was the nearest approach I saw in China to the Exeter Hall type of opium-eater, whose "wasted limbs and palsied hands" cry out against the sin of the opium traffic. Though a victim of the injustice of England, this man had never tasted Indian opium in his life, and, perishing as he was in body and soul, going "straight to eternal damnation," his "dying wail unheard," he yet undertook a journey that would have deterred the majority of Englishmen, and agreed to carry, at forced speed, a far heavier load than the English soldier is ever weighted with on march. The two coolies were to be paid 4 taels each (12*s.*) for the twenty stages to Singai, and had to find their own board and lodging. But I also stipulated to give them *churo* money (pork money) of 100 cash each at three places—Yungchang, Tengyueh, and Bhamo—100 cash each a day extra for every day that I detained them on the way, and, in addition, I was to reward them with 150 cash each a day for every day that they saved on the twenty days' journey, days that I rested not to count.

Of course none of the three men spoke a word of English. All were natives of the province of Szechuen, and all carried out their agreement to the letter.

On May 3rd I left Tali. The last and longest stage of all the journey was before me, a distance of some hundreds of miles, which I had to traverse before I could hope to meet another countryman or foreigner with whom I could converse. The two missionaries, Mr. Smith and Mr. Graham, kindly offered to see me on my way, and we all started together for Hsiakwan, leaving the men to follow.

Ten li from Tali we stopped to have tea at one of the many teahouses that are grouped round the famous temple to the Goddess of Mercy, the *Kwanyin-tang*. The scene was an animated one. The open space between the temple steps and the temple theatre opposite was thronged with Chinese of strange diversity of feature crying their wares from under the shelter of huge umbrellas. There is always a busy traffic to Hsiakwan, and every traveller rests here, if only for a few minutes. For this is the most famous temple in the valley of Tali. The Goddess of Mercy is the friend of travellers, and no thoughtful Chinese should venture on a journey without first asking the favour of the goddess and obtaining from her priests a forecast of his success. The temple is a fine specimen of Chinese architecture. It was built specially to record a miracle. In the chief court, surrounded by the temple buildings, there is a huge granite boulder lying in an ornamental pond. It is connected by marble approaches, and is surmounted by a handsome monument of marble, which is faced on all sides with memorial tablets. This boulder was carried to its present position by the goddess herself, the monument and bridges were built to detain it where it lay, and the temple afterwards erected to commemorate an event of such happy augury for the beautiful valley.

MEMORIAL IN THE TEMPLE OF THE GODDESS OF MERCY, NEAR TALIFU.

But the temple has not always witnessed only scenes of mercy. Two years ago a tragedy was enacted here of strange interest. At a religious festival held here in April, 1892, and attended by all the high officials and by a crowd of sightseers, a thief, taking advantage of the crush, tried to snatch a bracelet from the wrist of a young woman, and, when she resisted, he stabbed her. He was seized red-handed, dragged before the Titai, who happened to be present, and ordered to be beheaded there and then. An executioner was selected from among the soldiers; but so clumsily did he do the work, hacking the head off by repeated blows, instead of severing it by one clean cut, that the friends of the thief were incensed and vowed vengeance. That same night they lay in wait for the executioner as he was returning to the city, and beat him to death with stones. Five men were arrested for this crime; they were compelled to confess their guilt and were sentenced to death. As they were being carried out to the execution-ground, one of the condemned pointed to two men, who were in the crowd of sightseers, and swore that they were equally concerned in the murder. So these two men were also put on their trial, with the result that one was found guilty and was equally condemned to death. As if this were not sufficient, at the execution the mother of one of the prisoners, when she saw her son's head fall beneath the knife, gave a loud scream and fell down stone-dead. Nine lives were sacrificed in this tragedy: the woman who was stabbed recovered of her wound.

Hsiakwan was crowded, as it was market day. We had lunch together at a Chinese restaurant, and then, my men having come up, the kind missionaries returned, and I went on alone. A river, the Yangki River, drains the Tali Lake, and, leaving the south-west corner of the lake, flows through the town of Hsiakwan, and so on west to join the Mekong. For three days the river would be our guide. A mile from the town the river enters a narrow defile, where steep walls of rock rise abruptly from the banks. The road here passes under a massive gateway. Forts, now dismantled, guard the entrance; the pass could be made absolutely impregnable. At this point the torrent falls under a natural bridge of unusual beauty. We rode on by the narrow bank along the river, crossed from the left to the right bank, and continued on through a beautiful country, sweet with the scent of the honeysuckle, to the charming little village of Hokiangpu. Here we had arranged to stay. The inn was a large one, and very clean. Many of its rooms were already occupied by a large party of Cantonese returning home after the Thibetan Fair with loads of opium.

The Cantonese, using the term in its broader sense as applied to the natives of the province of Kuangtung, are the Catalans of China. They are as enterprising as the Scotch, adapt themselves as readily to circumstances, are enduring, canny, and successful; you meet them in the most distant parts of China. They make wonderful pilgrimages on foot. They have the reputation of being the most quick-witted of all Chinese. Large numbers come to Tali during the Thibetan Fair, and in the opium season. They bring all kinds of foreign goods adapted for Chinese wants—cheap pistols and revolvers, mirrors, scales, fancy pictures, and a thousand gewgaws useful as well as attractive—and they return with opium. They travel in bands, marching in single file, their carrying poles pointed with a steel spearhead two feet long, serving a double use—a carrying pole in peace, a formidable spear in trouble.

Everywhere they can be distinguished by their dress, by their enormous oiled sunshades, and by their habit of tricing their loads high up to the carrying pole. They are always well clad in dark blue; their heads are always cleanly shaved; their feet are well sandalled, and their calves neatly bandaged. They have a travelled mien about them, and carry themselves with an air of conscious superiority to the untravelled savages among whom they are trading. To me they were always polite and amiable; they recognised that I was, like themselves, a stranger far from home.

This is the class of Chinese who, emigrating from the thickly-peopled south-eastern provinces of China, already possess a predominant share of the wealth of Borneo, Sumatra, Java, Timor, the Celebes and the Philippine Islands, Burma, Siam, Annam and Tonquin, the Straits Settlements, Malay Peninsula, and Cochin China. "There is hardly a tiny islet visited by our naturalists in any part of these seas but Chinamen are found." And it is this class of Chinese who have already driven us out of the Northern Territory of Australia, and whose unrestricted entry into the other colonies we must prevent at all hazards. We cannot compete with Chinese; we cannot intermix or marry with them; they are aliens in language, thought, and customs; they are working animals of low grade but great vitality. The Chinese is temperate, frugal, hard-working, and law-evading, if not law-abiding—we all acknowledge that. He can outwork an Englishman, and starve him out of the country—no one can deny that. To compete successfully with a Chinaman, the artisan or labourer of our own flesh and blood would require to be degraded into a mere mechanical beast of labour, unable to support wife or family, toiling seven days in the week, with no amusements, enjoyments, or comforts of any kind, no interest in the country, contributing no share towards the expense of government, living on food that he would now reject with loathing, crowded with his fellows ten or fifteen in a room that he would not now live in alone, except with repugnance. Admitted freely into Australia, the Chinese would starve out the Englishman, in accordance with the law of currency—that of two currencies in a country the baser will always supplant the better. "In Victoria," says Professor Pearson, "a single trade—that of furniture-making—was taken possession of and ruined for white men within the space of something like five years." In the small colony of Victoria there are 9377 Chinese in a population of 1,150,000; in all China, with its population of 350,000,000, there are only 8081 foreigners (Dyer Ball), a large proportion of whom are working for China's salvation.

There is not room for both in Australia. Which is to be our colonist, the Asiatic or the Englishman?

In the morning we had another beautiful walk round the snow-clad mountains to the village of Yangpi, at the back of Tali. There was a long delay here. News of my arrival spread, and the people hurried along to see me. No sooner was I seated at an inn than two messengers from the yamen called for my passport. They were officious young fellows, sadly wanting in respect, and they asked for my passport in a noisy way that I did not like, so I would not understand them. I only smiled at them in the most friendly manner possible. I kept them for some time in a fever of irritation at their inability to make me understand; I listened with imperturbable calmness to their excited phrases till they were nearly dancing. Then I leisurely produced my passport, as if to satisfy a curiosity of my own, and began scanning it. Seeing this, they rudely thrust forth their hands to seize it; but I had my eye on them. "Not so quick, my friends," I said, soothingly. "Be calm; nervous irritability is a fruitful source of trouble. See, here is my passport; here is the official seal, and here the name of your unworthy servant. Now I fold it up carefully and—put it back in my pocket. But here is a copy, which is at your service. If you wish to show the original to the magistrate, I will take it to his honour myself, but out of my hands it does not pass." They looked puzzled, as they did not understand English; they debated a minute or two, and then went away with the copy, which in due time they politely returned to me.

If you wish to travel quickly in China, never be in a hurry. Appear unconscious of all that is passing; never be irritated by any delay, and assume complete indifference, even when you are really anxious to push on. Emulate, too, that leading trait in the Chinese character, and never understand anything which you do not wish to understand. No man on earth can be denser than a Chinaman, when he chooses.

Let me give an instance. It was not so long ago, in a police court in Melbourne, that a Chinaman was summoned for being in possession of a tenement unfit for human habitation. The case was clearly proved, and he was fined £1. But in no way could John be made to understand that a fine had been inflicted. He sat there with unmoved stolidity, and all that the court could extract from him was: "My no savvy, no savvy." After saying this in a voice devoid of all hope, he sank again into silence. Here rose a well-known lawyer. "With your worship's permission, I think I can make the Chinaman understand," he said. He was permitted to try. Striding fiercely up to the poor Celestial, he said to him in a loud voice, "John, you are fined two pounds." "No dam fear! Only *one*!"

Crossing now the river by a well-constructed suspension bridge, we had a fearful climb of 2000 feet up the mountain. My coolie "Bones" nearly died on the way. Then there was a rough descent by a jagged path down the rocky side of the mountain-river to the village of Taiping-pu. It was long after dark when we arrived; and an hour later stalked in the gaunt form of poor "Bones," who, instead of eating a good meal, coiled up on the *kang* and smoked an opium-pipe that he borrowed from the chairen. All the next day, and, indeed, for every day till we reached Tengyueh, our journey was one of the most arduous I have ever known. The road has to surmount in succession parallel ridges of mountains. The road is never even, for it cannot remain where travelling is easiest, but must continually dip from the crest of the ranges to the depths of the valleys.

Shortly before reaching Huanglien-pu my pony cast a shoe, and it was some time before we were able to have it seen to; but I had brought half a dozen spare shoes with me, and by-and-by a muleteer came along who fixed one on as neatly as any farrier could have done, and gladly accepted a reward of one halfpenny. He kept the foot steady while shoeing it by lashing the fetlock to the pony's tail.

Caravans of cotton coming from Burma were meeting us all day. Miles away the booming of their gongs sounded in the silent hills; a long time afterwards their bells were heard jingling, and by-and-by the mules and horses appeared under their huge bales of cotton, the foremost decorated with scarlet tufts and plumes of pheasant tails, the last carrying the saddle and bedding of the headman, as well as the burly headman himself, perched above all. A man with a gong always headed the way; there was a driver to every five animals. In the sandy bed of the river at one place a caravan was resting. Their packs were piled in parallel rows; their horses browsed on the hillside. I counted 107 horses in this one caravan.

. The prevailing pathological feature of the Chinese of Western Yunnan is the deformity goitre. It may safely be asserted that it is as common in many districts as are the marks of small-pox. Goitre occurs widely in Annam, Siam, Upper Burma, the Shan States, and in Western China as far as the frontier of Thibet. It is distinctly associated with cretinism and its interrupted intellectual development. And the disease must increase, for there is no attempt to check it. To be a "thickneck" is no bar to marriage on either side. The goitrous intermarry, and have children who are goitrous, or, rather, who will, if exposed to the same conditions as their parents, inevitably develop goitre. Frequently the disease is intensified in the offspring into cretinism, and I can conceive of no sight more disgusting than that which so often met our view, of a goitrous mother suckling her imbecile child. On one afternoon, among those who passed us on the road, I counted eighty persons with the deformity. On another day nine adults were climbing a path, by which we had just descended, every one of whom had goitre. In one small village, out of eighteen full-grown men and women whom I met in the street down which I rode, fifteen were affected. My diary in the West, especially from Yunnan City to Yungchang, after which point the cases greatly diminished in number, became a monotonous record of cases. At the mission in Tali three women are employed, and of these two are goitrous; the third, a Minchia woman, is free from the disease, and I have been told that among the indigenes the disease is much less common than among the Chinese. On all sides one encounters the horrible deformity, among all classes, of all ages. The disease early manifests itself, and I have often seen well-marked enlargement in children as young as eight. Turn any street corner in any town of importance in Western Yunnan and you will meet half a dozen cases; there must be few families in the western portion of the province free from the taint.

On a day, for example, like this (May 5th), when the road was more than usually mountainous, though that may have been an accident, my chairen was a "thickneck" and my two soldiers were "thicknecks." At the village of Huanglien-pu, where I had lunch, the landlady of the inn had a goitrous neck that was swelled out half-way to the shoulder, and her son was a slobbering-mouthed cretin with the intelligence of an animal. And among the people who gathered round me in a dull, apathetic way every other one was more or less marked with the disease and its attendant mental phenomena. Again, at the inn in a little mountain village, where we stopped for the night, mother, father, and every person in the house, to the number of nine, above the age of childhood was either goitrous or cretinous, dull of intelligence, mentally verging upon dementia in three cases, in two of which physical growth had been arrested at childhood.

Rarely during my journey to Burma was I offended by hearing myself called "*Yang kweitze*" (foreign devil), although this is the universal appellation of the foreigner wherever Mandarin is spoken in China. To-day, however, (May 6th), I was seated at the inn in the town of Chutung when I heard the offensive term. I was seated at a table in the midst of the accustomed crowd of Chinese. I was on the highest seat, of course, because I was the most important person present, when a bystander, seeing that I spoke no Chinese, coolly said the words "*Yang kweitze*" (foreign devil). I rose in my wrath, and seized my whip. "You Chinese devil" (*Chung kweitze*), I said in Chinese, and then I assailed him in English. He seemed surprised at my warmth, but said nothing, and, turning on his heel, walked uncomfortably away.

I often regretted afterwards that I did not teach the man a lesson, and cut him across the face with my whip; yet, had I done so, it would have been unjust. He called me, as I thought, "*Yang kweitze*," but I have no doubt, having told the story to Mr. Warry, the Chinese adviser to the Government of Burma, that he did not use these words at all, but others so closely resembling them that they sounded identically the same to my untrained ear, and yet signified not "foreign devil," but "honoured guest." He had paid me a compliment; he had not insulted me. The Yunnanese, Mr. Warry tells me, do not readily speak of the devil for fear he should appear.

On my journey I made it a rule, acting advisedly, to refuse to occupy any other than the best room in the inn, and, if there was only one room, I required that the best bed in the room, as regards elevation, should be given to me. So, too, at every inn I insisted that the best table should be given me, and, if there were already Chinese seated at it, I gravely bowed to them, and by a wave of my hand signified that it was my pleasure that they should make way for the distinguished stranger. When there was only the one table, I occupied, as by right, its highest seat, refusing to sit in any other. I required, indeed, by politeness and firmness, that the Chinese take me at my own valuation. And they invariably did so. They always gave way to me. They recognised that I must be a traveller of importance, despite the smallness of my retinue and the homeliness of my attire; and they acknowledged my superiority. Had I been content with a humbler place, it would quickly have been reported along the road, and, little by little, my complacence would have been tested. I am perfectly sure that, by never verging from my position of superiority, I gained the respect of the Chinese, and it is largely to this I attribute the universal respect and attention shown me during the journey. For I was unarmed, entirely dependent upon the Chinese, and, for all practical purposes, inarticulate. As it was, I never had any difficulty whatever.

Chinese etiquette pays great attention to the question of position; so important, indeed, is it that, when a carriage was taken by Lord Macartney's Embassy to Peking as a present, or, as the Chinese said, as tribute to the Emperor Kienlung, great offence was caused by the arrangement of the seats requiring the driver to sit on a higher level than His Majesty. A small enough mistake surely, but sufficient to mar the success of an expedition which the Chinese have always regarded as "one of the most splendid testimonials of respect that a tributary nation ever paid their Court."

On the morning of May 7th, as we were leaving the village where we had slept the night before, we were witnesses of a domestic quarrel which might well have become a tragedy. On the green outside their cabin a husband with goitre, enraged against his goitrous wife, was kept from killing her by two elderly goitrous women. All were speaking with horrible goitrous voices as if they had cleft palates, and the husband was hoarse with fury. Jealousy could not have been the cause of the quarrel, for his wife was one of the most hideous creatures I have seen in China. Throwing aside the bamboo with which he was threatening her, the husband ran into the house, and was out again in a moment brandishing a long native sword with which he menaced speedy death to the joy of his existence. I stood in the road and watched the disturbance, and with me the soldier-guard, who did not venture to interfere. But the two women seized the angry brute and held him till his wife toddled round the corner. Now, if this were a determined woman, she could best revenge herself for the cruelty that had been done her by going straightway and poisoning herself with opium, for then would her spirit be liberated, ever after to haunt her husband, even if he escaped punishment for being the cause of her death. If in the dispute he had killed her, he would be punished with "strangulation after the usual period," the sentence laid down by the law and often recorded in the *Peking Gazette* (*e.g.*, May 15th, 1892), unless he could prove her guilty of infidelity, or want of filial respect for his parents, in which case his action would be praiseworthy rather than culpable. If, however, in the dispute the wife had killed her husband, or by her conduct had driven him to suicide, she would be inexorably tied to the cross and put to death by the "*Ling chi*," or "degrading and slow process." For a wife to kill her husband has always been regarded as a more serious crime than for a husband to kill his wife; even in our own highly favoured country, till within a few years of the present century, the punishment for the man was death by hanging, but in the case of the woman death by burning alive.

Let me at this point interpolate a word or two about the method of execution known as the *Ling chi*. The words are commonly, and quite wrongly, translated as "death by slicing into 10,000 pieces"— a truly awful description of a punishment whose cruelty has been extraordinarily misrepresented. It is true that no punishment is more dreaded by the Chinese than the *Ling chi*; but it is dreaded, not because of any torture associated with its performance, but because of the dismemberment practised upon the body which was received whole from its parents. The mutilation is ghastly and excites our horror as an example of barbarian cruelty: but it is not cruel, and need not excite our horror, since the mutilation is done, not before death, but after. The method is simply the following, which I give as I received it first-hand from an eye-witness:—The prisoner is tied to a rude cross: he is invariably deeply under the influence of opium. The executioner, standing before him, with a sharp sword makes two quick incisions above the eyebrows, and draws down the portion of skin over each eye, then he makes two more quick incisions across the breast, and in the next moment he pierces the heart, and death is instantaneous. Then he cuts the body in pieces; and the degradation consists in the fragmentary shape in which the prisoner has to appear in heaven. As a missionary said to me: "He can't lie out that he got there properly when he carries with him such damning evidence to the contrary."

THE DESCENT TO THE RIVER MEKONG.

In China immense power is given to the husband over the body of his wife, and it seems as if the tendency in England were to approximate to the Chinese custom. Is it not a fact that, if a husband in England brutally maltreats his wife, kicks her senseless, and disfigures her for life, the average English bench of unpaid magistrates will find extenuating circumstances in the fact of his being the husband, and will rarely sentence him to more than a month or two's hard labour?

CHAPTER XIX.

The Mekong and Salween Rivers—How to Travel in China.

To-day, May 7th, we crossed the River Mekong, even at this distance from Siam a broad and swift stream. The river flows into the light from a dark and gloomy gorge, takes a sharp bend, and rolls on between the mountains. Where it issues from the gorge a suspension bridge has been stretched across the stream. A wonderful pathway zigzags down the face of the mountain to the river, in an almost vertical incline of 2000ft. At the riverside an embankment of dressed stone, built up from the rock, leads for some hundreds of feet along the bank, where there would otherwise have been no foothold, to the clearing by the bridge. The likin-barrier is here, and a teahouse or two, and the guardian temple. The bridge itself is graceful and strong, swinging easily 30ft. above the current; it is built of powerful chains, carried from bank to bank and held by masses of solid masonry set in the bedrock. It is 60 yards long and 10ft. wide, is floored with wood, and has a picket parapet supported by lateral chains. From the river a path led us up to a small village, where my men rested to gather strength. For facing us were the mountain heights, which had to be escaladed before we could leave the river gulch. Then with immense toil we climbed up the mountain path by a rocky staircase of thousands of steps, till, worn out, and with "Bones" nearly dead, we at length reached the narrow defile near the summit, whence an easy road brought us in the early evening to Shuichai (6700ft.).

In the course of one afternoon we had descended 2000ft. to the river (4250ft. above the sea), and had then climbed 2450ft. to Shuichai. And the ascent from the river was steeper than the descent into it; yet the railway which is to be built over this trade-route between Burma and Yunnan will have other engineering difficulties to contend with even greater than this.

My soldier to-day was a boy of fifteen or sixteen. He was armed with a revolver, and bore himself valiantly. But his revolver was more dangerous in appearance than in effect, for the cylinder would not revolve, the hammer was broken short off, and there were no cartridges. Everywhere the weapon was examined with curiosity blended with awe, and I imagine that the Chinese were told strange tales of its deadliness.

Next morning we continued by easy gradients to Talichao (7700ft.), rising 1000ft. in rather less than seven miles. It was bitterly cold in the mists of the early morning. But twenty miles further the road dipped again to the sunshine and warmth of the valley of Yungchang, where, in the city made famous by Marco Polo, we found comfortable quarters in an excellent inn.

Yungchang is a large town, strongly walled. It is, however, only a remnant of the old city, acres of houses having been destroyed during the insurrection, when for three years, it is said, Imperialists and Mohammedans were contending for its possession. There is a telegraph station in the town. The streets are broad and well-paved, the inns large, and the temples flourishing. One fortunate circumstance the traveller will notice in Yungchang—there is a marked diminution in the number of cases of goitre. And the diminution is not confined to the town, but is apparent from this point right on to Burma.

Long after our arrival in Yungchang my opium-eating coolie "Bones" had not come, and we had to wait for him in anger and annoyance. He had my hamper of eatables and my bundle of bedding. Tired of waiting for him, I went for a walk to the telegraph office and was turning to come back, when I met the faithful skeleton, a mile from the inn, walking along as if to a funeral, his neck elongating from side to side like a camel's, a lean and hungry look in his staring eyes, his bones crackling inside his skin. Continuing in the direction that he was going when I found him, he might have reached Thibet in time, but never Burma. I led him back to the hotel, where he ruefully showed me his empty string of cash, as if that had been the cause of his delay; he had only 6 cash left, and he wanted an advance.

This was the worst coolie I had in my employ during my journey. But he was a good-natured fellow and honest. He was better educated, too, than most of the other coolies, and could both read and write. His dress on march was characteristic of the man. He was nearly naked; his clothes hardly hung together; he wore no sandals on his feet; but round his neck he carried a small earthenware phial of opium ash. In the early stages he delayed us all an hour or two every day, but he improved as we went further. And then he was so long and thin, so grotesque in his gait, and afforded me such frequent amusement, that I would not willingly have exchanged him for the most active coolie in China.

INSIDE VIEW OF A SUSPENSION BRIDGE IN FAR WESTERN CHINA.

On the 9th we had a long and steep march west from the plain of Yungchang. At Pupiao I had a public lunch. It was market day, and the country people enjoyed the rare pleasure of seeing a foreigner feed. The street past the inn was packed in a few minutes, and the innkeeper had all he could do to attend to the many customers who wished to take tea at the same time as the foreigner. I was now used to these demonstrations. I could eat on with undisturbed equanimity. On such occasions I made it a practice, when I had finished and was leaving the inn, to turn round and bow gravely to the crowd, thanking them in a few kindly words of English, for the reception they had accorded me. At the same time I took the opportunity of mentioning that they would contribute to the comfort of future travellers, if only they would pay a little more attention to their table manners. Then, addressing the innkeeper, I thought it only right to point out to him that it was absurd to expect that one small black cloth should wipe all cups and cup-lids, all tables, all spilt tea, and all dishes, all through the day, without getting dirty. Occasionally, too, I pointed out another defect of management to the innkeeper, and told him that, while I personally had an open mind on the subject, other travellers might come his way who would disapprove, for instance—he would pardon my mentioning it—of the manure coolie passing through the restaurant with his buckets at mealtime, and halting by the table to see the stranger eat.

When I spoke in this way quite seriously and bowed, those whose eyes met mine always bowed gravely in return. And for the next hour on the track my men would tell each other, with cackles of laughter, how Mô Shensen, their master, mystified the natives.

From Pupiao we had a pleasant ride over a valley-plain, between hedges of cactus in flower and bushes of red roses, past graceful clumps of bamboo waving like ostrich feathers. By-and-by drizzling rain came on and compelled us to seek shelter in the only inn in a poor out-of-the-way hamlet. But I could not stop here, because the best room in the inn was already occupied by a military officer of some distinction, a colonel, on his way, like ourselves, to Tengyueh. An official chair with arched poles fitted for four bearers was in the common-room; the mules of his attendants were in the stables, and were valuable animals. The landlord offered me another room, an inferior one; but I waved the open fingers of my left hand before my face and said, "*puyao! puyao!*" (I don't want it, I don't want it). For I was not so foolish or inconsistent as to be content with a poorer quarter of the inn than that occupied by the officer, whatever his button. I could not acknowledge to the Chinese that any Chinaman travelling in the Middle Kingdom was my equal, let alone my superior. Refusing to remain, I waited in the front room until the rain should lift and allow us to proceed. But we did not require to go on. It happened as I expected. The Colonel sent for me, and, bowing to me, showed by signs that one half his room was at my service. In return for his politeness he had the privilege of seeing me eat. With both hands I offered him in turn every one of my dishes. Afterwards I showed him my photographs—I treated him, indeed, with proper condescension.

On the 10th we crossed the famous River Salween (2600 ft.). Through an open tableland, well grassed and sparsely wooded, we came at length to the cleft in the hills from which is obtained the first view of the river valley. There was a small village here, and, while we were taking tea, a soldier came hurriedly down the road, who handed me a letter addressed in Chinese. I confess that at the moment I had a sudden misgiving that some impediment was to be put in the way of my journey. But it was nothing more than a telegram from Mr. Jensen in Yunnan, telling me of the decision of the Chinese Government to continue the telegraph to the frontier of Burma. The telegram was written by the Chinese operator in Yungchang in a neat round hand, without any error of spelling; it had come to Yungchang after my departure, and had been courteously forwarded by the Chinese manager. The soldier who brought it had made a hurried march of thirty-eight miles before overtaking me, and deserved a reward. I motioned Laotseng, my cash-bearer, to give him a present, and he meanly counted out 25 cash, and was about to give them, when I ostentatiously increased the amount to 100 cash. The soldier was delighted; the onlookers were charmed with this exhibition of Western munificence. Suppose a rich Chinese traveller in England, who spoke no English, were to offer Tommy Atkins twopence halfpenny for travelling on foot thirty-eight miles to bring him a telegram, having then to walk back thirty-eight miles and find himself on the way, would the English soldier bow as gratefully as did his perishing Chinese brother when I thus rewarded him?

We descended by beautiful open country into the Valley of the Shadow of Death—the valley of the River Salween. No other part of Western China has the evil repute of this valley; its unhealthiness is a by-word. "It is impossible to pass," says Marco Polo; "the air in summer is so impure and bad and any foreigner attempting it would die for certain."

The Salween was formerly the boundary between Burma and China, and it is to be regretted that at the annexation of Upper Burma England did not push her frontier back to its former position. But the delimitation of the frontier of Burma is not yet complete. No time could be more opportune for its completion than the present, when China is distracted by her difficulties with Japan. China disheartened could need but little persuasion to accede to the just demand of England that the frontier of Burma shall be the true south-western frontier of China—the Salween River.

There are no Chinese in the valley, nor would any Chinaman venture to cross it after nightfall. The reason of its unhealthiness is not apparent, except in the explanation of Baber, that "border regions, 'debatable grounds,' are notoriously the birthplace of myths and marvels." There can be little doubt that the deadliness of the valley is a tradition rather than a reality.

By flights of stone steps we descended to the river, where at the bridge-landing, we were arrested by a sight that could not be seen without emotion. A prisoner, chained by the hands and feet and cooped in a wooden cage, was being carried by four bearers to Yungchang to execution. He was not more than twenty-one years of age, was well-dressed, and evidently of a rank in life from which are recruited few of the criminals of China. Yet his crime could not have been much graver. On the corner posts of his cage white strips of paper were posted, giving his name and the particulars of the crime which he was so soon to expiate. He was a burglar who had escaped from prison by killing his guard, and had been recaptured. Unlike other criminals I have seen in China, who laugh at the stranger and appear unaffected by their lot, this young fellow seemed to feel keenly the cruel but well-deserved fate that was in store for him. Three days hence he would be put to death by strangulation outside the wall of Yungchang.

THE RIVER SALWEEN, THE FORMER BOUNDARY BETWEEN CHINA AND BURMA.

Another of those remarkable works which declare the engineering skill of the Chinese, is the suspension bridge which spans the Salween by a double loop—the larger loop over the river, the smaller one across the overflow. A natural piece of rock strengthened by masonry, rising from the river bed, holds the central ends of both loops. The longer span is 80 yards in length, the shorter 55; both are 12ft. wide, and are formed of twelve parallel chain cables, drawn to an appropriate curve. A rapid river flows under the bridge, the rush of whose waters can be heard high up the mountain slopes.

None but Shans live in the valley. They are permitted to govern themselves under Chinese supervision, and preserve their own laws and customs. They have a village near the bridge, of grass-thatched huts and open booths, where travellers can find rest and refreshment, and where native women prettily arrayed in dark-blue, will brew you tea in earthenware teapots. Very different are the Shan women from the Chinese. Their colour is much darker; their head-dress is a circular pile formed of concentric folds of dark-blue cloth; their dress closely resembles with its jacket and kilt the bathing dress of civilisation; their arms are bare, they have gaiters on their legs, and do not compress their feet. All wear brooches and earrings, and other ornaments of silver filigree.

From the valley the main road rises without intermission 6130 feet to the village of Fengshui-ling (8730 feet), a climb which has to be completed in the course of the afternoon. We were once more among the trees. Pushing on till I was afraid we should be benighted, we reached long after dark an encampment of bamboo and grass, in the lonely bush, where the kind people made us welcome. It was bitterly cold during the night, for the hut I slept in was open to the air. My three men and the escort must have been even colder than I was. But at least we all slept in perfect security, and I cannot praise too highly the constant care of the Chinese authorities to shield even from the apprehension of harm one whose only protection was his British passport.

All the way westward from Yunnan City I was shadowed both by a yamen-runner and a soldier; both were changed nearly every day, and the further west I went the more frequently were they armed. The yamen-runner usually carried a long native sword only, but the soldier, in addition to his sword, was on one occasion, as we have seen, armed with the relics of a revolver that would not revolve. On May 10th, for the first time, the soldier detailed to accompany me was provided with a rusty old musket with a very long barrel. I examined this weapon with much curiosity. China is our neighbour in Eastern Asia, and is, it is often stated, an ideal power to be intrusted with the government of the buffer state called for by French aggression in Siam. In China, it is alleged, we have a prospective ally in Asia, and it is preferable that England should suffer all reasonable indignities and humilities at her hands rather than endanger any possible relations, which may subsequently be entered into, with a hypothetically powerful neighbour.

On my arrival in Burma I was often amused by the serious questions I was asked concerning the military equipment of the Chinese soldiers of Western Yunnan. The soldier who was with me to-day was a type of the warlike sons of China, not only in the province bordering on Burma, but, with slight differences, all over the Middle Kingdom. Now, physically, this man was fit to be drafted into any army in the world, but, apart from his endurance, his value as a fighting machine lay in the weapon with which the military authorities had armed him. This weapon was peculiar; I noted down its peculiarities on the spot. In this weapon the spring of the trigger was broken so that it could not be pulled; if it had been in order, there was no cap for the hammer to strike; if there had been a cap, it would have been of no use because the pinhole was rusted; even if the pinhole had been open, the rifle would still have been ineffective because it was not loaded, for the very good reason that the soldier had not been provided with powder, or, if he had, he had been compelled to sell it in order to purchase the rice which the Emperor, "whose rice he ate," had neglected to send him.

An early start in the morning and we descended quickly to the River Shweli.

THE RIVER SHWELI AND ITS SUSPENSION BRIDGE.

The Salween River is at an elevation of 2600 feet. Forty-five li further the road reaches at Fengshui-ling a height of 8730, from which point, in thirty-five li, it dips again to the River Shweli, 4400 feet above sea level. There was the usual suspension bridge at the river, and the inevitable likin-barrier. For the first time the

Customs officials seemed inclined to delay me. I was on foot, and separated from my men by half the height of the hill. The collectors, and the underlings who are always hanging about the barriers, gathered round me and interrogated me closely. They spoke to me in Chinese, and with insufficient deference. The Chinese seem imbued with the mistaken belief that their language is the vehicle of intercourse not only within the four seas, but beyond them, and are often arrogant in consequence. I answered them in English. "I don't understand one word you say, but, if you wish to know," I said, energetically, "I come from Shanghai." "Shanghai," they exclaimed, "he comes from Shanghai!" "And I am bound for Singai" (Bhamo);—"Singai," they repeated, "he is going to Singai!"—"unless the Imperial Government, suspicious of my intentions, which the meanest intelligence can see are pacific, should prevent me, in which case England will find a coveted pretext to add Yunnan to her Burmese Empire." Then, addressing myself to the noisiest, I indulged in some sarcastic speculations upon his probable family history, deduced from his personal peculiarities, till he looked very uncomfortable indeed. Thereupon I gravely bowed to them, and, leaving them in dumb astonishment, walked on over the bridge. They probably thought I was rating them in Manchu, the language of the Emperor. Two boys staggering under loads of firewood did not escape so easily, but were detained and a log squeezed from each wherewith to light the likin fires.

A steep climb of another 3000 or 4000 feet over hills carpeted with bracken, with here and there grassy swards, pretty with lilies and daisies and wild strawberries, and then a quick descent, and we were in the valley of Tengyueh (5600ft.). A plain everywhere irrigated, flanked by treeless hills; fields shut in by low embankments; villages in plantations round its margin; black-faced sheep in flocks on the hillsides; and, away to the right the crenellated walls of Tengyueh. A stone-flagged path down the centre of the plain led us into the town. We entered by the south gate, and, turning to the left, were conducted into the telegraph compound, where I was to find accommodation, the clerk in charge of the operators being able to speak a few words of English. I was an immediate object of curiosity.

CHAPTER XX.

THE CITY OF TENGYUEH—THE CELEBRATED WUNTHO SAWBWA—SHAN SOLDIERS.

I was given a comfortable room in the telegraph offices, but I had little privacy. My room was thronged during all the time of my visit. The first evening I held an informal and involuntary reception, which was attended by all the officials of the town, with the dignified exception of the Brigadier-General. The three members of the Chinese Boundary Commission, which had recently arranged with the British Commission the preliminaries to the delimitation of the boundary between Burma and China, were here, disputing with clerks, yamen-runners, and chair-coolies for a sight of my photographs and curiosities. The telegraph Manager Pen, Yeh (the magistrate), and a stalwart soldier (Colonel Liu), formed the Commission, and they retain hallowed recollections of the benignity of the Englishmen, and the excellence of their champagne. Colonel Liu proved to be the most enlightened member of the party. He is a tall, handsome fellow, fifty years of age, a native of Hunan, the most warlike and anti-foreign province in China. He was especially glad to see a foreign doctor. The gallant Colonel confided to me a wish that had long been uppermost in his heart. From some member, unknown, of the British Commission he had learnt of the marvellous rejuvenating power of a barbarian medicine—could I get him some? *Could I get him a bottle of hair-dye?* Unlike his compatriots, who regard the external features of longevity as the most coveted attribute of life, this gentleman, in whose brain the light of civilisation was dawning, wished to frustrate the doings of age. Could I get him a bottle of hair-dye? He was in charge of the fort at Ganai, two days out on the way to Bhamo, and would write to the officer in charge during his absence directing him to provide me with an escort worthy of my benefaction.

One celebrity, who lives in the neighbourhood of Tengyueh, did not favour me with a visit. That famous dacoit, the outlawed Prince of Wuntho—the Wuntho Sawbwa—lives here, an exile sheltered by the Chinese Government. A pure Burmese himself, the father-in-law of the amiable Sawbwa of Santa, he is believed by the Government of Burma to have been "concerned in all the

Kachin risings of 1892-1893." A reward of 5000 rupees is offered for his head, which will be paid equally whether the head be on or off the shoulders. Another famous outlaw, the Shan Chief Kanhliang, is also believed to be in hiding in the neighbourhood of Tengyueh. The value of *his* head has been assessed at 2000 rupees.

Tengyueh is more a park than a town. The greater part of the city within the walls is waste land or gardens. The houses are collected mainly near the south gate, and extend beyond the south gate on each side of the road for half a mile on the road to Bhamo. There is an excellent wall in admirable order, with an embankment of earth 20ft. in width. But I saw no guns of any kind whatever, nor did I meet a single armed man in the town or district.

Tengyueh is so situated that the invading army coming from Burma will find a pleasant pastime in shelling it from the open hills all around the town. This was the last stronghold of the Mohammedans. It was formerly a prosperous border town, the chief town in all the fertile valley of the Taiping. It was in the hands of the rebels till June 10th, 1873, when it was delivered over to the Imperialists to carnage and destruction. The valley is fertile and well populated, and prosperity is quickly returning to the district.

There is only one yamen in Tengyueh of any pretension, and it is the official residence of a red-button warrior, the Brigadier-General (*Chentai*) Chang, the successor, though not, of course, the immediate successor, of Li-Sieh-tai, who was concerned in the murder of Margary and the repulse of the expedition under Colonel Horace Browne in 1875. A tall, handsome Chinaman is Chang, of soldierly bearing and blissful innocence of all knowledge of modern warfare. Yungchang is the limit of his jurisdiction in one direction, the Burmese boundary in the other; his only superior officer is the Titai in Tali.

The telegraph office adjoins the City Temple and Theatre of Tengyueh. At this time the annual festival was being celebrated in the temple. Theatrical performances were being given in uninterrupted succession daily for the term of one month. Play began at sunrise, and the curtain fell, or would have fallen if there had been a curtain, at twilight. Day was rendered hideous by the clangour of the instruments which the blunted senses of Chinese have been misguided into believing are musical. Already the play, or succession of plays, had continued fifteen days, and another thirteen days had yet to be endured before its completion. Crowds occupied the temple court during the performance, while a considerable body of dead-heads witnessed the entertainment from the embankment and wall overlooking the open stage. My host, the telegraph Manager Pen, and his two friends Liu and Yeh, were given an improvised seat of honour outside my window, and here they sat all day and sipped tea and cracked jokes. No actresses were on the stage; the female parts were taken by men whose make-up was admirable, and who imitated, with curious fidelity, the voice and gestures of women. The dresses were rich and varied. Scene-shifters, band, supers, and friends remained on the stage during the performance, dodging about among the actors. There is no drop curtain in a Chinese theatre, and all scenes are changed on the open stage before you. The villain, whose nose is painted white, vanquished by triumphant virtue, dies a gory death; he remains dead just long enough to satisfy you that he *is* dead, and then gets up and serenely walks to the side. There is laughter at sallies of indecency, and the spectators grunt their applause. The Chinaman is rarely carried away by his feelings at the theatre; indeed, it may be questioned if strong emotion is ever aroused in his breast, except by the first addresses of the junior members of the China Inland Mission, the thrilling effect of whose Chinese exhortations is recorded every month in *China's Millions*.

The Manager of the telegraph, to show his good feeling, presented me with a stale tin of condensed milk. His second clerk and operator was the most covetous man I met in China. He begged in turn for nearly every article I possessed, beginning with my waterproof, which I did not give him, and ending with the empty milk tin, which I did, for "Give to him that asketh," said Buddha, "even though it be but a little." The chief operator in charge of the telegraph offices speaks a little English, and is the medium by which English messages and letters are translated into Chinese for the information of the officials. His name is Chueh. His method of translation is to glean the sense of a sentence by the probable meaning, derived from an inaccurate Anglo-Chinese dictionary, of the separate words of the sentence. He is a broken reed to trust to as an interpreter. Chueh is not an offensively truthful man. When he speaks to you, you find yourself wondering if you have ever met a greater liar than he. "Three men's strength," he says, "cannot prevail against truth;" yet he is, I think, the greatest liar I have met since I left Morocco. Indeed, the way he spoke of my head boy Laotseng, who was undoubtedly an honest Chinese, and the opinion Laotseng emphatically held of Chueh, was a curious repetition of an experience that I had not long ago in Morocco. I was living in Tangier, when I had occasion to go to Fez and Mequinez. My visit was arranged so hurriedly that I had no means of learning what was the degree of personal esteem attaching to the gentleman, a resident of Tangier, who was to be my companion. I accordingly interrogated the hotel-keeper, Mr. B. "What kind of a man is D.?" I asked. "Not a bad fellow," he replied, "if he wasn't such a blank, blank awful liar!" On the road to Wazan I became very friendly with D., and one day questioned him as to his private regard for Mr. B. of the hotel. "A fine fellow B. seems," I said, "very friendly and entertaining. What do you think of him?" "What do I think of him?" he shouted in his falsetto. "I *know* he's the biggest blank liar in Morocco." It was pleasant to meet, even in Morocco, such a rare case of mutual esteem.

My pony fared badly in Tengyueh. There was a poor stable in the courtyard with a tiled roof that would fall at the first shower. There were no beans. The pony had to be content with rice or paddy, which it disliked equally. The rice was 1-1/2*d.* the 7-1/2lbs. There was no grass, Chueh said, to be obtained in the district. He assured me so on his honour, or its Chinese equivalent; but I sent out and bought some in the street round the corner.

Silver in Tengyueh is the purest Szechuen or Yunnanese silver. Rupees are also current, and at this time were equivalent to 400 cash—the tael at the same time being worth 1260 cash. Every 10 taels, costing me 30*s.* in Shanghai, I could exchange in Tengyueh for 31 rupees. Rupees are the chief silver currency west from Tengyueh into Burma.

On May 31st I had given instructions that we were to leave early, but my men, who did not sleep in the telegraph compound, were late in coming. To still further delay me, at the time of leaving no escort had made its appearance. I did not wait for it. We marched out of the town unaccompanied, and were among the tombstones on the rise overlooking the town when the escort hurriedly overtook us. It consisted of a quiet-mannered chairen and two soldiers, one of whom was an impudent cub that I had to treat with every indignity. He was armed with a sword carried in the folds of his red cincture, in which was also concealed an old muzzle-loading pistol, formidable to look at but unloaded. This was one of the days on my journey when I wished that I had brought a revolver, not as a defence in case of danger, for there was no danger, but as a menace on occasion of anger.

Rain fell continuously. At a small village thronged with muleteers from Bhamo we took shelter for an hour. The men sipping tea under the verandahs had seen Europeans in Bhamo, and my presence evoked no interest whatever. Many of these strangers possessed an astonishing likeness to European friends of my own. Contact with Europeans, causing the phenomena of "maternal impression," was probably in a few cases accountable for the moulding of their features, but the general prevalence of the European type has yet to be explained. "My conscience! Who could ever have expected to meet *you* here?" I was often on the point of saying to some Chinese Shan or Burmese Shan in whom, to my confusion, I thought I recognised a college friend of my own.

Leaving the village, we followed the windings of the River Taiping, coasting along the edge of the high land on the left bank of the river.

THE SUBURB BEYOND THE SOUTH GATE OF TENGYUEH.
(Stalls under the Umbrellas.)

Rain poured incessantly; the creeks overflowed; the paths became watercourses and were scarcely fordable. "Bones," my opium-eating coolie with the long neck, slipped into a hole which was too deep even for his long shanks, and all my bedding was wetted. It was ninety li to Nantien, the fort we were bound to beyond Tengyueh, and we finished the distance by sundown. The town is of little importance. It is situated on an eminence and is surrounded by a wall built, with that strange spirit of contrariness characteristic of the Chinese, and because it incloses a fort, more weakly than any city wall. It is not more substantial nor higher than the wall round many a mission compound. Some 400 soldiers are stationed in the fort, which means that the commander draws the pay for 1000 soldiers, and represents the strength of his garrison as 1000. Their arms are primitive and rusty muzzle-loaders of many patterns; there are no guns to be seen, if there are any in existence—which is doubtful. The few rusty cast-iron ten-pounders that lie *hors de combat* in the mud have long since become useless. There may be ammunition in the fort; but there is none to be seen. It is more probable, and more in accordance with Chinese practice in such matters, that the ammunition left by his predecessor (if any were left, which is doubtful) has long ago been sold by the colonel in command, whose perquisite this would naturally be.

The fort of Nantien is a fort in name only—it has no need to be otherwise, for peace and quiet are abroad in the valley. Besides, the mere fact of its being called a fort is sufficiently misleading to the neighbouring British province of Burma, where they are apt to picture a Chinese fort as a structure seriously built in some accordance with modern methods of fortification.

I was given a comfortable room in a large inn already well filled with travellers. All treated me with pleasant courtesy. They were at supper when I entered the room, and they invited me to share their food. They gave me the best table to myself, and after supper they crowded into another room in order to let me have the room to myself.

Next day we continued along the sandy bed of the river, which was here more than a mile in width. The river itself, shrunk now into its smallest size, flowed in a double stream down the middle. Then we left the river, and rode along the high bank flanking the valley. All paved roads had ended at Tengyueh, and the track was deeply cut and jagged by the rains. At one point in to-day's journey the road led up an almost vertical ascent to a narrow ledge or spur at the summit, and then fell as steeply into the plain again. It was a short-cut, that, as you would expect in China, required five times more physical effort to compass than did the longer but level road which it was intended to save. So narrow is the ridge that the double row of open sheds leaves barely room for pack mules to pass. The whole traffic on the caravan route to Burma passes by this spot. The long bamboo sheds with their grass roofs are divided into stalls, where Shan women in their fantastic turbans, with silver bracelets and earrings, their lips and teeth stained with betel-juice, sit behind the counters of raised earth, and eagerly compete for the custom of travellers. More than half the women had goitre. Before them were laid out the various dishes. There were pale cuts of pork, well soaked in water to double their weight, eggs and cabbage and salted fish, bean curds, and a doubtful tea flavoured with camomile and wild herbs. There were hampers of coarse grass for the horses, and wooden bowls of cooked rice for the men, while hollow bamboos were used equally to bring water from below, to hold sheaves of chopsticks where the traveller helped himself, and to receive the cash. Trade was busy. Muleteers are glad to rest here after the climb, if only to enjoy a puff of tobacco from the bamboo-pipe which is always carried by one member of the party for the common use of all.

Descending again into the river valley, I rode lazily along in the sun, taking no heed of my men, who were soon separated from me. The broad river-bed of sand was before me as level as the waters of a lake. As I was riding slowly along by myself, away from all guard, I saw approaching me in the lonely plain a small body of men. They were moving quickly along in single file, and we soon met and passed each other. They were three Chinese Shan officers on horseback, dressed in Chinese fashion, and immediately behind them were six soldiers on foot, who I saw were Burmese or Burmese Shans. They were smart men, clad in loose jerseys and knickerbockers, with sun-hats and bare legs, and they marched like soldiers. Cartridge-belts were over their left shoulders, and Martini-Henry rifles, carried muzzle foremost, on their right. I took particular note of them because they were stepping in admirable order, and, though small of stature, I thought they were the first armed men I had met in all my journey across China who could without shame be presented as soldiers in any civilised country.

They passed me, but seemed struck by my appearance; and I had not gone a dozen yards before they all stopped by a common impulse, and when I looked back they were still there in a group talking, with the officers' horses turned towards me; and it was very evident I was the subject of their conversation. I was alone at the time, far from all my men, without weapon of any kind. I was dressed in full Chinese dress and mounted on an unmistakably Chinese pony. I rode unconcernedly on, but I must confess that I did not feel comfortable till I was assured that they did not intend to obtrude an interview upon me. At length, to my relief, the party continued on its way, while I hurried on to my coolies, and made them wait till my party was complete. I was probably alarmed without any reason. But it was not till I arrived in Burma that I learnt that this was the armed escort of the outlawed Wuntho Sawbwa, the dacoit chief who has a price set on his head. The soldiers' rifles and cartridge-belts had been stripped from the dead bodies of British sepoys, killed on the frontier in the Kachin Hills.

My men, when we were all together again, indicated to me by signs that I would shortly meet an elephant, and I thought that at last I was about to witness the realisation of that story, everywhere current in Western China, of the British tribute from Burma. Sure enough we had not gone far when, at the foot of a headland which projected into the plain, we came full upon a large elephant picking its way along the margin of the rocks—a remarkable sight to my Chinese. Its scarlet howdah was empty; its trappings were scarlet; the mahout was a Shan. It was the elephant of the Wuntho Prince—a little earlier and I might have had the privilege of meeting the dacoit himself. The elephant passed unconcernedly on, and we continued down the plain of sand to the village of Ganai, where we were to stay the night.

It was market-day in the town. A double row of stalls extended down the main street, each stall under the shelter of a huge umbrella. Japanese matches from Osaka were for sale here, and foreign nick-nacks, needles and braid and cotton, and Manchester dress stuffs mixed with the multitudinous articles of native produce. This is a Shan town, but large numbers of native women—Kachins—were here also with their ugly black faces, and coarse black fringes hiding their low foreheads. Far away from the town an obliging Shan had attached himself to us as guide. He was dressed in white cotton jacket and dark-blue knickerbockers, with a dark-blue sash round his waist. He was barelegged, and rode as the Chinese do, and as you would expect them to do who do everything *al reves*, with the heel in the stirrup instead of the toe. His turban was dark-blue, and the pigtail was coiled up under it, and did not hang down from under the skull cap as with the Chinese. When I rode into the town accompanied by the guide, all the people forsook the market street and followed the illustrious stranger to the inn which had been selected for his resting-place. It was a favourite inn, and was already crowded. The best room was in possession of Chinese travellers, who were on the road like myself. They were dozing on the couches, but what must they do when I entered the room but, thinking that I should wish to occupy it by myself, rise and pack up their things, and one after another move into another apartment adjoining, which was already well filled, and now became doubly so. Their thoughtfulness and courtesy charmed me. They must have been more tired than I was, but they smiled and nodded pleasantly to me as they left the room, as if they were grateful to me for putting them to inconvenience. They may be perishing heathen, I thought, but the average deacon or elder in our enlightened country could scarcely be more courteous.

- Ganai is a mud village thatched with grass. It is a military station under the command of the red-button Colonel Liu, whom I met in Tengyueh. The Colonel had earned his bottle of hair-dye. He had written to have me provided with an escort, and by-and-by the two officers who were to accompany me on the morrow came in to see me. As many spectators as could find elbow-room squeezed into my room behind them. Both were gentlemanly young fellows, very amiable and inquisitive, and keenly desirous to learn all they could concerning my honourable family. Their curiosity was satisfied. By the help of my Chinese phrase-book I gave them all particulars, and a few more. You see it was important that I should leave as favourable an impression as possible for the benefit of future travellers. More than one of my ancestors I brought to life again and endowed with a patriarchal age and a beard to correspond. As to my own age they marvelled greatly that one so young-looking could be so old, and when, in answer to their earnest question, I modestly confessed that I was already the unhappy possessor of two unworthy wives, five wretched sons, and three contemptible daughters, their admiration of my virtue increased tenfold.

The officers left me after this, but till late at night I held *levées* of the townsfolk, our landlady, who was most zealous, no sooner dismissing one crowd than another pressed into its place. The courtyard, I believe, remained filled till early in the morning, but I was allowed to sleep at last.

A large crowd followed me out of the town in the morning, and swarmed with me across the beautiful sward, as level as the Oval, which here widens into the country. No guest was ever sped on his way with a kindlier farewell. The fort is outside the town; we passed it on our left; it is a square inclosure of considerable size, inclosed by a mud wall 15 feet high; it is in the unsheltered plain, and presents no formidable front to an invader. At each of the four corners outside the square are detached four-sided watch-towers. No guns of any kind are mounted on the walls, and there are no sentries; one could easily imagine that the inclosure was a market-square, but imagination could never picture it as a serious obstacle to an armed entry into Western China. The river was well on our right. The plain down which we rode is of exceeding richness and highly cultivated, water being trained into the paddy-fields in the same way that everywhere prevails in China proper. Buffaloes were ploughing—wearily plodding through mud and water up to their middles. We were now among the Shans, and those working in the fields were Shans, not Chinese. Ganai, Santa, and other places are but little principalities or Shan States, governed by hereditary princelets or Sawbwas, and preserving a form of self-government under the protection of the Chinese. There are no more charming people in the world than the Shans. They are courteous, hospitable, and honest, with all the virtues and few of the vices of Orientals. "The elder brothers of the Siamese, they came originally from the Chinese province of Szechuen, and they can boast of a civilisation dating from twenty-three centuries B.C." So Terrien de Lacouperie tells us, who had a happy faculty of drawing upon his imagination for his facts.

Under the wide branches of a banyan tree I made my men stop, for I was very tired, and while they waited I lay down for an hour on the grass and had a refreshing sleep. While I slept, the rest of the escort sent to "*sung*" me to Santa arrived. Within a few yards of my resting place there is a characteristic monument, dating from the time when Burma occupied not only this valley but the fertile territory beyond it, and beyond Tengyueh to the River Salween. It is a solid Burmese pagoda, built of concentric layers of brick and mortar, and surmounted with a solid bell-shaped dome that is still intact. It stands alone on the plain near a group of banyans, and its erection no doubt gained many myriads of merits for the conscience-stricken Buddhist who found the money to build it. All goldleaf has been peeled off the pagoda years ago.

It was a picturesque party that now enfiladed into the wide stretch of sand which in the rainy season forms the bed of the river. Mounted on his white pony, there was the inarticulate European who had discarded his Chinese garb and was now dressed in the æsthetic garments of the Australian bush; there were his two coolies and Laotseng his boy, none of whom could speak any English, the two officers in their loose Chinese clothes, mounted on tough little ponies, and eight soldiers. They were Shans of kindly feature, small and nimble fellows, in neat uniforms—green jackets edged with black and braided with yellow, yellow sashes, and loose dark-blue knickerbockers—the uniform of the Sawbwa of Ganai. They were armed with Remington rifles, carried their cartridges in bandoliers, and seemed to be of excellent fighting material. All their accoutrements were in good order.

Now we had to cross the broad stream, here running with a swift current over the sand, in channels of varying depths that are frequently changing. For the width of nearly half a mile at the crossing place the water was never shallower than to my knee, nor deeper than to my waist. We all crossed safely, but, to my tribulation, the soldier who was carrying my two boxes tripped in the deepest channel and let both boxes slip from the carrying pole into the water. All the notes and papers upon which this valuable record is founded were much damaged. But it might have been worse. I had a presentiment that an accident would happen, and had waded back to the channel and was standing by at the time. But for this the papers might have been floated down to the Irrawaddy and been lost to the world—loss irreparable!

The sun was very hot. I laid out my things on the bank and dried them. Long and narrow dugouts, as light and swift as the stringtest gigs of civilisation, paddled or poled, were gliding with extraordinary speed down the channel near the bank. Riding then a little way, we dismounted under a magnificent banyan tree, one of the finest specimens, I should think, in the world. Ponies and men were dwarfed into Lilliputians under the amazing canopy of its branches. A number of villagers, come to see the foreigner, were clambering like monkeys over its roots, which "writhed in fantastic coils" over half an acre. Their village was hard by, a poor array of mud houses; the teak temple to which we were conducted was raised on piles in the centre of the village. The temple was lumbered like an old curiosity shop with fragmentary gods and torn missals. Yet the ragged priest in his smirched yellow gown, and shaven head that had been a week unshaven, seemed to enjoy a reputation for no common sanctity, to judge by the reverence shown him by my followers, and the contemptuous indifference with which he regarded their obeisance. He was club-footed and could only hobble about with difficulty—an excuse he would, no doubt, urge for the disorder of his sanctuary. To me, of course, he was very polite, and gave me the best seat he had, while Laotseng prepared me a bowl of cocoa. Then we rode along the right bank of the river, but kept moving away from the stream till in the distance across the plain at the foot of the hills, we saw the Shan town of Santa, the end of our day's stage.

Native women, returning from the town, were wending their way across the plain—lank overgrown girls with long thin legs and overhanging mops of hair like deck-swabs. They were a favourite butt of my men, who chaffed them in the humorous Eastern manner, with remarks that were, I am afraid, more coarse than witty. Kachins are not virtuous. Their customs preclude such a possibility. No Japanese maiden is more innocent of virtue than a Kachin girl.

CHAPTER XXI.

THE SHAN TOWN OF SANTA, AND MANYUEN, THE SCENE OF CONSUL MARGARY'S MURDER.

It was market day in Santa, and the accustomed crowd gathered round me as I stood in the open square in front of the Sawbwa's yamen. I was hot and hungry, for it was still early in the afternoon, and the attentions of the people were oppressive. Presently two men pushed their way through the spectators, and politely motioning to me to follow them, they led me to a neighbouring temple, to the upper storey, where the side pavilion off the chief hall was being prepared for my reception. My quarters overlooked the main court; the pony was comfortably stabled in the corner below me. Nothing could have been pleasanter than the attention I received here. Two foreign chairs were brought for my use, and half a dozen dishes of good food and clean chopsticks were set before me. The chief priest welcomed me, whose smiling face was good-nature itself. With clean-shaven head and a long robe of grey, with a rosary of black and white beads hung loosely from his neck, the kind old man moved about my room giving orders for my comfort. He held authority over a number of priests, some in black, others in yellow, and over a small band of choristers. Religion was an active performance in the temple, and the temple was in good order, with clean matting and well-kept shrines, with strange pictures on the walls of elephants and horses, with legends and scrolls in Burmese as well as in Chinese.

Towards evening the Santa Sawbwa, the hereditary prince (what a privilege it was to meet a prince! I had never met even a lord before in my life, or anyone approaching the rank of a lord, except a spurious Duke of York whom I sent to the lunatic asylum), the *Prince* of Santa paid me a State call, accompanied by a well-ordered retinue, very different indeed from the ragged reprobates who follow at the heels of a Chinese grandee when on a visit of ceremony. The Sawbwa occupied one chair, his distinguished guest the other, till the chief priest came in, when, with that deep reverence for the cloth which has always characterised me, I rose and gave him mine. He refused to take it, but I insisted; he pretended to be as reluctant to occupy it as any Frenchman, but I pushed him bodily into it, and that ended the matter.

A pleasant, kindly fellow is the Prince; even among the Shans he is conspicuous for his courtesy and amiability. He was a great favourite with the English Boundary Commission, and in his turn remembers with much pleasure his association with them. Half a dozen times, when conversation flagged, he raised his clasped hands and said "Warry *Ching, ching!*" and I knew that this was his foolish heathen way of sending greeting to the Chinese adviser of the Government of Burma. The Shan dialect is quite distinct from the Chinese, but all the princes or princelets dress in Chinese fashion and learn Mandarin, and it was of course in Mandarin that the Santa Sawbwa conversed with Mr. Warry. This Sawbwa is the son-in-law of the ex-Wuntho Sawbwa. He rules over a territory smaller than many squatters' stations in Victoria. He is one of the ablest of Shans, and would willingly place his little principality under the protection of England. He is thirty-five years of age, dresses in full Chinese costume, with pigtail and skullcap, is pock-marked, and has incipient goitre. He is polite and refined, chews betel nut "to stimulate his meditative faculties," and expectorates on the floor with easy freedom. I showed him my photographs, and he graciously invited me to give him some. I nodded cheerfully to him in assent, rolled them all up again, and put them back in my box. He knew that I did not understand.

We had tea together, and then he took his leave, "Warry *Ching, ching!*" being his parting words.

As soon as he had gone the deep drum—a hollow instrument of wood shaped like a fish—was beaten, and the priests gathered to vespers, dressed in many-coloured garments of silk; and, as evening fell, they intoned a sweet and mournful chant.

The service over, all but the choristers entered the room off the gallery in which I was lying, where, looking in, I saw them throw off their gowns and coil themselves on the sleeping benches. Opium-lamps were already lit, and all were soon inhaling opium; all but one who had rheumatism, and who, lying down, stretched himself at full length, while a brother priest punched him all over in that primitive method of massage employed by every native race the wide world over.

In the City Temple some festival was being celebrated, and night was turbulent with the beating of gongs and drums and the bursting of crackers. Long processions of priests in their yellow robes were passing the temple in the bright moonlight. Priests were as plentiful as blackberries; if they had been dressed in black instead of yellow, the traveller might have imagined that he was in Edinburgh at Assembly time.

In the morning another escort of half a dozen men was ready to accompany me for the day's stage to Manyuen. They were in the uniform of the Santa Sawbwa, in blue jackets instead of green. They were armed with rusty muzzle-loaders, unloaded, and with long Burmese swords (*dahs*). They were the most amiable of warriors, both in feature and manner, and were unlike the turbaned braves of China, who, armed no better than these men, still regard, as did their forefathers, fierceness of aspect as an important factor in warfare (*rostro feroz ao enemigo!*)—an illusion also shared in the English army, where monstrous bearskin shakos were introduced to increase the apparent height of the soldiers. The officer in command was late in overtaking me. As soon as he came within horse-length he let down his queue and bowed reverently, and I could see pride lighting his features as he confessed to the honour that had been done him in intrusting such an honourable and illustrious charge to the mean and unworthy care of so contemptible an officer.

The country before us was open meadow-land, pleasant to ride over, only here and there broken by a massive banyan tree. Herds of buffaloes were grazing on the hillsides. The mud villages were far apart on the margin of the river-plain, inclosed with superb hedges of living bamboo.

Thirty li from Santa is the Shan village of Taipingkai. It was market-day, and the broad main street was crowded. We were taken to the house of an oil-merchant, who kindly asked me in and had tea brewed for me. Earthenware jars of oil were stacked round the room. The basement opened to the street, and was packed in a moment. "*Dzo! Dzo!*" (Go! go!) cried the master, and the throng hustled out, to be renewed in a minute by a fresh body of curious who had waited their turn.

Then we rode on, over a country as beautiful as a nobleman's park, to the town of Manyuen. Every here and there by the roadside there are springs of fresh water, where travellers can slake their thirst. Bamboo ladles are placed here by devotees, whose action will be counted unto them for righteousness, for "he that piously bestows a little water shall receive an ocean in return." And, where there are no springs, neat little bamboo stalls with shelves are built, and in the cool shelter pitchers of water and bamboo cups are placed, so that the thirsty may bless the unknown hand which gives him to drink.

Manyuen—or, to use the name by which it is better known to foreigners, Manwyne—is a large and straggling town overlooking the river-plain. It was here that Margary, the British Consular Agent, was murdered in 1875. I had a long wait at the yamen gate while they were arranging where to send me, but by-and-by two yamen-runners came and conducted me to the City Temple. It was the same temple that Margary had occupied. Many shaven-pated Buddhist priests were waiting for me, and received me kindly in the temple hall. A table was brought for me and the only foreign chair, and Laotseng was shown where to spread my bedding in the temple hall itself. And here I held *levées* of the townspeople of all shades of colour and variety of feature—Chinese, Shan, Burmese, Kachin, and hybrid. The people were very amiable, and I found on all sides the same courtesy and kindliness that Margary describes on his first visit. But the crowd was quiet for only a little while; then a dispute arose. It began in the far corner, and the crowd left me to gather round the disputants. Voices were raised, loud and excited, and increased in energy. A deadly interest seemed to enthral the bystanders. It was easy to imagine that they were debating to do with me as they had done with Margary. The dispute waxed warmer. Surely they will come to blows? When suddenly the quarrel ceased as it had begun, and the crowd came smiling back to me. What was the dispute? The priests were cheapening a chicken for my dinner.

The temple was built on teak piles, and teak pillars supported the triple roof. It was like a barn or lumber room but for the gilt Buddhas on the altar and the gilt cabinets by its side, containing many smaller gilt images of Buddha and his disciples. Umbrellas, flags, and the tawdry paraphernalia used in processions were hanging from the beams. Sacerdotal vestments of dingy yellow— the yellow of turmeric—were tumbled over bamboo rests. When the gong sounded for prayers, men you thought were coolies threw these garments over the left shoulder, hitched them round the waist, and were transformed into priests, putting them back again immediately after the service. Close under the tiles was a paper sedan-chair, to be sent for the use of some rich man in heaven. Painted scrolls of paper were on the walls, and on old ledges were torn books in the Burmese character, which a few boys made a pretence of reading. Where I slept the floor was raised some feet from the ground, and underneath, seen through the gaping boards—though previously detected by another of the senses—were a number of coffins freighted with dead, waiting for a fit occasion for interment. Heavy stones were placed on the lids to keep the dead more securely at rest. The lucky day for burial would be determined by the priests—it would be determined by them as soon as the pious relatives had paid sufficiently for their fears. So long, then, as the coffins remained where they were, they might be described as capital invested by the priests and returning heavy interest; removed from the temple, they ceased to be productive.

As is the case in so many temples, there is an opium-room in the temple at the back of the gilded shrine, where priests and neophytes, throwing aside their office, can while away the licentious hours till the gong calls them again to prayers.

In the early morning, while I was still lying in my pukai on the floor, I saw many women, a large proportion of whom were goitrous, come to the hall, and make an offering of rice, and kneel down before the Buddha. As time went on, and more kept coming in, small heaps of rice had collected in front of the chief altar and before the cabinets. And when the women retired, a chorister came round and swept with his fingers all the little heaps into a basket. To the gods the spirit! To the priests the solid remains!

It was in Manyuen, as I have mentioned, that Margary met his death on February 21st, 1875. He had safely traversed China from Hankow to Bhamo, had been everywhere courteously treated by the Chinese and been given every facility and protection on his journey. He had passed safely through Manyuen only five weeks before, and had then written: "I come and go without meeting the slightest rudeness among this charming people, and they address me with the greatest respect." And yet five weeks later he was killed on his return! Even assuming that he was killed in obedience to orders issued by the cruel Viceroy at Yunnan City, the notorious

Tsen Yü-ying, and not by a lawless Chinese train-band which then infested the district and are believed by Baber to have been the real murderers, the British Government must still be held guilty of contributory negligence. Margary, having passed unmolested to Bhamo, there met the expedition under Colonel Horace Browne, and returned as its forerunner to prepare for its entry into China by the route he had just traversed. The expedition was a "peace expedition" sent by the Government of Burma, and numbered only "fifty persons in all, together with a Burmese guard of 150 armed soldiers."

Seven years before, an expedition under Major Sladen had advanced from Burma into Western China as far as Tengyueh; had remained in Tengyueh from May 25th to July 13th, 1868; had entered into friendly negotiations with the military governor and other Mohammedan officials in revolt against China; and had remained under the friendly protection of the Mohammedan insurgents who were then in possession of Western China from Tengyueh to near Yunnan City. "To what principles," it has been asked, "of justice or equity can we attribute the action of the British in retaining their Minister at the capital of an empire while sending a peaceful mission to a rebel in arms at its boundaries?"

The Mohammedan insurrection was not quelled till the early months of 1874. And less than a year later the Chinese learned with alarm that another peaceful expedition was entering Western China, by the same route, under the same auspices, and with the identical objects of the expedition which had been welcomed by the leaders of the insurrection.

The Chinese mind was incapable of grasping the fact that the second expedition was planned solely to discover new fields for international commerce and scientific investigation. Barbarians as they are, they feared that England thereby intended to "foster the dying embers of the rebellion." No time for such an expedition, a peaceful trade expedition, could have been more ill-chosen. The folly of it was seen in the murder of Margary and the repulse of Colonel Horace Browne, whose expedition was driven back at Tsurai within sight of Manyuen. And this murder, known to all the world, is the typical instance cited in illustration of the barbarity of the Chinese.

China may be a barbarous country; many missionaries have said so, and it is the fashion so to speak; but let us for a moment look at facts. During the last twenty-three years foreigners of every nationality and every degree of temperament, from the mildest to the most fanatical, have penetrated into every nook and cranny of the empire. Some have been sent back, and there has been an occasional riot with some destruction of property. But all the foreigners who have been killed can be numbered on the fingers of one hand, and in the majority of these cases it can hardly be denied that it was the indiscretion of the white man which was the exciting cause of his murder. In the same time how many hundreds of unoffending Chinese have been murdered in civilised foreign countries? An anti-foreign riot in China—and at what rare intervals do anti-foreign riots occur in its vast empire—may cause some destruction of property; but it may be questioned if the destruction done in China by the combined anti-foreign riots of the last twenty-three years equalled the looting done by the civilised London mob who a year or two ago on a certain Black Monday played havoc in Oxford-street and Piccadilly. "It is less dangerous," says one of the most accurate writers on China, the Rev. A. H. Smith, himself an American missionary, "for a foreigner to cross China than for a Chinese to cross the United States." And there are few who give the matter a thought but must admit the correctness of Mr. Smith's statement.

On May 17th I was on the road again. The fort of Manyuen is outside the town, and some little distance beyond it the dry creek bends into the pathway at a point where it is bordered with cactus and overshadowed by a banyan tree. This is said to be the exact spot where Margary was killed.

CHAPTER XXII.

CHINA AS A FIGHTING POWER—THE KACHINS—AND THE LAST STAGE INTO BHAMO.

We now left the low land and the open country, the pastures and meadows, and climbed up the jungle-clad spurs which form the triangular dividing range that separates the broad and open valley of the Taiping, where Manyuen is situated, from the confined and tropical valley of the Hongmuho, which lies at the foot of the English frontier fort of Nampoung, the present boundary of Burma. Two miles below Nampoung the two rivers join, and the combined stream flows on to enter the Irrawaddy a mile or two above Bhamo.

No change could be greater or more sudden. We toiled upwards in the blazing sun, and in two hours we were deep in the thickest jungle, in the exuberant vegetation of a tropical forest. We had left the valley of the peaceful Shans and were in the forest inhabited by other "protected barbarians" of China—the wild tribes of Kachins, who even in Burma are slow to recognise the beneficent influences of British frontier administration. Nature serenely sleeps in the valley; nature is throbbing with life in the forest, and the humming and buzzing of all insect life was strange to our unaccustomed ears.

A well-cut path has been made through the forest, and caravans of mules laden with bales of cotton were in the early stages of the long overland journey to Yunnan. Their bells tinkled through the forest, while the herd boy filled the air with the sweet tones of his bamboo flute, breathing out his soul in music more beautiful than any bagpipes. Cotton is the chief article of import entering China by this highway. From Talifu to the frontier a traveller could trace his way by the fluffs of cotton torn by the bushes from the mule-packs.

The road through the forest reaches the highest points, because it is at the highest points that the Chinese forts are situated, either on the road or on some elevated clearing near it.

The forts are stockades inclosed in wooden palisades, and guarded by *chevaux de frise* of sharp-cut bamboo. The barracks are a few native straw-thatched wooden huts. Perhaps a score or two of men form the garrison of each fort; they are badly armed, if armed at all. There are no guns and no store supplies. Water is trained into the stockades down open conduits of split bamboo. To anyone who has seen the Chinese soldiers at home in Western China, it is diverting to observe the credence which is given to Chinese statements of the armed strength of Western China. How much longer are we to persist in regarding the Chinese, as they now are, as a warlike power? In numbers, capacity for physical endurance, calm courage when well officered, and powers unequalled by any other race of mankind of doing the greatest amount of labour on the smallest allowance of food, their potential strength is stupendous. But they are not advancing, they are stationary; they look backwards, not forwards; they live in the past. Weapons with which their ancestors subdued the greater part of Asia they are loath to believe are unfitted for conducting the warfare of to-day. Should Japan bring China to terms, she can impose no terms that will not tend towards the advancement of China. Victories such as Japan has won over China might affect any other nation but China; but they are trifling and insignificant in their effect upon the gigantic mass of China. Suppose China has lost 20,000 men in this war, in one day there are 20,000 births in the Empire, and I am perfectly sure that, outside the immediate neighbourhood of the seat of operations, the Chinese as a nation, apart from the officials, are profoundly ignorant that there is even a war, or, as they would term it, a rebellion, in progress. Trouble, serious trouble, will begin in China in the near future, for the time must be fast approaching when the effete and alien dynasty now reigning in China—the Manchu dynasty—shall be overthrown, and a Chinese Emperor shall rule on the throne of China.

At a native village called Schehleh there is a likin-barrier. The yellow flag was drooping over the roadway in the hot sun. The customs officer, an amiable Chinese Shan, invited me in to tea, and brought his pukai for me to lie down upon. Like thousands of his countrymen, he had played for fortune in the Manila lottery. Two old lottery tickets and the prize list in Chinese were on one wall of his room, on the other were a number of Chinese visiting cards, to which I graciously permitted him to add mine.

Soldiers accompanied me from camp to camp, Chinese soldiers from districts many hundreds of miles distant in China. Some were armed, some were unarmed, and there was equal confidence to be reposed in the one as in the other; but all were civil, and watched me with a care that was embarrassing.

At the first camp beyond Schehleh the gateway was ornamented with trophies of valour. From two bare tree-trunks baskets of heads were hanging, putrefying in the heat. They were the heads of Kachin dacoits. And thus shall it be done with all taken in rebellion against the Son of Heaven, whose mighty clemency alone permits the sun to shine on any kingdom beyond his borders. Kachin villages are scattered through the forest, among the hills. You see their native houses, long bamboo structures raised on piles and thatched with grass, with low eaves sloping nearly to the ground. In sylvan glades sacred to the *nats* you pass wooden pillars erected by the roadside, rudely cut, and rudely painted with lines and squares and rough figures of knives, and close beside them conical grass structures with coloured weathercocks. Split bamboos support narrow shelves, whereon are placed the various food-offerings with which is sought the goodwill of the evil spirits.

The Kachin men we met were all armed with the formidable *dah* or native sword, whose widened blade they protect in a univalvular sheath of wood. They wore Shan jackets and dark knickerbockers; their hair was gathered under a turban. They all carried the characteristic embroidered Kachin bag over the left shoulder.

The Kachin women are as stunted as the Japanese, and are disfigured with the same disproportionate shortness of legs. They wear Shan jackets and petticoats of dark-blue; their ornaments are chiefly cowries; their legs are bare. Unmarried, they wear no head-dress, but have their hair cut in a black mop with a deep fringe to the eyebrows. If married, their head-dress is the same as that of the Shan women—a huge dark-blue conical turban. Morality among the Kachin maidens, a missionary tells me, is not, as we understand the term, believed to exist. There is a tradition in the neighbourhood concerning a virtuous maiden; but little reliance can be placed on such legendary tales. Among the Kachins each clan is ruled by a Sawbwa, whose office "is hereditary, not to the eldest son, but to the youngest, or, failing sons, to the youngest surviving brother." (Anderson.) All Kachins chew betel-nut and nearly all smoke opium—men, women and children. Goitre is very prevalent among them; in some villages Major Couchman believes that as many as 25 per cent. of the inhabitants are afflicted with the disease. They have no written language, but their spoken language has been romanised by the American missionaries in Burma.

We camped within five miles of the British border at the Chinese fortlet of Settee, a palisaded camp whose gateway also was hung with heads of dacoits. A Chinese Shan was in command, a smart young officer with a Burmese wife. He was active, alert, and intelligent, and gave me the best room in the series of sheds which formed the barracks. I was made very comfortable. There were between forty and fifty soldiers stationed in the barracks—harmless warriors—who were very attentive. At nightfall the tattoo was beaten. The gong sounded; its notes died away in a distant murmur, then brayed forth with a stentorian clangour that might wake the dead. At the same time a tattoo was beaten on the drum, then a gun was fired and the noise ceased, to be repeated again during the night at the change of guard. All foes, visible and invisible, were in this way scared away from the fort.

Hearing that I was a doctor, the commandant asked me to see several of his men who were on the sick list. Among them was one poor young fellow dying, in the next room to mine, of remittent fever. When I went to the bedside the patient was lying down deadly ill, weak, and emaciated; but two of his companions took him by the arms, and, telling him to sit up, would have pulled him into what they considered a more respectful attitude. In the morning I again went to see the poor fellow. He was lying on his side undergoing treatment. An opium-pipe was held to his lips by one comrade, while another rolled the pellet of opium and placed it heated in the pipe-bowl, so that he might inhale its fumes.

In the morning the officer accompanied me to the gate of the stockade and bade me good-bye, with many unintelligible expressions of good will. His eight best soldiers were told off to escort me to the frontier, distant only fifteen li. It was a splendid walk through the jungle across the mountains to the Hongmuho. We passed the outlying stockade of the Chinese, and, winding along the spur, came full in view of the British camp across the valley, half-way up the opposite slope. By a very steep path we descended through the forest to the frontier fort of the Chinese, and emerged upon the grassy slope that shelves below it to the river.

There are a few bamboo huts on the sward, and here the Chinese guard left me; for armed guards are allowed no further. I was led to the ford, my pony plunged into the swift stream, and a moment or two later I was on British soil and passing the Sepoy outpost, where the guard, to my great alarm, for I feared being shot, turned out and saluted me. Then I climbed up the steep hill to the British encampment, where the English officer commanding, Captain R. G. Iremonger, of the 3rd Burma Regiment, gave me a kind reception, and congratulated me upon my successful journey. He telegraphed to headquarters the news of my arrival. It was of no earthly interest to anybody that I, an unknown wanderer, should pass through safely; but it was of interest to know that anyone could pass through so easily. Reports had only recently reached the Government that Western China was in a state of disaffection; that a feeling strongly anti-foreign had arisen in Yunnan; and that now, of all times, would it be inexpedient to despatch a commission for the delimitation of the boundary. My quiet and uninterrupted journey was in direct conflict with all such reports.

The encampment of Nampoung is at an elevation of 1500 feet above the river. It is well exposed on all sides, and has been condemned by military experts. But the law of fortifications which applies to any ordinary frontier does not apply to the frontier of China, where there is no danger whatsoever. The palisade is irregularly made, and is not superior, of course, to any round the Chinese stockades.

The houses are built of bamboo, are raised on piles, and thatched with grass. A company of the 3rd Burma Regiment is permanently stationed here under an English officer, and consists of 100 men, who are either Sikhs or Punjabis, all of splendid stature and military bearing. A picket of six men under a non-commissioned native officer guards the ford, and permits no armed Chinese to cross the border.

There are numbers of transport mules and ponies. In the creek there are plenty of fish; the rod, indeed, is the chief amusement of the officers who are exiled on duty to this lonely spot to pass three months in turn in almost uninterrupted solitude. There is a telegraph line into Bhamo, and it is at this point that connection will be made with the Imperial Chinese Telegraphs.

At the ford from fifty to one hundred loaded pack-animals, mostly carrying cotton, cross into China daily. A toll of six annas is levied upon each pack-animal, the money so collected being distributed by the Government among those Kachin Sawbwas who have an hereditary right to levy this tribute. The money is collected by two Burmese officials, and handed daily to the officer commanding. No duty is paid on entering Burma. Chinese likin-barriers begin to harass the caravans at Schehleh.

Beautiful views of the surrounding hills, all covered with "lofty forest trees, tangled with magnificent creepers, and festooned with orchids," are obtained from the camp. All the country round is extremely fertile, yielding with but little labour three crops a year. Cultivation of the soil there is none. Fire clears the jungle, and the ashes manure the soil; the ground is then superficially scratched, and rice is sown. Nothing more is done. Every seed germinates; the paddy ripens, and, where one basketful is sown, five hundred basketfuls are gathered. And the field lies untouched till again covered with jungle. Thus is the heathen rewarded five-hundred-fold in accordance with the law of Nature which gives blessing to the labour of the husbandman inversely as he deserves it.

In the evening the officer walked down with me to the creek, where I bathed in the shadow of the bank, in a favourite pool for fishing. As we crossed the field on our return, we met the two Burmese tribute-gatherers. They had occasion to speak to the officer, when, instead of standing upright like a stalwart and independent Chinaman, they squatted humbly on their heels, and, resting their elbows on their knees in an attitude of servility, conversed with their superior. How different the Chinaman, who confesses few people his superior, and none of any race beyond the borders of China!

From Nampoung to Bhamo is an easy walk of thirty-three miles. This is usually done in two stages, the halting place being the military station of Myothit, which is fourteen miles from Nampoung. On leaving Nampoung, an escort of a lance-corporal and two soldiers was detailed to accompany me. They were Punjabis, men of great stature and warlike aspect; but they were presumably out of training, for they arrived at Myothit, limp and haggard, an hour or more after we did. There is an admirable road through the jungle, maintained in that excellent order characteristic of military roads under British supervision. My Chinese from time to time questioned me as to the distance. We had gone fifteen li when Laotseng asked me how much farther it was to Santien (Myothit). "Three li," I said. We walked ten li further. "How far is it now?" he asked. "Only five li further," I replied, gravely. We went on another six li, when again he asked me: "Teacher Mô, how many li to Santien?" "Only eight more li," I said, and he did not ask me again. I was endeavouring to give him information in the fashion that prevails in his own country.

At Myothit we camped in the dâk bungalow, an unfurnished cottage kept for the use of travellers. The encampment is on the outskirts of a perfectly flat plain, skirted with jungle-clad hills and covered with elephant grass. Through the plain the broad river Taiping flows on its muddy way to the Irrawaddy. One hundred sepoys are stationed here under a native officer, a Sirdar, Jemadar, or Subadar (I am not certain which), who called upon me, and stood by me as I ate my tiffin, and, to my great embarrassment, saluted me in the most alarming way every time my eye unexpectedly caught his. I confess that I did not know the gentleman from Adam. I mistook him for an ornamental head-waiter, and, as I regarded him as a superfluous nuisance, I told him not to stand upon the order of his going but go. I pointed to the steps; and he went, sidling off backwards as if from the presence of royalty. Drawing his heels together, he saluted me at the stair-top and again at the bottom, murmuring words which were more unintelligible to me even than Chinese.

During the night our exposed bungalow was assailed by a fearful storm of wind and rain, and for a time I expected it to be bodily lifted off the piles and carried to the lee-side of the settlement. The roof leaked in a thousand places, rain was driven under the walls, and everything I had was soaked with warm water.

Next day we had a pleasant walk into Bhamo, that important military station on the left bank of the Irrawaddy. We crossed the Taiping at Myothit by a bridge, a temporary and very shaky structure, which is every year carried away when the river rises, and every year renewed when the caravans take the road after the rains.

Bhamo is 1520 miles by land from Chungking; and it is an equal distance further from Chungking to Shanghai. The entire distance I traversed in exactly one hundred days, for I purposely waited till the hundredth day to complete it. And it surely speaks well of the sense of responsibility innate in the Chinese that, during all this time, I never had in my employ a Chinese coolie who did not fulfil, with something to spare, all that he undertook to do. I paid off my men in Bhamo. To Laotseng I gave 400 cash too many, and asked him for the change. At once with much readiness he ranged some cash on the table in the form of an abacus, and, setting down some hieroglyphics on a sheet of paper, he worked out a calculation, by which he proved that I owed *him* 400 cash, and, therefore, the accounts were now exactly balanced. For my own expenses I gave him 1175 cash in Tengyueh and 400 more in Bhamo, so that my entire personal expenses between two points nine days distant from each other were rather more than 3*s*. My entire journey from Shanghai to Bhamo cost less than £20 sterling, including my Chinese outfit. Had I travelled economically, I estimate that the journey need not have cost me more than £14. Had I carried more silver with me, I would still further have reduced the total cost of my tour. The gold I bought in Yunnan with my surplus silver, I sold in Burma for 20 per cent. profit, the rupees which I purchased in Tengyueh for 11*d.* were worth 13*d.* in Bhamo. For some curios which I purchased in the interior for £2 5*s*. I was offered when I reached civilisation £14. Without doubt the journey across China is the cheapest that can be done in all the world.

I was sorry to say good-bye to my men, who had served me so faithfully. And I cannot speak more highly of the pleasure of my journey than to declare that I felt greater regret when it was finished than I ever felt on leaving any other country. The men all through had behaved admirably, and it is only fair to add that mine was the common experience of travellers in far Western China. Thus a very great traveller in China and Thibet (W. W. Rockhill), writing in the *Century*, April, 1894, on the discomforts of his recent journey, says:

"But never a word of complaint from either the Thibetans or my Chinese. They were always alert, always good-tempered, always attentive to me, and anxious to contribute to my comfort in every way in their power. And so I have ever found these peoples, with whom I am glad to say, after travelling over 20,000 miles in their countries, I have never exchanged a rough word, and among whom I think I have left not one enemy and not a few friends."

Two days after their arrival in Bhamo my three men started on their return journey to Talifu. They were laden with medicines, stores, newspapers, and letters for the mission in Tali, which for months had been accumulating in the premises of the American Mission in Bhamo, the missionary in charge, amid the multifarious avocations pertaining to his post, having found no time to forward them to their destination to his lonely Christian brother in the far interior. And, had I not arrived when I did, they could not have been sent till after the rains. A coolie will carry eighty pounds weight from Bhamo to Tali for 12*s*.; and I need hardly point out that a very small transaction in teak would cover the cost of many coolies. Besides, any expenditure incurred would have been reimbursed by the Inland Mission. My three men were pursued by cruel fate on their return; they all were taken ill at Pupiao. Poor "Bones" and the pock-marked coolie died, and Laotseng lay ill in the hotel there for weeks, and, when he recovered sufficiently to go on to Tali, he had to go without the three loads, which the landlord of the inn detained, pending the payment of his board and lodging and the burial expenses of his two companions.

CHAPTER XXIII.

BHAMO, MANDALAY, RANGOON, AND CALCUTTA.

The finest residence in Bhamo is, of course, the American mission. America nobly supports her self-sacrificing and devoted sons who go forth to arrest the "awful ruin of souls" among the innumerable millions of Asia, who are "perishing without hope, having sinned without law." The missionary in charge told me that he labours with a "humble heart to bring a knowledge of the Saving Truth to the perishing heathen among the Kachins." His appointment is one which even a worldly-minded man might covet. I will give an instance of his methods. This devoted evangelist told me that a poor woman, a Kachin Christian, in whose welfare he felt deep personal interest, was, he greatly feared, dying from blood-poisoning at a small Christian village one hour's ride up the river from Bhamo; and he had little doubt that some surgical interference in her case would save her life. I at once offered to go and see her. I had received great kindness from many American missionaries in China, and it would give me great pleasure, I said, if I could be of any service.

The missionary professed to be grateful for my offer, but, instead of arranging to go that afternoon, named seven o'clock the following morning as the hour when he would call for me to take me to the village. At the time appointed I was ready; I waited, but no missionary came. There was a slight drizzle, sufficient to prevent his going to the sick woman but not sufficient to deter him from going to market to the Irrawaddy steamer, where I accidentally met him. So far from being abashed when he saw me, he took the occasion to tell me what he will, I know, pardon me for thinking an inexcusable untruth. He had written, he said, to the poor woman telling her, dying as he believed her to be, to come down to Bhamo by boat to see me.

In Bhamo I stayed in the comfortable house of the Deputy Commissioner, and was treated with the most pleasant hospitality. To my regret, the Deputy Commissioner was down the river, and I did not see him. He is regarded as one of the ablest men in the service. His rise has been rapid, and he was lately invested with the C.I.E.—there seems, indeed, to be no position in Burma that he might not aspire to. In his absence his office was being administered by the Assistant Commissioner, a courteous young Englishman, who gave me my first experience of the Civil Service. I could not but envy the position of this young fellow, and marvel at the success which attends our method of administering the Indian Empire. Here was a young man of twenty-four, acting as governor with large powers over a tract of country of hundreds of square miles—a new country requiring for its proper administration a knowledge of law, of finance, of trade, experience of men, and ability to deal with the conflicting interests of several native races. Superior to all other authorities, civil and military, in his district, he was considered fit to fill this post—and success showed his fitness—because a year or two before he had been one of forty crammed candidates out of 200 who had taken the highest places in a series of examinations in Latin, English, mathematics, &c. With the most limited experience of human life, he had obtained his position in exactly the same way that a Chinese Mandarin does his—by competitive examination in subjects which, even less than in the case of the Chinese, had little bearing upon his future work; and now, like a Chinese Mandarin, "there are few things he isn't."

On the face of it no system appears more preposterous; in its results no system was ever more successful. The Assistant Commissioner early learns self-reliance, decision, and ability to wield authority; and he can always look forward to the time when he may become Chief Commissioner.

There is a wonderful mixture of types in Bhamo. Nowhere in the world, not even in Macao, is there a greater intermingling of races. Here live in cheerful promiscuity Britishers and Chinese, Shans and Kachins, Sikhs and Madrasis, Punjabis, Arabs, German Jews and French adventurers, American missionaries and Japanese ladies.

There are many ruined pagodas and some wooden temples which, however, do not display the higher features of Burmese architecture. There is a club, of course; a polo and football ground, and a cricket ground. Inside the fort, among the barracks, there is a building which has a double debt to pay, being a theatre at one end and a church at the other, the same athletic gentleman being the chief performer at both places. But, at its best, Bhamo is a forlorn, miserable, and wretched station, where all men seem to regard it as their first duty to the stranger to apologise to him for being there.

The distinguished Chinese scholar and traveller, E. Colborne Baber, who wrote the classic book of travel in Western China, was formerly British Resident in Bhamo. He spoke Chinese unusually well and was naturally proud of his accomplishment. Now the ordinary Chinaman has this feature in common with many of the European races, that, if he thinks you cannot speak his language, he *will* not understand you, even if you speak to him with perfect correctness of idiom and tone. And Baber had an experience of this which deeply hurt his pride. Walking one day in the neighbourhood of Bhamo, he met two Chinese—strangers—and began speaking to them in his best Mandarin. They heard him with unmoved stolidity, and, when he had finished, one turned to his companion and said, as if struck with his discovery, "the language of these foreign barbarians sounds not unlike our own!"

In Bhamo I had the pleasure of meeting the three members of the Boundary Commission who represented us in some preliminary delimitation questions with the Chinese Government. A better choice could not have been made. M. Martini, a Frenchman, has been twenty years in Upper Burma, and is our D.S.P. (District Superintendent of Police). Mr. Warry, the Chinese adviser to the Burmese Government, is one of the ablest men who ever graduated from the Consular Staff in China; while Captain H. R. Davies, of the Staff Corps, who is on special duty in the Intelligence Department, is not only an exceptionally able officer, but is the most accomplished linguist of Upper Burma. These were the three representatives.

I sold my pony in Bhamo. I was exceedingly sorry to part with it, for it had come with me 800 miles in thirty days, over an unusually difficult road, at great variations of altitude, and amid many changes of climate. And it was always in good spirit, brave and hardy, carrying me as surely the last twenty miles as it had the first twenty. Yet, when I came to sell it, I was astonished to learn how many were its defects. Its height, which was 12.3 in Nampoung, had shrunk three days later to 11.3 in Bhamo. This one subaltern told me who came to look at the pony with the view, he said, of making me an offer. Another officer proved to me that the off foreleg was gone hopelessly; a third confirmed this diagnosis of his friend, and in a clinical lecture demonstrated that the poor beast was spavined, and that its near hind frog was rotten, "as all Chinese ponies' are," he added. One of the mounted constabulary, a smart officer, fortunately discovered in time that the pony was a roarer; while the Hungarian Israelite who lends help on notes of hand, post-obits, personal applications, and other insecurities, and is on terms of friendly intimacy with most of the garrison, when about to make an offer, found, to his great regret, that the pony's hind legs were even more defective than the fore. The end of it was that I had to sell the pony—for what it cost me. I am indebted to the Reverend Mr. Roberts, of the American Baptist Mission, for helping me to sell my pony. Mr. Roberts has a pious gift for buying ponies and selling them—at a profit. He offered me 40 rupees for my pony. I mentioned this offer at the Bhamo Club, when a civilian present at once offered me 50 rupees for the pony; he did not know the pony, he explained, but—he knew Roberts.

In a steamer of the Irrawaddy Flotilla Company I came down the river from Bhamo to Mandalay. When I left the Commissioner's bungalow, the entire staff of the establishment and of some neighbouring bungalows assembled to do me honour, creeping up to me, and with deep humility carrying each an article of my possessions from my room down to the porch. There were the *dhobie* and *bearer*, the waterman with his goatskin waterbag, the washerman who washed my blue Chinese garments as white as his own, the *syce* who did not collect grass, the cook who sent me ten bad eggs in three days, and the Christian Madrasi, the laziest rascal in Bhamo, who early confessed to me his change of faith and the transformation it had effected in the future prospects of his soul. There was the Burmese watchman, and the English-speaking Burmese clerk, and the coolie who went to the bazaar for me, and many others. They lined the stairs as I came out, and placed their hands reverently to their foreheads when I passed by. It was pleasant to see such disinterested evidence of their good will, and my only regret was that I could not reward them according to their deserts. But to the Chinese coolie who was grinning to see my paltry outfit carried by so many hands, and who gathered together all I possessed and swung off with it down past the temples to the steamer landing in the native city, I gave a day's pay, and cheerfully—though he then asked for more.

In Mandalay I was taken to the club, and passed many hours there reading the home papers and wandering through its gilded halls. Few clubs in the world have such a sumptuous setting as this, for it is installed in the throne-room and chambers and reception-halls of the palace of King Theebaw.

In the very centre of the building is a seven-storeyed spire, "emblematic of royalty and religion," which the Burmese look upon as the "exact centre of creation." The reception-hall at the foot of the throne is now the English chapel; the reading-room with its gilded daïs where the Queen sat on her throne, with its lofty roof, its pillars of teak, and walls all ablaze with gilding, was the throne-room of Theebaw's chief Queen.

Mandalay is largely Chinese, and on the outskirts of the city there is a handsome temple which bears the charming inscription, so characteristic of the Chinese, "enlightenment finds its way even among the outer barbarians."

There is a military hospital with two nursing sisters, highly trained ladies from Bart.'s. Australians are now so widely distributed over the world that it did not surprise me to find that one of the two sisters comes from Melbourne.

From Mandalay I went by train to Rangoon, where I lived in a pretty villa among noble trees on the lower slope of the hill which is crowned with the famous golden pagoda, the "Shway-dagon," the most sacred temple of Indo-China. We looked out upon the park and the royal lake. I early went to the Intelligence Department and saw Major Couchman. In his office I met the chief Chinese interpreter, a Chinaman with a rare genius for languages. He is a native of Fuhkien province, and, of course, speaks the Fuhkien dialect; he knows also Cantonese and Mandarin. In addition, he possesses French, Hindustani, Burmese, Shan, and Sanscrit, and, in an admirable translation which he has made of a Chinese novel into English, he frequently quotes Latin. Fit assistant he would make to Max Müller; his services command a high salary.

The Chinese in Rangoon are a predominating force in the prosperity of the city. They have deeply impressed their potentiality upon the community. "It seems almost certain," says a great authority, perhaps *the* greatest authority on Burma—J. G. Scott (Shway Yoe)—"that in no very long time Burma, or, at any rate, the large trading towns of Burma, will be for all practical purposes absorbed by the Chinese traders, just as Singapore and Penang are virtually Chinese towns. Unless some marvellous upheaval of energy takes place in the Burmese character, the plodding, unwearying Chinaman is almost certainly destined to overrun the country to the exclusion of the native race."

The artisans of Rangoon are largely Chinese, and the carpenters exclusively so. The Chinese marry Burmese women, and, treating their wives with the consideration which the Chinaman invariably extends to his foreign wife in a foreign country, they are desired as husbands even above the Burmans. Next to the British, the only indispensable element in the community is now the Chinese.

The best known figure in Burma is the Reverend John Ebenezer Marks, D.D., Principal of the St. John's College of the S.P.G. Dr. Marks has been thirty-five years in Burma, is still hale and hearty, brimful of reminiscences, and is one of the most amusing companions in the world. I think it was he who converted King Theebaw to Christianity. His school is a curiosity. It is an anthropological institute with perhaps the finest collection of human cross-breeds in existence. It is away out beyond the gaol, in large wooden buildings set in extensive playgrounds. Here he has 550 students, all but four of whom are Asiatics of fifteen different nationalities—Chinese, Karens, Kachins, Shans, and a varied assortment of Hindoos and Malays, both pure and blended with the native Burmese. All the different races represented in Burma have intermarried with the native Burmese, and the resulting half-breeds have crossed with other half-breeds. Most of the better class Eurasian boys (European-Asian) are educated here, some being supported by their fathers, some not. The former Dr. Marks ingeniously calls after their mothers; the latter, who have been neglected, retain the names (when they are known), of their fathers. It is amusing to meet among the latter the names of so many brave Englishmen who, in the earlier days when morals had not attained the strictness that now characterises them, gallantly served their country in Burma.

No woman in the world is more catholic in her tastes than the Burmese. She bestows her loves as variously as the Japanese. She marries with equal readiness Protestant or Catholic, Turk, Infidel, or Jew. She clings cheerfully to whichever will support her; but above all she desires the Chinaman. No one treats her so well as the Chinaman. If she is capable of experiencing the emotion of love for any being outside her own race, she feels it for the Chinaman, who is of a cognate race to her own, is hard-working, frugal, and industrious, permits her to live in idleness, and delights her with presents, loving her children with that affection which the Chinaman has ever been known to bestow upon his offspring. The Chino-Burmese is not quite the equal of his father, but he is markedly superior to the Burmese. The best half-caste in the East is, of course, the Eurasian of British parentage. Englishmen going to Burma are, as a rule, picked men, physically powerful, courageous, energetic, and enterprising; for it is the possession of these qualities which has sent them to the East, either for business or in the service of their country. And their Burmese companions—of course I speak of a condition of things which is gradually ceasing to exist—are all picked women, selected for the comeliness of their persons and the sweetness of their manners.

After a stay of two or three weeks in Rangoon, I went round by the British India steamer to Calcutta. Ill fortune awaited me here. The night after my arrival I was laid down with remittent fever, and a few days later I nearly died. The reader will, I am sure, pardon me for obtruding this purely personal matter. But, as I opened this book with a testimony of gratitude to the distinguished surgeon who cut a spear point from my body, where nine months before it had been thrust by a savage in New Guinea, so should I be sorry to close this narrative without recording a word of thanks to those who befriended me in Calcutta.

I was a stranger, knowing only two men in all Calcutta; but they were friends in need, who looked after me during my illness with the greatest kindness. A leading doctor of Calcutta attended me, and treated me with unremitting attention and great skill. To Mr. John Bathgate and Mr. Maxwell Prophit and to Dr. Arnold Caddy I owe a lasting debt of gratitude. And what shall I say of that kind nurse—dark of complexion, but most fair to look upon—whose presence in the sick room almost consoled me for being ill? Bless her dear heart! Even hydrochlorate of quinine tasted sweet from her fingers.

Lightning Source UK Ltd.
Milton Keynes UK
UKHW04f0626150718
325723UK00001B/71/P